The Political Economy of Food and Finance

The financialization, globalization, and industrialization of our food systems make it increasingly difficult to access quality fresh food. In fact, the industrialized global food system is creating products that are less food-like, engendering growing questions about the health and safety of our food supply. In addition, the bio-engineering of food commodities is another factor influencing the growth of industrial farming for an increasingly homogenized, globalized market.

This book describes the financialization process in commodity futures markets which transformed commodities into an asset class. Incorporated into the portfolio decisions of investors, commodity prices now behave like all asset prices, becoming more volatile and subject to periodic bubbles. As commodity prices were driven higher in the 2000s, farmland became more valuable, setting off a global land grab by investors, nations, and corporations. More recently, under the financialization food regime, slow growth and low returns encouraged merger activity driven by private equity firms, with food industry corporations as prime targets, leading to increased industry concentration.

With government policy focused on supporting corporate interests, there has been a global reaction to the current food system. The food sovereignty movement is taking on the interests behind the global land grab, and the regional food movement in cities across the United States is hitting corporations at the bottom line. Food corporations are listening. Is the food movement winning?

This book is of interest to those who study political economy, financialization, and agriculture and related studies, as well as food systems and commodity future markets.

Ted P. Schmidt is Associate Professor of Economics & Finance at SUNY Buffalo State, New York, USA.

Routledge Frontiers of Political Economy

The Political Economy of Food and Finance

Ted P. Schmidt

Routledge
Taylor & Francis Group

LONDON AND NEW YORK

First published 2016 by Routledge

2 Park Square, Milton Park, Abingdon, Oxon OX14 4RN
711 Third Avenue, New York, NY 10017, USA

Routledge is an imprint of the Taylor & Francis Group, an informa business

First issued in paperback 2017

British Library Cataloguing in Publication Data
A catalogue record for this book is available from the British Library

Library of Congress Cataloging in Publication Data
Schmidt, Ted P., author.
The political economy of food and finance / Ted Schmidt.
pages cm
1. Agriculture—Economic aspects—United States. 2. Agriculture—United
States—Finance. 3. Agricultural industries—United States. 4. Commodity
exchanges—United States. I. Title.
HD1761.S2523 2016
338.1'9—dc23
2015025827

ISBN: 978-1-138-83822-2 (hbk)
ISBN: 978-1-138-29937-5 (pbk)

Typeset in Times New Roman
by Book Now Ltd, London

To my wife Elizabeth and children Adam, John, and Louisa

Contents

Contents

Figures

Tables

Tables

Acronyms

AHR	Adjusted Hedge Ratio
ARC	Agriculture Risk Coverage program
BHC	Bank Holding Company
BIS	Bank for International Settlements
BLS	Bureau of Labor Statistics
CBOT	Chicago Board of Trade
CEA	Commodity Exchange Act of 1936
CEC	Commodity Exchange Commission
CFMA	Commodity Futures Modernization Act of 2000
CFTC	Commodity Futures Trading Commission
CIF	Commodity Index Fund
CME	Chicago Mercantile Exchange
COT	Commitment of Traders report
CRB	Commodity Research Bureau
CSA	Community Supported Agriculture
DCOT	Disaggregated Commitment of Traders report
DGAC	Dietary Guidelines Advisory Committee
ETF	Exchange Traded Fund
FAO	Food and Agriculture Organization of the United Nations
FHC	Financial Holding Company
FPC	Food Policy Councils
FRB	Federal Reserve Board of the United States
GE	Genetically Engineered
GLBA	Gramm–Leach–Bliley Act of 1999
GMO	Genetically Modified Organisms
HRW	Hard Red Winter wheat
ICE	Intercontinental Exchange
ISDS	Investor-State Dispute Settlement
KCBOT	Kansas City Board of Trade
LBO	Leveraged Buyout
M&A	Mergers and Acquisitions
MAP	Massachusetts Avenue Project
MMT	Managed Money Traders

NFC   National Financial Complex
NYMEX New York Mercantile Exchange
NYSE   New York Stock Exchange
OECD   Organization for Economic Co-operation and Development
OTC   Over-the-Counter markets
PE   Private Equity
PLC   Price Loss Coverage program
REIT   Real Estate Investment Trust
SCIT   Supplemental Commodity Index Trader report
SEC   Securities and Exchange Commission
SNAP   Supplemental Nutrition Assistance Program
SOR   US Senate Oil Report
SP-GSCI Standard & Poor's Goldman Sachs Commodity Index
SRW   Soft Red Winter wheat
SSA   Social Structure of Accumulation Theory
SWR   US Senate Wheat Report
TTIP   Trans-Atlantic Trade and Investment Partnership trade agreement
TTP   Trans-Pacific Partnership trade agreement
UN   The United Nations
USDA   United States Department of Agriculture
VAR   Vector Auto-Regression model
WTI   West Texas Intermediate crude oil
WTO   World Trade Organization

1 Introduction
Food and finance

In 2008, skyrocketing food prices were the source of riots and destabilization in almost thirty countries around the globe. From Haiti to Egypt to Panama and the Philippines, rising food prices created turmoil for countries reliant on imported foodstuffs. Was this the specter of Parson Malthus? Had global population finally outpaced our ability to produce food? Or was it simply the workings of a commodity *super-cycle* brought on by growing global demand from the BRICK countries (Brazil, Russia, India, China, and Korea) combined with supply disruptions from poor harvests?

From 2002 to 2008 the nominal value of the FAO Food Price Index increased by 125 percent, and the most dramatic increases occurred in 2007 and 2008, with prices rising by 26 percent per year in nominal terms and 18 percent in real terms (Figure 1.1). Attempts to explain the cause of higher food prices have primarily laid blame on a super-cycle driven by global demand from China, with secondary causes attributed to biofuel mandates, supply disruptions, a decline in the US

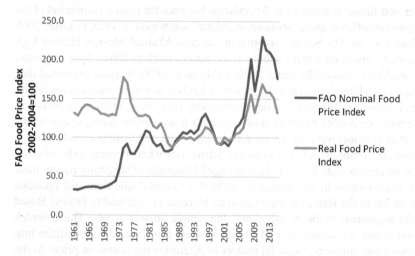

Figure 1.1 FAO Food Price Index.

Source: Food and Agriculture Organization of the United Nations.

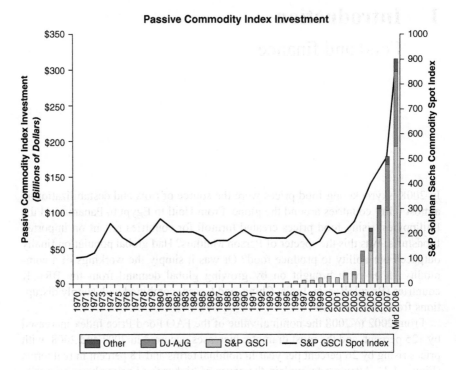

Figure 1.2 Commodity index investments and commodity prices.
Source: Better Markets, 2011. Reproduced with permission.

dollar, and financial speculation. Speculation has been the most controversial of the explanations offered, and a "speculation debate" was triggered when, in a May 2008 testimony to the US Senate, investment manager Michael Masters blamed high commodity prices on a price bubble in the futures markets driven by a new class of speculators, *commodity index traders* (Masters, 2008). Masters presented data (Figure 1.2) which showed that the growth of funds flowing into passive commodity index investments mirrored the rise in commodity spot prices. Investment flows into these new commodity-based financial products from pension funds, endowments, and other investors were driving up commodity prices, and therefore food prices.

Masters' testimony set off a vigorous debate over what appeared to be an obvious relationship. Was it a statistical mirage? Hundreds of academic papers have since been written in an attempt to settle this "simple" question: did financial speculation in the futures market cause an increase in commodity prices? Based on the arguments made in this work, the simple answer is yes. The complex answer is that *financialization* of futures markets transformed commodities into an asset class, allowing financial traders to determine the course of prices in the short run: financialization of commodity markets explains how, but not the extent to which, financial speculators contributed to the 2008 food price bubble.

The main argument in this work is that financial interests, large Wall Street banks, used a financial innovation to circumvent regulations and break down barriers to entry in the regulated commodity futures markets; then, through political influence, the innovations were codified through a deregulatory act. This *financialization process* resulted in a "flipping of the markets," where financial traders, previously restrained, now dominate markets and determine the direction of prices in the short term. Financialization has transformed commodities into an asset, and like all asset prices, commodity prices have become more volatile and they are subject to periodic bubbles.

Financialization of physical things creates new markets and profit opportunities for financial traders, and volatility is good for profits because it increases the demand for financial products used to hedge against price movements. In a low-yield environment, or what former PIMCO managing director Bill Gross (Gross, 2009) called the *New Normal*, investors are motivated to find new, alternative investment outlets. With trillions of dollars chasing yield, commodities, farmland, water, climate, utilities, and even sewage disposal are fair game.

The term financialization has been used to describe this encroachment by finance into new markets and its influence over the broader economy. While there are several definitions, the one most often cited is Epstein (Epstein, 2005), "Financialization refers to the increasing importance of financial markets, financial motives, financial institutions, and financial elites in the operation of the economy and its governing institutions, both at the national and international level" (p. 3). Financialization is one of several institutional forces that have shaped the US economy over the past forty years, and food prices, industries, and food systems have not been immune from its influence.

This influence of finance along with the re-emergence of market fundamentalism and trade liberalization are characteristics of what has been described as the *neoliberal* capital accumulation regime by Regulation and Social Structure of Accumulation (SSA) schools of thought (Kotz, 2010). In these approaches, the accumulation process under capitalism is characterized by regimes, or institutional arrangements, that emerge to facilitate long periods of capital accumulation. Neoliberalism, then, is the set of forces that arose out of an accumulation crisis in the late 1970s, and these forces have established new institutional arrangements which govern the current accumulation process. However, as we discuss, financialization has become the dominant force regulating the accumulation process since 2000.

As argued in this work, financialization of commodity markets allows financial traders to determine prices in the short run, and it is one of several factors underlying the 2008 food price bubble. However, as one of the forces under the neoliberal accumulation regime, financialization helps explain broader long-term changes in the US and global economies. As a process, financialization has directly impacted commodity markets and food prices; however, as a broader force, it has influenced food markets and systems in other, less obvious, ways. Neoliberalism and financialization have literally changed the shape of American society and its people.

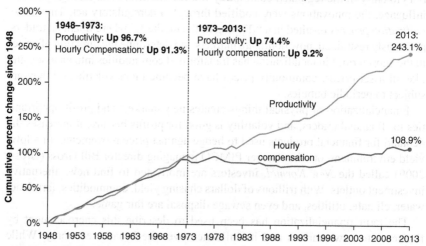

Workers produced much more, but typical workers' pay lagged far behind
Disconnect between productivity and typical worker's compensation, 1948–2013

1948–1973:
Productivity: **Up 96.7%**
Hourly Compensation: **Up 91.3%**

1973–2013:
Productivity: **Up 74.4%**
Hourly compensation: **Up 9.2%**

2013:
243.1%

Productivity

Hourly
compensation

108.9%

Figure 1.3 Productivity and worker compensation.

Source: Figure 2 in Mishel et al., 2015. Reproduced with permission.

The main goal of neoliberal policies was restoring profitability through deregulating markets, expanding trade, eliminating barriers to capital mobility, and eroding the social safety net. In addition, at the level of the firm, a revolution in shareholder activism led to management compensation policies that produced a focus on short-term value creation. The result of these policies was the breakdown in the post-war social compact tying wage gains to productivity, as shown in Figure 1.3. The loss of high-wage union jobs to low-wage competitors and the erosion of the social safety net reduced labor's bargaining power, which allowed the gains from productivity to flow to shareholders and managers in the form of higher profits and stock prices.

Neoliberal supply-side economic policies were used to justify tax cuts for capital and high-income earners, which saw the top marginal tax rate in the US lowered from 70 percent in 1980 to a post-war low of 28 percent in 1988. As more income flowed to the top, measured inequality worsened (Figure 1.4). From 1980 to 2013, the share of family income received by the top quintile increased from 41.1 to 48.8 percent, with over 90 percent of the gains going to the top 5 percent, increasing their share from 14.6 to 21.1 percent.

As the structure of the US economy was changing, so too was the social structure. As wages stagnated, two-income families became the norm. From 1967 to 1990, the number of families with two-income earners increased from 43.6 percent in 1967 to 59 percent in 1990. As financial duress increased, the divorce rate increased in the 1970s and 1980s, and the number of households headed by a single parent doubled from 11.9 percent in 1970 to 24.3 percent in 1988 (Current Population Survey).

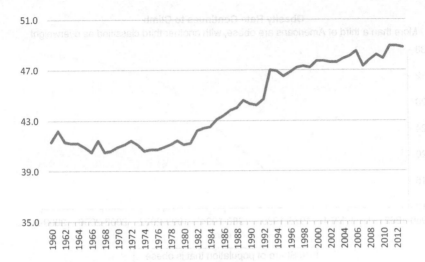

Figure 1.4 Share of family income, top 20 percent.

Source: US Census Bureau.

These economic and social changes, in turn, helped transform the US food system and Americans themselves. With less time and money, the American diet has shifted toward cheap and convenient in the form of fast, processed food, leading to what Eric Schlosser called the *Fast Food Nation* (Schlosser, 2012). Small fast-food joints became big global fast-food chains which required food sources of equal size. Large industrial farms were needed to feed the sugar to Pepsi and Coke and the tomatoes for the 25,000 global pizza locations of Dominos and Pizza Hut (Kaufman, 2012). These changes are not without consequences.

The trends in wages, inequality, and family structure that began in the 1970s have a counterpart in our health. Americans have become increasingly obese, and it is by no means a coincidence that the trend in obesity (Figure 1.5) mirrors the trends in stagnant wages and inequality – economic variables influence obesity (Courtemanche *et al.*, 2015). Obesity is associated with serious health conditions including high blood pressure, Type 2 diabetes, heart disease, stroke, and cancer among others (Center for Disease Control and Prevention, 2015). Obesity also creates significant economic costs in the form of lower productivity and higher medical costs, and it was estimated that widespread obesity increased medical spending in the US by $316 billion in 2010 (Stilwell, 2015).

The US spends more money on healthcare than any other advanced nation, yet it ranks near the bottom among advanced nations in health rankings. A recent report by the National Research Council and Institute of Medicine ranked the US last out of 17 advanced countries, and Americans were in poorer health across the lifespan, from infancy to old age (Rubenstein, 2013). We have more and better healthcare, but the number of Americans reporting they are healthy has dropped

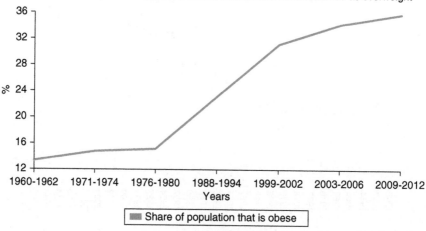

Figure 1.5 US obesity rate (share of population).

Source: Stilwell, 2015. Used with permission of Bloomberg Finance LP.

from 39 percent in 1982 to 28 percent in 2006 (Grabmeier, 2015). In many cases, food is literally killing us:

> Food sickens 48 million Americans a year, with 128,000 hospitalized and 3,000 killed, the Centers for Disease Control and Prevention estimates. The rate of infections linked to foodborne salmonella, which causes the most illnesses and deaths, rose 10 percent from 2006 to 2010.
>
> (Armour *et al.*, 2012)

As more people awaken to the connections between food and health, reactions to the globalized, industrialized, financialized food production system are growing.

In this book we attempt to illuminate some of the main connections between finance and food. In many cases the connections are clear, as in the financialization of commodity markets; in other cases, they are less so, since finance is a broad force which influence many aspects of economic activity. In the next section we outline the path taken in this work.

Outline of the book

The purpose of this work is to describe the ways in which financialization has influenced the US food system; however, as the largest market in the world, the US food system, in turn, influences the global food system. We focus on three primary finance–food connections. First, we described the financialization of commodity futures markets which has transformed food into an asset. Since asset prices are subject to the whims of investors, they are more volatile than goods' prices and are prone to bubbles. The second area of interest, connected to the first, the long-term rise in agriculture commodity prices from the early 2000s to 2012 has increased the value of farmland, and investors in search of yield in the New Normal environment are buying up farmland around the globe. Third, one of the most important agents of change in the financialization regime is the private equity (PE) firm, and the PE industry has fueled a merger and acquisition (M&A) boom through leveraged buyouts (LBO) that has raised corporate debt levels and increased concentration. While private equity deals influence all industries, the food industry has the characteristic that lends itself to takeovers, stable growth that generates steady cash flows.

The food system is a complex organism, and describing the forces that have shaped it over time is no easy task. As a way to incorporate the development of food systems over time into the broader economic framework of accumulation theories, we adopt *food regime theory* (McMichael, 2009). Food regimes are the analogue of regulation and SSA theories, and we introduce this framework in Chapter 2. While food regime theorists identify two clear regimes covering the period from 1850 to 1970, there is less agreement in describing the period that begins with the emergence of neoliberalism (Burch and Lawrence, 2009). For purposes of this work, and as outlined in Chapter 2, we identify the late 1970s to 2000 as the neoliberal regime, and the post-2000 period as the financialization regime.

One of the main goals of Chapter 2 is to formalize the concept of financialization. While Epstein's definition may be cited most often, there are competing definitions, so we survey the literature to identify alternative concepts, then set out definitions of financialization used in this work. In modern heterodox literature financialization is viewed as a negative force which stands in contradistinction to the mainstream view of finance as a benign force. Finance is simply the set of institutions that efficiently allocate capital to promote economic growth. Before we establish a framework of analysis, then, we begin Chapter 2 by evaluating these opposing views of finance, raising a basic question, what is its social purpose?

Chapter 3 "sets the table" for the issues discussed throughout the text. There are three major sections in this chapter: the first section describes the development of the modern global food system within the food regime framework; the second section describes the development of the PE firm; and the third section discusses the functions and workings of modern futures markets. The development of modern food systems is essentially a story of the global wheat market, since wheat is the primary source of labor's *daily bread*. The food regime framework, for the most part, describes the wheat trade during the reign of two hegemonic powers, England and the US. However, globalization of the wheat market cannot take place without the development of institutions which *commodify* food; that is, in order to support the growth of the global wheat trade, wheat had to become a *fungible* commodity, and wheat cannot become fungible without development of the modern futures market. Chapter 3, then, begins with a brief history of the development of modern futures markets, with the details of futures trading, price relationships, and the role of speculation covered in the third section.

Historically, large Wall Street banks were the most important *agent of change* in the US financial sector; however, under financialization, a new agent of change has emerged in the form of the PE firm. The modern PE firm evolved out of the LBO associations that dominated 1980s finance, and the PE industry has been an important influence ever since. Chapter 3 (see section "Food regime III") describes the development, functions, and early influence of the PE industry.

A central tenet of this work is financialization of commodity futures markets allowed speculators to determine the course of short-run prices. How did finance take over the markets? Chapter 4 discusses the *financialization process* that occurred in the commodity futures markets which allowed finance to penetrate, then dominate the market. The financialization process begins with an innovation, the commodity index fund in this case, which allows finance to circumvent regulatory barriers; then, to complete the process, finance uses political influence to codify the innovation through a deregulatory act. As finance encroached on a market previously dominated by the large grain merchants, these corporations reacted by expanding their own financial activities. The behavior of commodity producers and Wall Street banks has become more alike than not.

Based on Masters' data (Figure 1.2), it appears that the link between speculation and commodity prices is clear; however, there is a group of (mainly) academics who stridently argue that speculation did not impact the 2008 price bubble. At the center of contention is the impact of commodity index funds, so we begin Chapter 5 with a look at the "speculation debate" in the world of academia. Much of the debate and discussion in Chapter 5 is focused on the oil and wheat markets, and one reason for this is that the US Senate, prompted by complaints of speculation by commercial interests, investigated both markets for price manipulation. A second motivation will be made clear through a survey of the evidence in the last section of the chapter: financialization of commodity markets has strengthened the connection between oil prices and food commodity prices.

The secular rise in commodity prices from the early 2000s through 2012 created a secondary impact: as the prices of wheat, corn, and soybeans increased, farmland became more valuable, leading to an avalanche of investments into global farmland, or what some have called the "global land grab." Not only are investors gobbling up global farmland, but nation-states, motivated by the 2008 food riots, are investing in foreign farmland in their effort to achieve *food security*. And, as this competition for global farmland increases, the global grain merchants must raise their efforts to secure future sources of supply. In Chapter 6 we discuss motivations behind the global farmland rush, separating the discussion into two sections, one focused on US farmland investments and one focused on global farmland investments.

The PE firm has been an important agent of change in the financialization regime; in fact, the M&A activity driven by PE from 2005 to 2007 has been described as the "golden age" of PE (Reuters, 2007). We begin Chapter 6 by examining PE's influence and impact on food industries under the financialization food regime. While the global financial crisis initially restrained merger and acquisition activity by PE firms, they are back with a vengeance. The escalation in M&A activity is significant, and activity in the food industry is no exception; in fact one of the largest mergers in the past year is 3G Capital's (Heinz) takeover of Kraft Foods. In the New Normal economy, with trillions of dollars chasing yield, and fewer opportunities for productive investment, financial activities take precedence. Despite the large, flashier deals by PE firms like 3G Capital, the majority of food industry M&A activity is being driven from within, as firms attempt to increase market control or gain access to a new market.

In Chapter 7 we look at policy changes related to food and finance. As part of the 2010 Dodd–Frank Act, the Commodity Futures Trading Commission (CFTC) was asked to impose new position limits on speculative trades, but they have yet to be effected some five years later. Will financial traders in commodity markets ever be reined in? US agriculture policy, which historically focused on income and price supports, made a significant change in the 2014 Farm Bill, moving away from income support toward crop insurance programs. We evaluate some of these policy changes in Chapter 7, including some very recent debates over upcoming trade agreements and the US dietary guidelines.

We conclude the book with a look at reactions to the current global food system. At the international level, non-governmental organizations (NGOs) are pressuring global corporations and institutional investors, trying to make them accountable for their actions which influence land grabs and agriculture policies. Millions of small producers and peasant farmers have formed a coalition to take on the vested interests behind industrial agriculture and the global land grab, establishing an alternative in the form of the *food sovereignty* movement. In the US, as we consumers – as we human beings – recognize the destructiveness of the current food system, and its impact on our health and environment, we are turning away from industrially produced food, going back to our roots, and reconnecting directly with producer-farmers. And, as these regional food movements in cities across the US make a dent in the corporate bottom line, corporations are starting to listen.

There are powerful vested interests backing the system: big US agriculture, producing commodities for global markets, is dependent on billions of dollars in government subsidies; and big finance in search of yield continues its expansion into new markets. Is it possible to overcome the power of vested interests? Feeling the pinch in their pocketbooks from these food movements, several food corporations recently announced plans to make their products healthier, so we end this work pondering a question recently debated among food activists and writers, is the food movement winning? More importantly, can food be a galvanizing issue that forms the basis of a broader political movement?

Finally, before turning to the meat of the discussion, a few caveats are in order. Food and finance are very broad topics, so it is difficult to do justice to all aspects. The main purpose of this work is to explain financialization of commodity futures markets and its impact, so much of the discussion on food is focused on the impact from the transformation of futures markets. Relatedly, while the case is made in this work that financial speculation was one of several factors behind the 2008 price bubble, the emphasis on financialization over other factors is not meant to imply it was the most important; it was not. However, in markets dominated by financial traders, it is also difficult to separate the extent to which prices are driven away from fundamentals, and the more dominant finance becomes, the greater the push by the herd.

As the reader will find, oil plays an important role in the speculation debate, and though it may appear at times that there is too much emphasis on this crude market, financialization of commodity markets has strengthened the relationship between oil and food prices. Unlike water and oil, food and oil are now mixed in a world of financialized food. Lastly, much of the discussion, as it unfolds, is chronological. For example, Chapter 3 discusses the developments in food and finance from the mid-nineteenth century through the early 2000s, where the neo-liberal regime ends and the financialization regime begins; whereas, Chapter 6 focuses specifically on the financialization regime of the 2000s. The purpose of this approach, and a goal of this book, is to explain how financialization of commodity markets influenced the upward trajectory in prices during this period; as a consequence, there is little discussion on the current downward trend in commodity prices. It should be clear, though, as OPEC suggests, speculation tends to cause overshooting in both directions (Boyle, 2014).

Bibliography

Armour, S., Lippert, J., and Smith, M.. (2012). Food sickens millions as company-paid checks find it safe. Retrieved May 15, 2015, from http://www.bloomberg.com/news/articles/2012-10-11/food-sickens-millions-as-industry-paid-inspectors-find-it-safe

Better Markets. (2011). Position limits for derivatives. *Comments*. Retrieved October 21, 2014 from https://www.bettermarkets.com/sites/default/files/CFTC%20Position%20Limits%20CL%20As%20Submitted%20Hi%20Res.pdf

Boyle, C. (2014). Oil price falls? Why you should relax: OPEC Head. Retrieved June 21, 2015, from http://www.cnbc.com/id/102163020

Burch, D., and Lawrence, G. (2009). Towards a third food regime: behind the transformation. *Agriculture and Human Values, 26*(4), 267–279.

Center for Diseases Control and Prevention. (2015). The health effects of overweight and obesity. Retrieved June 10, 2015, from http://www.cdc.gov/healthyweight/effects/

Courtemanche, C. J., Pinkston, J. C., Ruhm, C. J., and Wehby, G. (2015). *Can Changing Economic Factors Explain the Rise in Obesity?* (No. w20892). National Bureau of Economic Research.

Current Population Survey, *Living Arrangements of Children Under 18 Years Old: 1960 to Present*. Retrieved May 10, 2015 from: https://www.census.gov/hhes/families/data/children.html

Epstein, G. A. (2005). *Financialization and the World Economy*. Cheltenham: Edward Elgar Publishing.

Grabmeier, J. (2015). Medical expansion has led people worldwide to feel less healthy Retrieved May 2, 2015, from http://www.sciencedaily.com/releases/2015/03/150319104222.html

Gross, W. H. (2009). On the "course" to a new normal. *Investment Outlook*. Retrieved June 1, 2015 from http://www.pimco.com/en/insights/pages/gross%20sept%20on%20the%20course%20to%20a%20new%20normal.aspx

Kaufman, F. (2012). *Bet the Farm: How Food Stopped Being Food*. Hoboken, NJ: John Wiley & Sons.

Kotz, D. M. (2011). Financialization and neoliberalism. In G. Teeple and S. McBride (eds) *Relations of Global Power: Neoliberal Order and Disorder*, 1–18. Toronto: University of Toronto Press.

Masters, M. W. (2008). Testimony before the Committee on Homeland Security and Governmental Affairs. Washington, DC: US Senate, May 20.

McMichael, P. (2009). A food regime genealogy. *The Journal of Peasant Studies, 36*(1), 139–169.

Mishel, L., Gould, E., and Bivens, J. (2015). Wage stagnation in nine charts. Economic Policy Institute, January.

Reuters. (2007). "Golden age" of private equity is behind: Carlyle. Retrieved June 18, 2015, from http://www.reuters.com/article/2007/07/20/us-carlyle-rubenstein-idUSL20 29932520070720

Rubenstein, G. (2013). New health rankings: of 17 nations, U.S. is dead last. *The Atlantic*. Retrieved June 4, 2015 from http://www.theatlantic.com/health/archive/2013/01/new-health-rankings-of-17-nations-us-is-dead-last/267045/

Schlosser, E. (2012). *Fast Food Nation: The Dark Side of the All-American Meal*. New York: Houghton Mifflin Harcourt.

Stilwell, V. (2015). Obesity is hurting the U.S. economy in surprising ways. Retrieved March 7, 2015 from http://www.bloomberg.com/news/articles/2015-03-05/american-economy-has-a-weight-problem-as-costs-of-obesity-mount

2 Financialization

There and back again

The central issue addressed in this book is the financialization of commodity futures markets. Financialization of commodity markets in simplest terms means financial traders dominate trading, so prices behave more like assets than goods. The price of a good is determined by its cost of production, subject to short-term disturbances in supply or demand; the price of an asset is determined by the cash flows it generates, returns from other assets, its diversification properties, and psychological behavior of investors. Asset prices are more volatile and subject to speculative bubbles.

Financialization is a term that has been used increasingly to describe characteristics of the US economy. Much like the term globalization, financialization is an amorphous concept, difficult to put into concrete terms, which is evidenced by the disparate definitions found in the literature. The purpose of this chapter is to define financialization, explain how it will be used in this work, and set out a general framework of analysis for the discussion on the "financialization of food."

Before we can establish the framework used in this work, there are several other issues to address. First, in the mainstream literature, finance is viewed as a positive force that promotes economic growth; however, in the heterodox literature, more often than not, financialization carries a negative connotation, associated with lower growth. Which view is correct? Can finance be both good and bad? Second, in the modern heterodox financialization literature, it is characterized as a relatively recent force used to explain, for example, the current capital accumulation regime. However, the concept of finance as an institutional force of control in capitalism was first introduced by Hilferding (Hilferding and Bottomore, 1990) over one hundred years ago:

> Finance capital signifies the unification of capital. The previously separate spheres of industrial, commercial and bank capital are now brought under the common direction of high finance, in which the masters of industry and of the banks are united in a close personal association. The basis of this association is the elimination of free competition among individual capitalists by the large monopolistic combines. This naturally involves at the same time a change in the relation of the capitalist class to state power.
>
> (p. 301)

Given Hilferding's analysis over one hundred years ago, why did the concept of financialization disappear from the lexicon for nearly 80 years? Was Hilferding simply ignored and forgotten?

In order to understand these issues, we begin the chapter by addressing two questions. First, what is the role of finance in the economy? Is finance a benign force that supports the economic development process, or is it a pernicious force in need of control? Second, why did analysis of finance capital, or what is now called financialization, disappear from the literature? Understanding the reason for its disappearance and reemergence helps answer the first question, and we will answer the question by way of a historical discursion. With this understanding, we then turn to a survey of the modern financialization literature in order to determine how the concept is used and analyzed today, and from this review, we define a framework of analysis for this work.

The role of finance

In modern heterodox literature, financialization has taken on a negative, almost pejorative connotation. Does this suggest that finance is inherently bad? According to one mainstream textbook view:

> History shows that a strong financial system is a necessary ingredient for a growing and prosperous economy. Companies raising capital to finance capital expenditures and investors saving to accumulate funds for future use require well-functioning financial markets and institutions.
>
> (Brigham and Houston, 2013, p. 25)

The main purpose of financial markets and institutions in the mainstream view is to facilitate capital development of nations through allocating and channeling those savings toward productive investment. There are two important caveats here: first, financial markets must be "well-functioning" or efficient; and second, savings is the source of funding productive investment. In addition, Shaw (1973) suggested that financial sector growth could promote economic growth through what he called *financial deepening*, where growth of the financial sector, especially non-bank financial institutions, could promote economic growth by expanding the savings that would support capital formation in developing economies.

One of the important functions of financial markets and instruments, and a primary reason for the development of many financial markets, is risk management. Derivative instruments like futures contracts, options, and swaps were created so that market participants – like farmers and Arab sheiks – could hedge or insure themselves against unexpected and detrimental price changes. Derivative instruments allow commercial participants to transfer price risk to speculators who willingly take on that risk. Despite also carrying a negative connotation, speculators are necessary in derivative markets because they provide additional liquidity in what are characterized as "thin markets."

Let us compare this antiseptic mainstream view with a recent characterization by journalist Matt Taibbi (2009) who described Goldman Sachs (or finance in general) as "a great vampire squid wrapped around the face of humanity, relentlessly jamming its blood funnel into anything that smells of money" (p. 52). Is this simply the ranting of a gonzo journalist, or is there something inherently sinister about finance? In order for us to answer the question there are two interrelated issues we need to discuss. First, are financial institutions passive intermediaries that take in savings and lend those funds for productive investments? Second, are financial markets well-functioning and efficient as required in the mainstream view?

The mainstream view, more appropriately called the "academic" mainstream view, of finance is expressed by the term *financial intermediary*. Financial institutions are viewed as passive intermediaries that take in savings which are then loaned to borrowers in order to fund productive investment. In this view, bank lending is constrained by the savings that flow into institutions in the form of deposits; however, banks can also expand lending if the central bank takes action to increase bank reserves. In the latter case, the central bank expands reserves through buying a (government) security which allows the banking system to increase deposits by a multiple. The money supply, therefore, is viewed as exogenously controlled by the central bank. The growth of credit, and therefore the financial sector, is a function of two variables: one, the decisions of economic agents to save for future consumption; and two, the decision by the central bank to expand bank reserves.

In the alternative heterodox view, banks are described as dynamic profit-seeking enterprises that are given a government "license" to create (bank) money through loan creation. In this view, money is endogenously created by the banking system in response to economic activity. The implication of this endogenous money approach is that credit creation by the financial system is constrained only by the demand for loans. As Minsky (Minsky and Kaufman, 2008) stated, "money is created as bankers go about their business of arranging for the financing of trade, investment, and positions in capital assets" (p. 250). Minsky viewed finance as "a disruptive force that tends to induce and amplify instability even as it is an essential factor if investment and economic growth are to be financed" (pp. 255–256). In this view of finance, the banking system's ability to create money and credit is highly flexible, and it is not constrained by savings; rather, bank financing of investment creates the income and savings ex post. In the heterodox approach, the central bank attempts to constrain credit creation through an interest rate channel, and its most important function is to maintain stability of a highly elastic financial system through the lender of last resort function.

Which view is correct? While the debate over exogenous versus endogenous money dates back to the 1950s, a recent report by the Bank of England (McLeay *et al.*, 2014) concluded:

> In normal times, the central bank does not fix the amount of money in circulation, nor is central bank money 'multiplied up' into more loans and deposits ....
> Although commercial banks create money through lending, they cannot do so

freely without limit. Banks are limited in how much they can lend if they are to remain profitable in a competitive banking system.

(p. 1)

McLeay *et al.* provide support for the view that money is endogenously created, but they also acknowledge that individual banks cannot expand loans without limit, as the viability of a bank in a competitive system depends on creating loans for qualified customers (credit risk) and managing net liquidity flows. Ultimately, monetary policy limits money creation through an interest rate channel that influences loan demand. However, without other restraints, interest rates are a clumsy tool for restraining the credit-creating ability of the banking system.

Certainly the ability to create loans in and of itself does not create instability, rather instability can result if loan creation is not directed toward the proper social purpose of financing productive activities that promote economic growth. If credit creation by the financial system is used to support speculative or unproductive uses over productive uses, instability and mal-investment can result. The issue is best encapsulated by Keynes:

> Speculators may do no harm as bubbles on a steady stream of enterprise. But the position is serious when enterprise becomes the bubble on a whirl-pool of speculation. When the capital development of a country becomes the by-product of the activities of a casino, the job is likely to be ill-done. The measure of success attained by Wall Street, regarded as an institution of which the proper social purpose is to direct new investment into the most profitable channels in terms of future yield, cannot be claimed as one of the outstanding triumphs of *laissez-faire* capitalism – which is not surprising, if I am right in thinking that the best brains of Wall Street have been in fact directed towards a different object.
>
> (Keynes, 2006, p. 159)

In effect, when markets are dominated by speculative financial interests, they are not well-functioning or efficient; rather, they tend to generate greater volatility and a propensity for speculative bubbles, losing their social purpose.[1] In modern financial systems, banks play a special role in that they are given a government charter which allows them to create credit in order to finance productive investment – their proper social purpose. While Keynes described the basis for financial market instability, how do we ensure that finance, the banking system in particular, achieves its proper social purpose?

Hilferding (Hilferding and Bottomore, 1990) argued that finance and its attendant credit system was the mechanism through which capital worked to establish, ironically, a more stable economic environment by creating stable relations among and between oligopolistic corporations. Capitalism was being destroyed by its own regulating mechanism of competition, as the competitive struggle caused prices to decline over time which was the underlying cause of severe contractions in the form of debt deflations. If capitalism was to survive, large corporations required stable markets with stable prices. Finance capital could create stability through establishing controlling relationships over oligopolistic firms, and directing credit toward these large corporations, and away from nascent competitors. While oligopolistic industries controlled by finance created more stability, Hilferding argued that the system would create a greater burden on the working class:

> The more monopolization progresses the greater is the burden which extra profit imposes upon all other classes. The rise in the cost of living brought about by the trusts reduces living standards, and all the more so because the upward trend in food prices increases the cost of the most essential necessities of life.
>
> (pp. 368–369)

The less competitive oligopolistic structure would cause the price of necessities to be higher than those generated in a competitive market, thus creating a burden on workers if wages did not keep up with the cost of essentials. Hilferding concluded this "union of interests" was designed to create stability for the capitalist classes, both productive and financial, but it was to the detriment of the working class.[2]

In the history of economic ideas, Veblen (1978) provided another view of finance as a malevolent force, and he raised important questions about the purpose and efficiency of finance. Veblen was one of the earliest to describe the *capitalization* of physical assets, which allowed physical goods to be sold as representative values, or shares of stock. For Veblen, this form of financialization created a mechanism for the businessman/predator to manipulate financial values for gain. Since competition was constantly driving down prices and profits, one way to counteract falling profits was through manipulation of paper values, allowing businessmen to profit from both rising and falling markets. Capitalization of tangible things into representative paper values allowed financial interests to manipulate the underlying real assets for gain, and Veblen's predator, shunned in communal societies, was naturally attracted to this new form of extracting community wealth.

At the turn of the last century, which characterization of finance was correct? Was the financial system efficiently allocating capital to its highest return? Or, as Hilferding explained, was the financial system used as a mechanism to control competition through credit? Further, as Veblen explained, was finance susceptible to abuse through fraudulent manipulation of paper for gain? Real-world outcomes in the 1920s supported the views of Hilferding and Veblen. In one analysis, Eichengreen and Mitchener (2003) described the *Roaring Twenties* as a bank-financed, debt-fueled speculative bubble. While it is well known that bank-financed purchases of stocks on margin (often as high as 90 percent) fueled the stock market bubble, it is less known that bank lending fueled the economic bubble in other ways. For example, there was a real-estate bubble in the mid-1920s, and banks created the financial innovation of installment debt which helped expand the market for consumer durables. According to Eichengreen and

Mitchener, the 1920s expansion was a classic debt-fueled expansion that led to a great collapse and great depression.

As a result of the financial speculation and stock market crash in October 1929, the Senate launched an investigation into its causes. The outcome of this investigation was a 1934 US Senate report known as the *Pecora Commission Report* (US Senate, 1934). The Pecora report affirmed the views of Hilferding and Veblen, as it described the influence Wall Street banks wielded over large corporations through the formation of trusts and interlocking directorates. Some examples of the control and fraud included Albert Wiggin, president of Chase National Bank, who was listed as a director for 59 different corporations, many of which received favorable financing and were supposedly controlled by an "independent" Chase investment bank. Wiggin was forced to resign after it was discovered during the hearings that he shorted his own bank's stock during the crisis. In another case, Charles Mitchell, president of City National Bank (the precursor of Citibank) was forced to resign after the investigation found he eliminated his income tax liability in 1929 through the use of a loss taken on bank stock sold to his wife (Anonymous, 2010).

As a result of Pecora's ongoing public investigation, Congress passed the 1933 Banking Act, commonly known as the Glass–Steagall Act. In addition to the well-known law separating commercial and investment banking, the act included creation of the Federal Deposit Insurance Corporation (FDIC); creation of Regulation Q, which disallowed payment of interest on demand deposits and put an interest rate ceiling on savings deposits; creation of the Federal Open Market Committee (FOMC) in order to promote an independent monetary policymaking body; and restriction on the use of bank credit for speculative trading or carrying of securities, commodities, and real estate. Two other finance-related legislative acts were the 1934 Securities Exchange Act and the 1936 Commodities Exchange Act which provided oversight over security and commodity markets respectively.

Credit creation is the lifeblood of economies, and most governments have given this responsibility to private interests. Given the flexibility of the banking system, credit creation can easily be abused. The reason financialization disappeared from the lexicon for almost 80 years is because debt-financed speculation, instability, and the fraudulent behavior of bankers that preceded and helped cause the *Great Depression* created a backlash in the form of restrictive regulations. It is not that Hilferding was ignored and/or forgotten, rather banking and finance were severely regulated and constrained. And the result of this regulatory reform? One of the most stable periods of banking in the history of the United States: from 1946 to 1973 (the Bretton Woods era), the number of commercial bank failures averaged 3.8 per year. In comparison, since the first financial deregulatory act in 1980, the number of bank failures has averaged 100 per year (FDIC).

Finance did not go quietly, but the Roosevelt administration had an angry public on its side, fueled by Pecora's public dealings with Wall Street's titans. As Wall Street attempted to fight back and regain power in the late 1930s, Ferdinand Pecora published *Wall Street on Trial* in 1939 (Pecora, 1968), an account of his experiences, and in the preface he provided a premonition of what was to come:

Under the surface of the governmental regulations the same forces that produced the riotous speculative excesses of the wild bull market of 1929 still give evidences of their existence .... It cannot be doubted that, given a suitable opportunity, they would spring back into pernicious activity.

(p. ix)

The return of finance

A confluence of factors created significant economic turmoil in the 1970s: the breakdown of the Bretton Woods exchange rate system, increased global competition from rebuilt Europe and Japan, oil price spikes, and a secular decline in profits would all foster greater volatility and rising inflation. Economic turmoil and crisis created a "suitable opportunity."

Rising inflationary pressure in the 1970s caused market interest rates to rise above the ceilings imposed by Regulation Q, and the banking system began to experience an outflow of funds (*financial disintermediation*), putting strain on bank profitability. Banks responded with financial innovations that helped circumvent interest rate ceilings and subsequently began to push for deregulation. In March 1980, President Jimmy Carter signed the Depository Institutions Deregulation and Monetary Control Act which eliminated the interest rate ceiling on deposits. Over the next twenty years other components of the 1930s financial regulatory regime would be dismantled or eliminated. The Garn–St Germain Act of 1982 allowed Savings & Loans to offer competitive interest rates on savings deposits, expanded their loan portfolios into commercial real estate, and allowed all depository institutions to offer variable rate mortgages. The 1994 Riegle–Neal Act broke down barriers to interstate banking, and the 1999 Gramm–Leach–Bliley Act (GLBA) put an end to Glass–Steagall and the separation of investment and commercial banking. The last major piece of deregulation, to be discussed in greater detail in Chapter 4, was the Commodity Futures Modernization Act of 2000 which deregulated commodity markets.

As described in the Social Structure of Accumulation (SSA) literature, the turbulent 1970s and the concomitant fall in the rate of profit were the driving forces behind the transition from a state-supported accumulation system to one based on neoliberalism (Kotz, 2011). The institutional forces of neoliberalism include market liberalization, the belief in the power of unfettered markets; globalization, characterized by free trade agreements and breaking down barriers to free mobility of capital; and financialization, the reemergence of finance capital.[3]

What precisely is meant by financialization? Lapavitsas (2011) provided a comprehensive survey of the modern literature on financialization and noted that early ideas about the growth and influence of finance were developed in the 1970s by Harry Magdoff and Paul Sweezy, editors of the *Monthly Review*. Similar to the argument made in Baran and Sweezy's *Monopoly Capital* (Baran and Sweezy, 1969), Magdoff and Sweezy argued that the fundamental problem of monopoly capitalism was absorption of the surplus generated by large oligopolistic firms. While *military Keynesianism* was one outlet for the surplus, they argued that another was through the financial sphere, as large corporations began to establish financial subsidiaries which could support productive activities and generate additional profits.

Lapavitsas identified Arrighi (1994) as another early examination of the growing influence of finance. Arrighi analyzed the life-cycle of historical powers, and argued:

> Financialization represents the autumn of the hegemon as productive power declines and the sphere of finance expands. Genoa, the Netherlands, Britain and the USA entered financialization when they lost their prowess in production and trade. In decline, they became lenders, particularly to a younger power that emerged to overtake them.
>
> (As cited in Lapavitsas, 2011, p. 616)

While other strands of thought on financialization can be found during the deregulatory phase of finance from 1980 to 2000, one does not find systematic discussion as a framework of analysis until the late 1990s.[4] The Regulation and Social Structure of Accumulation (SSA) schools emerged in the late 1970s independently deriving frameworks of analysis to explain long periods of capital accumulation. Neoliberalism was viewed as a new accumulation regime, and financilization was one of several characteristics of the forces underlying neoliberalism.

By the late 1990s, financialization as a construct had once again entered the economic lexicon, especially within the heterodox literature. Its reemergence can be identified with the economic turmoil of the 1970s which gave rise to what has been identified as the neoliberal accumulation regime. In this work, we identify the date of its emergence with the first financial deregulatory act in 1980.

Modern definitions of financialization

In the recent literature, there are three complementary definitions of financialization, and they are presented from conceptually broadest to narrowest in scope. At the broadest level, Epstein (2005) states, "Financialization refers to the increasing importance of financial markets, financial motives, financial institutions, and financial elites in the operation of the economy and its governing institutions, both at the national and international level" (p. 3). Epstein's definition, while comprehensive, does not lend itself to operationalizing the concept. Blackburn (2006) tied this broader concept to a micro-level concept, "Financialization can most simply be defined as the growing and systemic power of finance and financial engineering" (p. 39). In this case, financial engineering can include both market- and firm-level financial mechanisms. McNally (2009) also defined financialization in a way that bridges the macro with the micro, and he provides a tangible way to measure the term:

> What the term 'financialization' should capture, in my view, is that set of transformations through which *relations between capitals and between capital*

and wage-labour have been increasingly financialised – that is, increasingly embedded in interest-paying financial transactions. Understanding this enables us to grasp how it is that financial institutions have appropriated ever larger shares of surplus-value.

(p. 56)

McNally's definition suggests that financialization is a process by which innovations are used to expand credit relations allowing finance to capture or capitalize a greater share of the surplus at the expense of workers and non-financial capitalists, and it can be measured by the growth of interest-paying transactions over time.

Krippner (2005) focused on the transformation of non-financial corporations from productive activities toward financial activities, describing financialization "as a pattern of accumulation in which profits accrue primarily through financial channels rather than through trade and commodity production" (p. 174). This suggests that financialization can be encapsulated through the way corporations have expanded their financial activities relative to productive activities.

The narrowest concept of financialization is discussed in the *market for corporate control* literature. Financialization is the change in corporate management incentive structures created to ensure that managers' interests coincide with shareholders' interests. Grabel (1997) incorporated forms of institutional control into what she called the National Financial Complex (NFC), "which refers to the constellation of institutions, practices, sectoral and state relations, and regulations that join a nation's savers, intermediaries and borrowers" (p. 252). The first, an Anglo-American form, is an arrangement where financial intermediation takes place mainly through competitive capital markets and managers are driven to focus on short-term profit goals by active shareholders; in a second, a Euro-Asian form, where corporations are closely aligned with oligopolistic banks, government typically plays a formal role in the guise of industrial policy, and all participants tend to focus on long-term decision-making and profitability.

Based on the definitions found in the literature we will attempt to operationalize the concept for this work. First, in its broadest form, financialization is an over-arching force that transforms nonfinancial corporations and markets. At this macroeconomic level, financialization represents a broad political-economic force that transforms the economy, reorienting it toward increased financial activities. One can measure financialization by variables that capture increased financial activity. In this context, financialization is one of the broad forces underlying the neoliberal regime of accumulation that emerged in the 1970s. Second, a concept that bridges the macro with the micro, financialization is a control mechanism. Specifically, under the Anglo-American NFC, financialization is the process that shapes or "controls" corporate behavior, causing managers to focus on shareholder returns. In this form, financialization influences individual corporate behavior, but as a pervasive force described as an NFC, it influences corporate behavior in general.

Third, at the microeconomic level, financialization is a process that transforms nonfinancial corporations and markets, which increases the level of financial activity. That is, financialization is the process of transforming markets in order to increase financial sector profits, and this process can include innovations which capitalize a greater share of labor and capital income, or innovations that transform physical products into capitalized financial assets.

Evidence of financialization

Before we describe how these forms of financialization are used in this work, we look at some of the evidence that has been used to describe the financialization of the US economy. Krippner (2005) quantified financialization through corporate cash-flow variables. First Krippner found that the ratio of portfolio income (interest, dividend, and realized capital gains) to corporate cash flow was three to five times higher for the 1980s and 1990s than the 1950s and 1960s. The second measure used was the ratio of financial to non-financial profits, which assessed increased financial activity *within* firms, and she found that this ratio changed in a similar manner.

Giovannoni *et al.* (2014) provided evidence on income shares, specifically evaluating the functional share of income. Since 1980, the share of labor income in the US had fallen by 5 percent, and, when one excludes the top 1 percent, labor's share decreased by 15 percent. To explain the cause, Giovannoni (2014) surveyed the functional distribution literature and found three competing theories to explain the decline: technology, trade liberalization, and financialization. Based on the empirical literature review, the evidence suggested that financialization and trade liberalization were the two most important forces of change. In one study cited, which used a sample of 71 countries, financialization (46 percent) and globalization (19 percent) were responsible for the majority of the observed decline in the wage share. Giovannoni (2014) also analyzed data for the US economy, and found that the share of compensation in manufacturing decreased by 14 percent from 1977 to 2007, while the share of the finance, insurance, and real estate (FIRE) sectors increased by 18 percent. Additionally, he stated, had it not been for increased participation of women in the labor force, labor's share of income would have experienced greater deterioration.

Hudson and Bezemer (2012) argued that growth of the FIRE sector is the modern day equivalent of the *rentier*, and financialization of the economy reduces growth and promotes financial bubbles. Along these lines, Epstein and Crotty (2012) posed the question how big is too big (for finance)? They evaluated a combination of balance sheet and profit data, and found:

> The financial sector's total financial assets grew from about one-third of total assets in the U.S. economy during the post-World War II decades to 45 percent of total assets by 2010. The value of the financial sector assets was approximately equal to the U.S. Gross Domestic Product (GDP) in the early 1950s, whereas now it amounts to 4.5 times the U.S. GDP. Financial sector profit has grown from about 10 percent of total domestic profits in the 1950–60s to 40 percent in the early 2000s.
>
> (p. 4)

Their answer to "what level of finance is too big" was

> the financial sector in the United States is extracting 2–4 times as much
> income relative to the services it provides the real sector in the decade of the
> 2000's as it did during the high growth period of the 1960's.
>
> (p. 13)

While their evidence tells us the financial sector is much bigger and garnering a
larger share of income, it does not explain what makes this too big. The financial
sector is bigger; so what?

How has financialization influenced the economy? Regarding the change in the
market for corporate control, Stockhammer (2004) found that, for the US, UK, and
France, the focus on shareholder returns led to a decline in real investment, which
came about from a greater emphasis on financial flows to investors through dividends and stock buybacks. Consistent with the decline in real investment, Palley
(2007) found that financialization was associated with tepid growth and slowdown
in trend. In the case of the US, per capita income averaged 2.2 percent from 1960 to
1979, then declined to 1.9 percent from 1979 to 2004. He also stated that financialization has contributed to income inequality and wage stagnation through decoupling
of wages from productivity gains, and it has increased financial fragility.

Recent empirical analysis from mainstream researchers provides additional
support. The global financial crisis instigated mainstream researchers to raise the
same question: what level is too big? An IMF study (Sahay *et al.*, 2015) provided
one method for answering this important question, focusing more specifically on
two issues: does too much finance impede growth and increase instability? Sahay
et al. evaluated the relationship between finance and growth with data from over
170 countries, and they constructed a Financial Development Index to measure
the depth, access, and efficiency of both financial institutions and markets. The
index was normalized to establish a minimum value of 0 and maximum value of 1.
They found a bell shape or "inverted U" relationship, showing that growth of
finance supported economic growth up to a point; but beyond a certain range,
economic growth slowed as financial development expanded. Specifically, there
is a range along the curve, from 0.5 to 0.7, where expansion of finance transitions
from growth promotion to growth reduction; and beyond the 0.7 level, expansion
of finance unquestionably reduces growth.

Sahay *et al.* also found that increased financial development did not impede
the capital formation process, but it was associated with a decrease in productive
efficiency, or total factor productivity. This is supportive of Giovanni's research,
and is suggestive that excessive financial development promotes bubbles. Capital
formation is the expansion of savings and financial capital, which creates the
potential to increase investment in real capital and boost factor productivity, but it
has not. Rather, the capital "formed" has sought out alternative investment outlets
like real estate and commodities.

Of the factors measured by the index, they found that depth, increased size,
and liquidity of institutions and markets are more closely associated with slower

growth and financial instability, and that an effective, not necessarily larger, regulatory environment could improve growth and stability. One can interpret these findings as, there is a point on the curve (0.7 on their scale) where growth of the financial sector exceeds the ability to fund new productive opportunities, and expansion of finance beyond this point is associated with extractive, rentier capitalism, which reduces growth. The index value for the US was close to 0.8.

Two Bank of International Settlement studies derive similar results. In the first, Cecchetti and Kharroubi (2012), using different measures, also found an inverted U-shape relationship between financial sector growth and economic growth. Over the period from 1980 to 2009, they used the ratio of the "five-year average in private credit growth to GDP" and evaluated its impact on five-year average productivity growth. They found productivity growth is reduced when the private credit ratio exceeds 100 percent of GDP. For the US:

> Where private credit grew to more than 200% of GDP by the time of the financial crisis. Reducing this to a level closer to 100% would, by our estimates, yield a productivity growth gain of more than 150 basis points.
>
> (p. 5)

They constructed a second measure using the five-year average of the financial sector's share of total employment to productivity, and found similar results: the turning point for growth was associated with a financial sector employment level of 3.9 percent of the total. The second paper by Cecchetti and Kharroubi (2015) explained that the decline in productivity and economic growth was due to the financial sector hiring away skilled workers, which created negative externalities for other productive sectors of the economy that rely on those workers. They concluded:

> This evidence, together with recent experience during the financial crisis, leads us to conclude that there is a pressing need to reassess the relationship of finance and real growth in modern economic systems. More finance is definitely not always better.
>
> (Cecchetti and Kharroubi, 2012, p. 14)

To sum up the issues, at the turn of the last century, Hilferding described finance capital as a coordinating mechanism which helped prevent the destructiveness of price competition in oligopolistic industries, and corporations were tied to large banks that controlled competition through control of credit. After the Pecora Commission found financial manipulation by the banking system was a central cause of the speculative stock market frenzy leading to the *Great Depression*, the Roosevelt administration was able to push significant regulatory legislation through Congress which would restrain finance for nearly thirty years. Relative financial calm was the result, and discussions about the power and influence of finance all but disappeared. Economic turbulence during the 1970s created an opportunity for the resurgence of finance. From 1980 to 2000, finance was deregulated, global capital controls were eliminated, and the influence of finance expanded. The result? Finance has captured a growing share of profits at the expense of labor income, and the economy has experienced periodic bubbles, greater volatility, and slower growth. Within heterodox academic research, the result has been a reemergence of analyses concerning the power and influence of finance capital or what we now call financialization of the economy.

Framework of analysis

This book attempts to answer two main questions regarding financialization of food. First, how does financialization of commodity futures markets influence food prices? Second, how has the broader force of financialization influenced US food systems in general? Financialization is a complementary force that emerged within the framework of neoliberalism. To capture Epstein's broad definition of financialization, we use the Social Structure of Accumulation/Regulation theory approach. Regulation and SSA theories categorize capitalism through broad, historical capital accumulation regimes, and there is an analogous concept developed in food systems literature, *food regime* theory. As a framework for describing the historical changes that have occurred in the organization of food systems, we use the food regime approach. According to Kotz (1994), SSA and Regulation theories seek

> to explain long-run patterns of capital accumulation by analyzing the relations between the capital accumulation process and a set of social institutions which affect that process. The central idea of both is that crucial feature of the trajectory of the capital accumulation process, over a long time period, are the product of the supporting role played a set of social institutions.
>
> (p. 86)

Kotz stated that both frameworks have foundations in Marxian long-run accumulation and crisis theories, but SSA theory tends to lean toward Keynesian views about the institutions necessary to support long-term investment decisions made under uncertainty, whereas regulation theory focuses on the Marxian concept of the rate of profit and realization of value. Regarding the latter, regimes or modes of regulation are categorized through either extensive or intensive accumulation. Extensive refers to an accumulation regime that relies on extending a particular accumulation process by expanding a given production technique and hiring more labor to expand markets. Intensive refers to an accumulation regime that relies upon improving a technique, and raising productivity. For example, theorists in both schools suggest that the regime associated with industrialization in the nineteenth century was governed by a competitive process relying on extensive accumulation; a second inter-war regime was associated with intensive accumulation without mass consumption; and a third post-World War II regime, *Fordism*, characterized by intensive accumulation with State-governed institutions supporting mass consumption. SSA and Regulation school theorists have described the regime emerging out of the late 1970s with the neoliberalism moniker, which is characterized by competitive markets, globalization, and financialization, and these forces helped disconnect the wage–productivity relationship established as part of the Fordist regime. Transitions between regimes are characterized by a crisis in the accumulation process, and a new institutional framework emerges to support the next regime. While there are differences in approaches, for brevity's sake, we use the SSA acronym when discussing capital accumulation regimes.

Food regime theory categorizes the development of global food systems into regimes that are, for the most part, analogous to the periods of capitalist development defined by SSA theory. Friedmann (1993) defined a food regime as "a rule-governed structure of production and consumption of food on a world scale" (pp. 30–31). The first food regime (1850–1910) is associated with the competitive era of industrialization and colonization which served to support an extensive accumulation process through providing England, and the rest of Europe, with cheap agriculture products which reduced subsistence wages paid to the industrial army of labor; and the second food regime (1950–1970) describes the post-World War II era, which was dominated by the US through its food aid policy (McMichael, 2009). There is some controversy over characterizations of the current food regime, and some researchers have described it as neoliberalism, though regulated by financial forces (Burch and Lawrence, 2009). In fact, Burch and Lawrence argued that an alternative financialization regime has emerged, where finance capital has increasingly influenced the agri-food system. Their view is partially consistent with the argument made in this work, which defines the period from 1980 to 2000 as the neoliberal food regime, and the post-2000 period as the financialization food regime. Chapter 3 describes the development of US and global food systems within the framework of food regime theory, focusing on the period from 1850 to 2000. Chapter 6 focuses on the financialization regime in the post-2000 period.

Where Hilferding focused on the unification of monopolized industries through the control of large banks, the most dynamic force – the *agent of change* – in the modern era of financialization has been the private equity firm. Leveraged buyouts and the emergence of private equity firms have changed corporate structure and behavior through emphasis on maximization of shareholder value and returns. Twenty-five years ago, Jensen (1997) predicted that the leveraged buyout association, what we now call private equity (PE) firms, would be the end of publicly held corporations in many industries. In fact, Jensen waxed nostalgic that the changes PE would bring about represented:

> Rediscovering the role played by active investors prior to 1940, when Wall Street banks such as J.P. Morgan and Co. were directly involved in the strategy and governance of the public corporations they helped create . . . Morgan and his small group of partners served on the boards of U.S. Steel, International Harvester, First National Bank of New York, and host of railroads, and were a powerful management force in these and other companies.
>
> (Jensen, 1997, p. 7)

Private equity is the agent of change in the Anglo-American NFC. Applebaum and Batt (2014) described the emergence and transition from the old management-controlled regime to the new financial-dominated firm:

> The shareholder-value model of business organization and management emerged and prospered during the 1970s and 1980s owing to transformative changes in the governance of the American corporation. Declines in financial and labor market regulations created a new regulatory regime. The rise of institutional investors, the formation of new financial engineering strategies and intermediaries, and the activist elaboration of academic theories combined to provide the institutional opportunity structure for Wall Street to replace the management-controlled firm with the finance-controlled firm.
>
> (p. 28)

The private equity firm emerged in the 1980s in the form of the leveraged buyout, and its influence during the 1980s is covered in Chapter 3. The post-2000 period has been described as the *golden era* of private equity, and the influence of PE during this financialization food regime era is discussed in Chapter 6.

In defining the forms of financialization, at the micro level, financialization is a process that transforms markets. The *financialization process*, then, we define as a process that breaks down barriers to entry, and allows finance to penetrate new markets to enhance or maintain profits. Chapter 4 discusses the financialization process that took place in commodity futures markets. The financialization process can be generalized, and the last section of this chapter provides some historical examples.

The framework of analysis then begins with the framework of SSA and food regime theory as a way to characterize long periods of development. Financialization emerges as one of several forces within the neoliberal accumulation regime, and we initially discuss financialization within this framework; however, as we will argue, after 2000, financialization became the dominant force in the economy, and this is expressed by the financialization process that took place in commodity futures markets and the influence of private equity firms on US and global food systems. We define and describe the financialization process in the last section of this chapter.

The financialization process

The financialization process describes the mechanism by which finance breaks down barriers to penetrate new markets in order to increase profits. The financialization process includes two phases: in phase one a financial innovation creates a mechanism to circumvent *barriers to entry* (regulations) or create new profit-generating products; in phase two, political influence is used to legitimize or legalize the innovations, which are then codified through an act of Congress. Examples of the financialization process include the effort to circumvent Regulation Q, interest rate ceilings, and the process that broke down the wall separating commercial and investment banking codified in the Glass–Steagall Act.

The first act of financial deregulation was a consequence of rising inflation in the 1970s which caused market interest rates to exceed the interest rate ceiling on savings deposits imposed by Regulation Q. While interest rate ceilings on savings accounts were raised, demand deposits were not. To counteract the loss of deposits to market-based instruments like Money Market Funds, savings banks in the northeast began to allow limited check-writing on savings accounts, known as Negotiable Ordered Withdrawal (NOW) accounts. Automatic Transfer from Savings (ATS) accounts were created by banks to automatically shift funds from interest bearing savings accounts into checking accounts when needed. The interest cap on savings accounts was phased out by the Depository Institutions Deregulation and Monetary Control Act of 1980.[5] The financialization process in this example was instigated as a response to loss of profits due to financial disintermediation, so innovations were designed to maintain market share and compete with non-regulated market-rate instruments held outside of the formal banking system.

A second example was the process that led to breakdown of the Glass–Steagall Act. Beginning in the 1980s, the banking industry was lobbying to eliminate the restriction between banking and commerce. According to Omarova (2013), bank lobbying efforts caused the Federal Reserve Board to relax restrictions, allowing subsidiaries of bank holding companies (BHC) "to underwrite securities, as long as these activities generated no more than five percent of such subsidiaries' revenues. By 1996, the Board increased the revenue ceiling to twenty-five percent, thus allowing many BHCs to acquire regional investment banking firms" (p. 279).

In April 1998, Citigroup announced a merger with Traveller's Insurance Group which had recently purchased the investment bank/financial services firm Salomon Smith Barney. However, given restrictions of the Glass–Steagall and Bank Holding Company Acts, Traveller's CEO Weill and Citigroup CEO Reed had to first meet with Federal Reserve Chairman Alan Greenspan for approval. Greenspan gave approval, with the following caveat:

> Unless Congress changed the laws and relaxed the restrictions, Citigroup would have two years to divest itself of the Travelers insurance business (with the possibility of three one-year extensions granted by the Fed) and any other part of the business that did not conform with the regulations. Citigroup was prepared to make that promise on the assumption that Congress would finally change the law – something it had been trying to do for 20 years – before the company would have to divest itself of anything.
>
> (National Public Radio, 2003)

For the next two years the financial industry intensely lobbied Congress to repeal Glass–Steagall, and their efforts were rewarded when President Bill Clinton signed the Financial Services Modernization Act in November 1999, commonly known as the Gramm–Leach–Bliley Act (GLBA). It is somewhat ironic that former (and now retired) CEO John Reed recently argued for reinstatement of

Glass–Steagall, citing the "clash of cultures" between investment banking and commercial banking (Authers, 2013).

Chapter 4 describes the financialization process that took place in the commodity futures markets. Deregulation of commodity markets was effected through the Commodity Futures Modernization Act (CFMA) of 2000, but, as we shall find, the GLBA also played an important part in financialization of commodities by allowing financial firms to engage in the physical trading of commodities. Before we discuss the financialization process, some background information on food and finance is necessary for the ensuing discussions throughout this book. In the next chapter we "set the table" with an overview of the development of the US food system, and a discussion of the development, operation, and functions of modern futures markets.

Notes

1 Behavioral finance explains how financial markets are often inefficient due to irrational investor actions, such as herd behavior related to momentum investment strategies.
2 Veblen (1978) described the collusive behavior behind price stability as "the great union of interests."
3 While some associate the neoliberal era with the elections of conservatives Ronald Reagan and Margaret Thatcher, the rise of these forces is really apolitical, as the first financial deregulatory act was signed by Jimmy Carter in 1980, and Bill Clinton pushed for and signed the North American Free Trade Agreement (NAFTA).
4 Lapavitsas (2011) mentions a 2001 issue of the journal *Economy and Society*, which devoted the issue to articles on financialization, as the beginning of systematic analyses the topic.
5 The interest ceiling on demand deposits would not be formally eliminated until 2011.

Bibliography

Anonymous. (June 2010). When Washington took on Wall Street. *Vanity Fair*, Issue 598, *156*.
Appelbaum, E., and Batt, R. (2014). *Private Equity at Work: When Wall Street Manages Main Street*. New York: Russell Sage Foundation.
Arrighi, G. (1994). *The Long Twentieth Century: Money, Power, and the Origins of Our Times*. New York: Verso.
Authers, J. (2013, September 8, 2013). Culture clash means banks must split, says former Citi chief. *Financial Times*.
Baran, P. A., and Sweezy, P. M. (1969). *Monopoly Capital*. New York: Monthly Review Press.
Blackburn, R. (2006). Finance's fourth dimension. *New Left Review, 39*, 39.
Brigham, E. F., and Houston, J. F. (2013). *Fundamentals of Financial Management*, 13th edition. Mason, OH: South-Western.
Burch, D., and Lawrence, G. (2009). Towards a third food regime: behind the transformation. *Agriculture and Human Values, 26*(4), 267–279.
Cecchetti, S. G., and Kharroubi, E. (2012). Reassessing the impact of finance on growth. BIS Working Paper No. 381. Retrieved June 12, 2015 from http://ssrn.com/abstract=2117753

Cecchetti, S. G., and Kharroubi, E. (2015). Why does financial sector growth crowd out real economic growth? BIS Working Paper No. 490. Retrieved June 18, 2015 from http://ssrn.com/abstract=2564267

Eichengreen, B., and Mitchener, K. (2003). The great depression as a credit boom gone wrong. BIS Working Paper No. 137.

Epstein, G. A. (2005). *Financialization and the World Economy*. Cheltenham: Edward Elgar Publishing.

Epstein, G., and Crotty, J. (2012). How big is too big? On the social efficiency of the financial sector in the United States. Paper presented at the INET conference, Berlin. Available at www. ineteconomics. org.

FDIC. Bank data and statistics. Retrieved October 23, 2014 from: https://www.fdic.gov/ bank/individual/failed/

Friedmann, H. (1993). The political economy of food: a global crisis. *New Left Review*, (197), 29–57.

Giovannoni, O. G. (2014). What do we know about the labor share and the profit share? Part I: Theories. Levy Economics Institute at Bard College Working Paper (803).

Giovannoni, O. G., Lu, L., Nguyen, D. L., and Xu, A. J. (2014). What do we know about the labor share and the profit share? Part II: Empirical studies. Levy Economics Institute at Bard College Working Paper (804).

Grabel, I. (1997). Savings, investment and functional efficiency: a comparative examination of national financial complexes. *The Macroeconomics of Saving, Finance, and Investment*. Ann Arbor: University of Michigan Press.

Hilferding, R., and Bottomore, T. B. (1990). *Finance Capital: A Study in the Latest Phase of Capitalist Development*. London: Routledge.

Hudson, M., and Bezemer, D. (2012). Incorporating the rentier sectors into a financial model. *World Economic Review, 1*(1), 1–12.

Jensen, M. C. (1997). Eclipse of the public corporation. *Harvard Business Review* (Sept.-Oct. 1989), 67(5), 61–74, revised.

Keynes, J. M. (2006). *General Theory of Employment, Interest and Money*. New Delhi: Atlantic Publishers & Dist.

Kotz, D. M. (1994). The regulation theory and the social structure of accumulation approach. In D. M. Kotz, T. McDonough, and M. Reich (eds) *Social Structures of Accumulation: The Political Economy of Growth and Crisis*, 85–97. New York: Cambridge University Press.

Kotz, D. M. (2010). Financialization and neoliberalism. In G. Teeple and S. McBride (eds) *Relations of Global Power: Neoliberal Order and Disorder*, 1–18. Toronto: University of Toronto Press.

Krippner, G. R. (2005). The financialization of the American economy. *Socio-Economic Review, 3*(2), 173–208.

Lapavitsas, C. (2011). Theorizing financialization. *Work, Employment & Society, 25*(4), 611–626.

McLeay, M., Radia, A., and Thomas, R. (2014). Money creation in the modern economy. *Bank of England Quarterly Bulletin*, Q1, 14–22.

McMichael, P. (2009). A food regime genealogy. *The Journal of Peasant Studies, 36*(1), 139–169.

McNally, D. (2009). From financial crisis to world-slump: Accumulation, financialization, and the global slowdown. *Historical Materialism, 17*(2), 35–83.

Minsky, H. P., and Kaufman, H. (2008). *Stabilizing an Unstable Economy* (Vol. 1). New York: McGraw-Hill.

National Public Radio. (2003). The long demise of Glass-Steagall. Retrieved October 21, 2014 from http://www.pbs.org/wgbh/pages/frontline/shows/wallstreet/weill/demise.html.

Omarova, S. T. (2013). The merchants of Wall Street: banking, commerce, and commodities. *Minnesota Law Review, 98*(1), 266–355.

Palley, T. I. (2007). Financialization: what it is and why it matters. Political Economy Research Institute Amherst, Working Paper No. 153.

Pecora, F. (1968). *Wall Street Under Oath*. London: Cresset Press.

Sahay, R., Čihák, M., Papa N'Diaye, A., Barajas, R. B., Ayala, D., Gao, Y. *et al.* (2015). *Rethinking Financial Deepening: Stability and Growth in Emerging Markets.* International Monetary Fund.

Shaw, E. S. (1973). *Financial Deepening in Economic Development* (Vol. 270). New York: Oxford University Press.

Stockhammer, E. (2004). Financialization and the slowdown of accumulation. *Cambridge Journal of Economics, 28*(5), 719–741.

Taibbi, M. (2009). The great American bubble machine. *Rolling Stone*, July 9, 52–61 and 98–101.

US Senate, Committee on Banking and Currency (1934). *Stock Exchange Practices* (1455). Retrieved October 23, 2015 from http://www.senate.gov/artandhistory/history/common/investigations/pdf/Pecora_FinalReport.pdf.

Veblen, T. (1978). *The Theory of Business Enterprise*. New Brunswick, NJ: Transaction Publishers.

3   Setting the table

To "set the table" for the main issues covered in this work, we need to provide some background on the development of global food markets. While we do not want to regurgitate a detailed history, it is necessary to briefly describe some of the forces that helped shape the modern global food systems. As outlined in Chapter 2, the discussion is framed within food regime theory as it provides a broad framework to describe changes in global food markets similar to capitalist accumulation regimes used in the SSA approach. In addition to summarizing the factors that shaped the modern food system, background is needed on the financial elements described throughout the book, namely development of modern futures markets and the private equity firm. The discussions in this chapter provide the foundation for material discussed in the remainder of the book.

Food regime theory identified two distinct historical periods of development: the first regime, from 1870 to 1930, was associated with industrialization and colonialism during Great Britain's reign as hegemonic power; the second, from 1950 to the early 1970s, associated with the rise of the US as hegemonic power and global markets were shaped by US food aid policy (McMichael, 2009). Food regime theorists are currently debating how to characterize a third regime that emerged along with neoliberalism in the early 1980s (Burch and Lawrence, 2009).

As Marx (1977) argued, profit-motivated capital accumulation is the driving force of capitalism. Labor power is the primary variable ingredient in capitalist reproduction, and food is the primary ingredient necessary for reproduction of labor power. Classical political economists were clear on the relationship between accumulation, wages, and food. Ricardo (Ricardo and Hartwell, 1971) was explicit in the connection, "profits depend on high or low wages, wages on the price of necessaries, and the price of necessaries chiefly on the price of food" (p. 71). Marx was equally clear that wages were subservient to capital, "the rate of accumulation is the independent, not the dependent, variable; the rate of wages, the dependent, not the independent, variable" (Marx 1977, p. 620). Profits drive the accumulation process, a high rate of profit depends upon keeping wages low, and wages are determined by the cost of subsistence, or labor's *daily bread*. Wages could only be pushed as low as the cost of labor's daily bread (and beer).

Since wheat was the primary source of subsistence, early development of the global food system, for the most part, coincided with development of the global wheat market. However, an important ingredient necessary for the development of national and global wheat markets was the complementary development of a financial institution that could facilitate extensive trade in wheat. That is, expansion of markets required the development of institutions that could transform wheat into a *fungible* commodity, one that is uniform and tradable. Futures markets are what transformed food into fungible commodities, so the growth and development of national and international grain markets could not occur until these financial institutions were created. Therefore, we begin the chapter with a discussion of the development of modern futures markets, with a focus on the first futures market organized in the US, the Chicago Board of Trade (CBOT).

Fungible food

Given the expanse and fertility of the soil, immigrant farmers in the US easily produced surplus output which they would transport to emerging urban centers for sale, or sell to traders who would ship the produce to eastern urban areas. Prior to the railroad, trading centers naturally arose along the main river ways and Great Lakes. With the opening of the Erie Canal in 1825, Buffalo, New York became the main hub for the export of immigrants west and the import of grain shipments east. In 1838, the steamer Great Western became the first ship to carry wheat from Chicago to Buffalo (Lewis and Brendon, 2003). As the Chicago wheat trade expanded, merchants realized the need for a formal trading center and the CBOT was formed in 1848. Trade grew rapidly, and the exchange was formally granted a charter by the state legislature in 1859 which allowed it to become a self-governing, member-owned institution.

As Midwest farmers brought their wheat to Chicago in mid-to-late summer, prices would be driven down by the glut of output, and much of it could not be sold. Rather than carting it home, farmers would simply dump the grain in Lake Michigan. This mismatch between supply and demand led to the first major development toward modern futures market, the creation of *to arrive* contracts in 1851. These contracts guaranteed farmers a given price for delivery of grain any time of the year; however, this new sale and delivery arrangement created another problem. To arrive contracts stated a given quantity was to be delivered, but not quality, so farmers and storage merchants would often deliver low-quality product to fulfill contracts. As a result, CBOT traders began to *grade out* the grains as early as 1858, and formally established contracts of a given quantity and quality to be delivered. Receipts designating a given quantity and quality of wheat meant warehouses no longer had to store grains by ownership, so wheat could be stored and shipped in bulk. It was not long before the receipts themselves were traded, and with the development of a highly liquid market for *paper wheat*, the transformation of wheat into a fungible commodity was complete. Tradable grain receipts were also acceptable as collateral by bankers, which provided farmers with a source capital.

Historians disagree on when modern futures markets started. The to arrive contracts were not yet equivalent to modern day futures contracts; and two other developments were needed to before they were equivalent. The first occurred during the US Civil War, when the Union quatermaster took control of the CBOT wheat market and procured wheat with contracts that postponed delivery until they were needed:

> These contracts created a market in "seller's" or "buyer's" options for the future delivery of commodities. Delivery before a date was "optional" because of the risks of transporting commodities to Chicago. Speculative purchases and sales of commodities were also inspired by these options. Regulations governing them were published by the Board of Trade in October 1865. These crude seller's or buyer's options evolved into "futures" contracts by the end of the 1870s.
>
> (Gregory, 2005, para. 5)

Second, in 1865 the CBOT began the first *clearing operation* requiring traders to post *performance bonds*, or margin accounts held by the exchange. The final piece was added in 1877, when the CBOT formally began publishing prices of its contracts (CMEGroup, 2015). As will be discussed in greater detail, the characteristics of modern futures contracts include margin accounts, publicly published prices, and traders have the ability to opt out of delivery on contracts.

The development of the Chicago Board of Trade facilitated growth of the wheat market by creating a fungible commodity. Futures contracts allowed farmers to hedge price risk, and production increased knowing there was always a price and market for grain throughout the year. Wheat and other grains (corn and oats were traded beginning in 1859) had become "goods," not unlike any other reproducible good created to generate revenue. As Morgan (2000) noted, "The grain exchanges that existed by the end of the century in Winnipeg, New York, Buenos Aires, and many European cities were a sign that the grain business was achieving a global organization and integration" (p. 60). The expansion of liquid markets for tradable receipts attracted "additional capital," and, as Veblen (1978) noted, once a physical good is *capitalized* into a tradable financial asset, it soon attracts the interest of financial traders. The last section of this chapter expands upon the function and mechanics of modern futures markets, including a discussion of the role and regulation of speculators.

Food regime I: Industrialization, 1850–1910

Historically, the global grain trade was driven by the need of empires to feed armies. With the movement of populations into large urban centers during the industrial revolution, a similar revolution was required in grain production and trade to supply the daily bread for a growing "industrial army" of labor. British policy in the early nineteenth century, however, was firmly entrenched in mercantilist philosophy which focused on protecting home industries and was supported by the vested interests of the landed aristocracy.

Mercantilism was epitomized through the *Corn Laws*, enacted in 1815 to place tariffs on imported wheat.[1] David Ricardo would lead the assault against mercantilist philosophy, using the logic underlying his *Corn model*. Ricardo argued that a growing population required cultivation of less fertile land, and diminishing returns from land of lesser quality increased the price of corn, increasing money wages, thus reducing profits. A second prong in his attack was the theory of *comparative advantage*, which explained that all nations gained from trade as long as their relative costs differed. A generation after his death in 1823, the Corn Laws would be repealed (in 1846) and Britain would adopt *laissez faire* free-trade policies.

Free trade would benefit Britain in two ways: first, cheap imports of wheat reduced the cost of wages by decreasing the cost of subsistence; second, it created new markets for its goods. The rapid development of the global wheat trade was a direct consequence of Britain adopting free-trade policies. The first food regime encompassed the era of the global wheat trade tied to feeding Britain's industrial army through its colonial relationships. In the SSA framework, the first food regime could be characterized by extensive capital accumulation, and growth under industrial capitalism required a large army of labor, which required an industrial-sized grain trade to provide that army's daily bread.

Morgan (2000) chronicled a history of the world's five great grain merchants that dominated the grain markets of the late nineteenth and early twentieth centuries. The trading houses of Andres, Bunge, Cargill, Continental, and Louis Dreyfus emerged in the mid-nineteenth century, and they would develop the global infrastructure that ensured their dominance of the world grain trade a century later.

The European trading houses sprouted from the grain trade that brought Russian and Eastern European wheat to Europe via the Rhine River. Charles Bunge's grain trading business began in Antwerp in 1859, but its significant growth came after son Ernesto moved operations to Argentina in 1876; George Andre founded the company bearing his name in Switzerland in 1877; Leopold Louis Dreyfus began trading out of Switzerland in 1852; Continental was founded in 1813 by the Fribourg family in Arlon, Belgium, but grain would not become a major focus until it moved to Antwerp in the 1850s (Morgan, 2000).

Cargill, now the world's largest grain merchant, is currently celebrating the 150th year since Scottish immigrant William Cargill bought his first grain elevators along a major railroad route in 1865. When William Cargill died in 1909, the company was over-indebted and struggled to survive, but son-in-law John McMillan turned it around, and created the foundation for the powerhouse company it is to this day.

The history and growth of these first transnational firms goes hand in hand with the history of the wheat trade developed to meet the needs of Great Britain and other industrializing nations of Europe. By the turn of the new century, wheat shipments were flowing into British harbors from Argentina and Australia in spring, Africa and India in early summer, and from Russia and America in late summer. The rapid growth of the wheat trade, necessary to feed a growing industrialized labor force, was facilitated by technological improvements in seed breeding, production, storage, and transportation. Jethro Tull's seed drill (1701),

McCormick's mechanical reaper (1831), and John Deere's steel plow (1837) increased wheat productivity dramatically in the nineteenth century: "In 1837 it took 148 man-hours to plant, cultivate, and harvest an acre of wheat; in 1890, it was down to only 37 hours" (Morgan 2000, p. 47).

An important development for the US market was the introduction of seeds that were suitable for the North American climate. Wheat has three defining characteristics: the season it is grown – winter or spring; the color – red, white, and amber (known as durum); and the texture of the ripened grain – hard or soft. Hard winter wheat has the highest gluten content which is best suited for bread, whereas soft wheat with lower gluten content is typically used for cookies, cakes, and pastas. Gluten – the protein power in wheat – combined with yeast is what gives rise to bread, and bread made with high gluten wheat has a longer shelf life, making it more profitable. Strands of hard red wheat first arrived in the US around 1880, and Hard Red Winter (HRW) wheat was prized in bread-making for its gluten content; the global demand for this variety helped establish Minneapolis, Minnesota as a major grain trading and processing center.

The nature of the global wheat market meant the grain companies' operations had to span nations, as their core business was buying in surplus markets, then transporting and selling in deficit markets, mainly the industrial powers of Europe. Toward the end of the nineteenth century, these companies expanded market power by vertically integrating and creating monopolies in the storing, milling, and transportation of the major grain crops. While price changes certainly influenced profitability, volume was more important, as much of their revenue was generated by the logistical elements of trade – they profited whether prices were high or low.

Wars, revolution, and depression created significant change in the global wheat trade. The *communist revolution* and world wars would end Russia's influence in the global wheat markets for the next one hundred years, and India, an early source of British grain, was forced to focus on domestic needs to meet its rapidly growing population. These developments meant the Americas would be the focal point of the twentieth-century global grain trade. A new food regime would emerge along with the emergence of the US as the new hegemonic power.

One of the characteristic of the second food regime was an expanded role for government in agriculture policy:

> The Depression forced governments all over the world to change course radically. And the 1930s marked a turning away from seventy-five years of a light government hand in the grain economies. It was a decade that saw more governmental intervention in the grain trade than there had been since the repeal of the British Corn Laws in 1846. The decade produced the New Deal farm programs; the Canadian Wheat Board, a quasi-government monopoly that replaced many functions of the private grain trade; comparable government boards in France, Norway, Italy, and the Netherlands .... The United States came out of the 1930s conditioned to farm price supports, wheat export

subsidies, and farm programs that regulated the amount of acreage planted to certain crops.

(Morgan 2000, p. 78)

Food regime II: The age of surplus, 1950–1970

Regulation theory described the post-war accumulation regime as Fordist, an accumulation process regulated by the state via *Keynesian demand management* policies, but also one characterized through the *compact* between capital and labor that tied wage increases to productivity gains. Capitalism had entered a new stage, one that created a surplus of output, and it would need to develop new institutions to manage the accumulation process.

The second food regime has been described as US centric, with global trade dominated by US food aid programs used as a geo-political weapon (McMichael, 2009). After World War II, US wheat output was significantly greater than domestic needs, and price support programs enacted in the 1930s, which created incentives for farmers to produce as much as possible, led to significant surpluses of wheat and other grains. The post-war food regime was one focused on state influence, and it became explicit US government policy to create and support export markets for its agriculture commodities. A symbiotic relationship was forged between government, through the USDA, and the grain merchants that controlled the US grain trade: "By the end of World War II, a period during which government and food producers worked together in the national interest, farmers and food producers had come to view USDA as *their* department and its secretary as *their* spokesman" (Nestle, 2013, p. 97).

The US food aid regime was facilitated through Public Law 480 passed in 1954 to allow exports of surplus agriculture to nations "friendly" to the US. Purchases were often financed with loans which could be paid back in the importing nation's currency, so many of these transactions effectively became outright grants since the US Treasury rarely utilized the currencies of poorer countries. In the 1960s, the Kennedy administration ramped up food aid with its *food for peace* program. Food aid programs were complemented with a tacit US strategy to "convert" countries to western-style diets:

> To strategists at the USDA, Cargill, and Continental, the solution to the surplus problem was self-evident. It was to get people in other countries to eat the way Americans did. A global economy in which millions of rice-eaters in Asia were converted to wheat bread was on that absorbed some of the perennial U.S. wheat surpluses. And a food system in which affluent countries bought billions of dollars of U.S corn and soybeans to feed their beef, hogs, and poultry every year was one that helped the American balance of payments and trade.
>
> (Morgan 2000, p. 99)

Another significant event in the 1960s that had shaped global agriculture was the *Green Revolution*. Biologist Norman Borlaug created a hybrid wheat seed that yielded three times as much as any current seed, which dramatically increased grain output in a world already characterized by excess supply. One problem with the hybrid seeds, though, was that the traits did not carry over to the next generation, so new seeds had to be purchased each growing season. A market for seeds was created that would eventually entice pharmaceutical and chemical companies into the seed engineering business.

Despite the perceived relative calm and stability of the US-dominated global economy and food regime of the 1950s and 1960s, instability was brewing. As a consequence of increased global competition, the breakdown of the Bretton Woods exchange rate system, and the first OPEC oil embargo, an accumulation crisis emerged in the early 1970s. Combined with Russian wheat deals that significantly reduced government stockpiles, commodity prices spiked in the early 1970s, and a period of increased price volatility ensued.

US farm policy was also changing. President Nixon's Agriculture Secretary Earl Butz was encouraging farmers to "get big or get out." Butz also urged farmers to grow global commodity crops and mechanize, because he believed bigger and more capital-intensive farms would reduce the need for farm support programs. Farmers certainly heeded the call, and high commodity prices in the 1970s supported debt-financed land acquisitions. However, when the Federal Reserve raised interest rates in 1981, a recession combined with declining export markets for grain, created the *1980s farm crisis*, which would lead to increased consolidation of the US farm sector. Crises and volatility are the forces that lead to the emergence of new accumulation regimes.

Food regime III: Neoliberalism and private equity

Within food regime theory, there is debate regarding how to characterize the institutional arrangements associated with the regulation regime that emerged out of the turbulence of the 1970s. What are the defining characteristics that describe the capital accumulation process and food system since 1980? McMichael described the system that emerged as a *corporate* food regime, "an ordering of the world food economy that combines state power, the price weapon, and corporate sourcing strategies" (McMichael and Patel, 2009, p. 16). Burch and Lawrence (2009), among others, have used neoliberalism to describe the system, but more recently have suggested that the current food regime is more accurately described by financialization.

As discussed, we use neoliberalism to describe the institutional structures that define the capital accumulation (and food) regime in existence since 1980. Neoliberalism incorporates market liberalization, trade liberalization (globalization), and financialization, all of the forces at work since 1980. The institutional arrangements that have dominated capital accumulation since 2000 are characterized by financialization. The remainder of this section discusses some changes in the US food system during the neoliberalism period, and Chapter 6 discusses changes that occurred during the period of financialization. Private equity firms that use leveraged buyouts (LBOs) in takeovers were dominant agents of change in the neoliberal and financialization regimes, and we discuss the emergence of this transformational force in the next section.

Private equity

Historically in the US the large Wall Street investment banking houses were the primary agents of change, especially with respect to the financialization process that broke down barriers for finance. However, in the age of financialization, a relatively new financial force has emerged in the form of the private equity firm. As the financialization process was breaking down old barriers, the pivotal event that signaled the rise and power of finance as a new regulatory force in accumulation was the hostile takeover engineered through LBO firms. In the early 1980s, Kohlberg, Kravis, and Roberts (KKR) began perfecting *the art of the deal*, and many of the takeovers were financed through funds raised by Michael Milken's firm Drexel Burnham Lambert. Milken raised a pool of funds used to fund takeovers by issuing low-grade debt instruments, or what are now commonly known as *junk bonds*. Milken himself viewed the development of junk bonds as helping break the financial monopoly of Wall Street financiers:

> As late as the 1960s, access to financial capital was controlled by relatively few bankers who dispensed it to privileged clients – a few hundred corporations with an investment-grade rating. Such companies, whose managements were almost all male, white, and part of the Establishment, were considered safe. This institutionalized the denial of capital to many entrepreneurs with great business ideas. Among its victims were minorities and women.

> Financial technology, including the prudent use of non-investment-grade debt and many other securities types, helped right that wrong. In the 1970s public and private markets started to replace banks and insurance companies as the main capital source. The results were revolutionary: From 1970 to 2000, these "junk" companies created 62 million net new jobs in America even as the large "investment-grade" businesses contracted by 4 million employees. The growing flexibility of the capital markets allowed many companies to recapitalize during the most recent economic downturn, proving once again that capital structure matters.

> (Milken, 2014)

Hilferding would have been proud. LBOs financed with junk bonds epitomized what Grabel (1997) described as the Anglo-American National Financial Complex. Certainly, this institutional arrangement was not created in some Machiavellian fashion; rather it was spawned by individual actors like Milken, Carl Icahn, and firms like KKR. The profits made by these early pioneers of LBOs and hostile takeovers laid the groundwork for the creation and development of what we know as the private equity (PE) firm, the institutional agent of change in the Anglo-American NFC model.

In 1989, Michael Jensen (1997) predicted that LBO firms like KKR would eventually dominate the financial landscape:

> The publicly held corporation, the main engine of economic progress in the United States for a century, has outlived its usefulness in many sectors of the economy and is being eclipsed. New organizations are emerging in its place – organizations that are corporate in form but have no public shareholders and are not listed or traded on organized exchanges. These organizations use public and private debt, rather than public equity, as their major source of capital. Their primary owners are not households but large institutions and entrepreneurs that designate agents to manage and monitor on their behalf and bind those agents with large equity interests and contracts governing the distribution of cash.
>
> (p. 1)

Was Jensen prophetic? His article was published the same year of the largest hostile takeover of the 1980s, KKR's bid for RJR Nabisco.[2] Jensen believed the structure of what he called the LBO Association – high leverage, performance pay, large equity stakes for managers and directors, and contracts with owners and creditors that would force the efficient use of free cash flows – would refocus companies toward value creation rather than maximizing growth and earnings per share. In his view, the old model of maximizing growth and earnings meant that managers were more inclined to retain poor-performing segments of the firm; whereas, PE managers would focus purely on return to capital invested. Many of today's well-known PE firms were founded in the 1980s: Bain Capital in 1984, Blackstone Group in 1985, and Carlyle Group in 1987.

The PE firm is a management company that creates and manages a limited liability fund used as a vehicle to purchase firms. The PE management firm is known as the general partner, and it provides a small portion of the equity to the PE fund. The majority of funds are provided by limited partners, who consist of pensions, (college) endowment funds, insurance companies, and wealthy individuals. The fund operates similar to a closed-end mutual fund, and investors must commit funds for a significant amount of time, usually about ten years (Kaplan and Strömberg, 2008, p. 5). The PE management firm receives a management fee (usually 2 percent of assets invested), and profits are typically split 20/80 between the firm and the limited partners, subject to meeting a minimum return on investment. The end goal of private equity takeovers is to raise the value of the firm through creating "efficiencies," then "exiting" at a higher value within the 5-10-year time frame. How are efficiencies created? The gains are separated into two types: gains from leverage and gains from "superior" management skills, though the latter are often separated into market timing and operational management.

Debt-financed deals generate returns through the tax advantage for debt financing. Interest payments on debt are paid prior to taxes, whereas dividends are paid after taxes. The tax advantage of debt can create significant value for shareholders. Modigliani and Miller (1963) showed formally that the tax differential on debt and equity created additional value through what they called the *debt tax shield*, given as $t \times D$, where t is the corporate tax rate and D is the amount of debt held by the firm. They showed the value of a levered firm was equal to the value of an unlevered firm plus the tax shield, with the increase in value accruing to the remaining shareholders, the PE firm and its limited partners.

With respect to a belief in superior management skills, gains are generated through the disposition of underperforming assets which existing management may have been reluctant to sell. It has also been argued that PE managers create value through market timing, though there is no reason to believe that PE managers can outperform the market through timing over the long run. Operational efficiencies are generated by lowering costs which can be done through layoffs, lowering wages, or cutting benefits for the existing workforce.

The ultimate goal of the PE fund is to sell or "exit" within about five years, selling the firm at a value higher than it was purchased for. While there may be a perception that exits are mainly done through Initial Public Offerings (IPO), the reality is different. According to Kaplan and Stromberg (2008), there were just over 17,000 LBO transactions worldwide from 1970 to mid-2007, of which 6 percent went bankrupt, 14 percent exited via an IPO, 38 percent were sold to a strategic buyer, and 24 percent were sold to a financial buyer, often another PE firm.

The evidence is mixed regarding efficiency gains, though Kaplan and Stromberg (2008) found the source of gains may have changed over time, with operational efficiency gains prevalent in the 1980s, but modest increases post-1980s. A report by The Boston Consulting Group (BCG) found that leverage was more important early on,

> even more important, the value created by private equity firms is less and less the result of debt arbitrage. Increasingly, private equity firms are creating value not through high leverage but through increases in fundamental value as a result of operational improvement and profitable growth.
>
> (Meerkatt *et al.*, 2008)

The BCG report included data categorizing returns from takeovers by decade based upon three major sources of returns: leverage (the tax shield), higher multiplies (associated with higher asset values and market timing), and earnings growth (operational efficiencies). For the 1980s, they found that 51 percent of the returns were attributed to the leverage effect, 31 percent to higher multiples, and 18 percent to earnings; for the 1990s, higher multiples and valuations were the source of 46 percent of the returns – which most likely was associated with the dot-com stock bubble, while leverage generated 32 percent, and earnings 22 percent; and in the 2000s, earnings growth increased to 36 percent, higher multiplies 39 percent, and leverage 25 percent. They suggested that this trend would continue, with gains from takeovers relying more on operational efficiencies and less from leverage and market timing. As we discuss in Chapter 6, the current spate of PE takeovers confirms the prediction; most value creation is expected to come from operational efficiencies.

How has private equity influenced the food industry during the neoliberal era? The activities associated with PE firms, LBOs and hostile takeovers, changed corporate behavior in general. Any firm is a potential target. To reduce the chances of a hostile takeover, firms have increased leverage. Some of the early takeovers in the 1980s, though not necessarily hostile, included food industry firms. For example, one of the first takeovers using a tender offer was KKR's bid for Malone and Hyde in 1984, a food distributor and supermarket chain. KKR stepped in as a *white knight* to help Safeway's management avoid a hostile bid from the Dart Group in 1986. After the takeover, assets were sold off to reduce debt, costs were reduced, and when profitability was restored, KKR took the company public.

KKR's hostile takeover of RJR Nabisco brought the 1980s LBO phase to a climactic end. With the indictment of Michael Milken, the first LBO phase seemingly faded away, but certainly did not die. Given the negative connotation associated with LBOs, the industry came up with the euphemistic use of PE, which became prevalent in the 1990s. While most of the takeovers that occurred in the 1990s focused on technology firms, there were some buyouts of food firms, including Thomas H. Lee Company's purchase of Snapple in 1992, and Bain Capital's acquisition of a stake in Domino's Pizza in 1998.

Neoliberalism 1980–2000

As Palley (2007) described, the neoliberal era was associated with stagnant wages, rising inequality, and slow growth, and these economic changes have had dramatic social consequences. As noted in Chapter 1, from the early 1970s to 1990 the number of two-income families increased from about 44 percent to 60 percent, and the number of children living with one parent doubled from about 10 percent to 20 percent (Current Population Survey). As the family structure has changed, so too has the food industry. Two-income and single-parent families have less time to prepare meals, which has increased the demand for prepared and "fast" foods. The US (along with other advanced countries) has become a *fast-food nation*, with food produced for the masses on the go, requiring industrial farms to supply that food. McDonald's, Domino's Pizza, Olive Gardens, and Kraft frozen dinners have literally shaped generations of Americans. Kaufman (2012) described how the global pizza trade, dominated by Domino's, Papa John's, Pizza Hut, and Little Caesar's, has changed the US and global food systems. Yum! Brands, Inc., which owns Pizza Hut, has 13,600 restaurants in 87 countries, not including operations in China and India. Big pizza needs big suppliers and food engineered to meet its needs. As Kaufman noted, tomato varietals have been created to meet the demands generated by global pizza, and large-scale industrial farms that produce for global pizza have driven out small farmers in many countries. Mozzarella is now the number one cheese consumed in the world, and 5–7 percent of the milk produced in the US "feeds the cheese." A USDA report (Dimitri *et al.*, 2005) characterized these changes somewhat more euphemistically:

Consumer influence in agricultural production has also grown over the years, as consumers have become more time-pressed and affluent, creating new pressures on the farming sector. Demand has shifted toward products that meet convenience, ethnic, and health-based preferences, while efforts to meet these new demands have led to new relationships between food producers, processors, and retailers. Contracting and vertical integration for supply and quality control, and development of special-use, high-value commodities, have changed the structure of agricultural markets, further increasing the specialization and scale, particularly of livestock and specialty crop operations.

(p. 7)

Globalization and free-trade agreements have been major forces of change in the global food system. Ricardo's comparative advantage argument has been used as the basis to open up global food markets to US and European food interests. Developing economies are urged to focus on their comparative advantage in low-wage labor and produce labor-intensive goods, opening up domestic markets to cheaper grains produced by more productive agriculture of the advanced economies. This policy shift has been characterized by some as the CASTE system: Comparative Advantage and economies of Scale justify global Trade and lead to greater Efficiency (Dancs and Sharber, 2015). According to Patel and McMichael (2009) the system was institutionalized through WTO agreements:

The WTO's Agreement on Agriculture outlawed artificial price support through trade restrictions, production controls, and state trading boards. While countries of the global South were instructed to open their farm sectors, those of the global North retained their huge subsidies. Decoupling subsidies from prices removed the price floor, establishing an artificially low 'world price' for agricultural commodities, which were dumped in Southern markets.

(p. 17)

During the 1960s and 1970s many developing nations pursued import-substitution strategies of growth, which included protection for domestic food industries dominated by small, peasant (mostly) women farmers. Under the direction of the WTO and other international organizations, trade liberalization has forced countries to open up markets and end government subsidies of domestic agricultural sectors. By one estimate, some 20–30 million people have lost their land from trade liberalization (Madeley, 2000, cited in Patel and McMichael, 2009, p. 17).

Increasing concentration of the food industry

Private equity through leveraged buyouts fueled the takeovers of the 1980s, which has increased industry concentration throughout the food supply chain. In capitalism, competition is the regulating force and it has always been viewed as good, at least for the other guy. Neoliberalism has certainly facilitated concentration of the global food supply chain. The trends from 1980 to the early 2000s indicate growing concentration throughout the entire food supply chain, from farmers to food retailers. The 1980 farm crisis kick-started the movement toward a more concentrated US farm sector, and though there are still some 2.1 million family farms in the US, the trend – started by Secretary Butz – is toward capital-intensive, industrial farms. From 1982 to 2007, the amount of land used in agriculture has dropped from 54 to 51 percent of total US land area, and farms use 30 percent less hired labor, and 40 percent less operator labor (O'Donoghue *et al.*, 2011). Over the same period, ownership structure has shifted from sole proprietorship to partnerships and corporations, as the percentage of farm sales by the latter two has increased from 34 to 43 percent. As the organizational structure has changed, there has also been an increased movement toward contract farming, with two forms of contracts: marketing contracts, where most of the decisions remain with the farmer; and production contracts, where the contracting firm dictates what will be produced, as well as the inputs and organization. In the latter case, farmers have once again become serfs who work the land.

One step up the food chain, the seed industry is dominated by a handful of global corporations. Patented genetically engineered (GE) seeds is a big, profitable business. While the Green Revolution created hybrid seeds through traditional cross-pollination methods, GE seeds, and genetically modified organisms (GMO) in general, are created by genetically implanting a specific trait into the seed. Some of the early genetic traits implanted were designed to combat pests and create resistance to herbicides. GE seeds have been designed to withstand the use of weedkillers, like Monsanto's *Roundup*, which allows farmers to kill weeds without damaging crops. In 2007, the top two GE seeds corporations (Monsanto and DuPont) captured 58 percent of the US corn seed market. Monsanto was the 2007 global market leader for acreage planted using GE seeds, controlling 90 percent of the market for corn, cotton, soybeans, and canola (Hendrickson and Heffernan, 2007). For all seeds sold globally, the top four firms (DuPont, Monsanto, Syngenta, and Limagrain) had about 29 percent of the market in 2006.

Moving up the food chain into processing, from 1982 to 2005, the top four flour millers increased market share from 40 to 63 percent (the top three, Cargill, ADM, and ConAgra control 55 percent); the top four soybean crushers increased market share from 54 to 80 percent (the top three are ADM, Bunge, Cargill with 71 percent). Finally, at the end of food chain, from 1997 to 2004, the top five supermarket chains almost doubled market share from 24 to 46 percent (Hendrickson and Hefferman, 2007).

Chapter 6 discusses recent developments in the food industry during the era of financialization, as mergers and acquisitions are being driven by a *hyper* private equity industry. The futures market is another area where financialization had a significant impact. Chapter 4 details the financialization process that occurred in futures markets, and Chapter 5 discusses the speculation debate. The next section introduces the basic operations of modern futures markets, the price relationship between futures and spot prices, and the role and regulation of speculators in these markets.

Commodity futures markets

Derivative instruments are designed to manage price risk. A commodity futures contract, in its simplest form, allows a producer-farmer to *lock-in* a price today, then deliver a specified quantity and quality of commodity at some point in the future. The reality is more complicated. Futures markets for agriculture commodities developed out of the need to reduce the chaotic nature of agriculture markets and prices caused by the seasonal nature of production or the vagaries of Mother Nature. CBOT futures contracts allowed producers to deliver product at several fixed dates throughout the year, so commodities like wheat could be stored locally, then delivered when needed. When discussing the role of futures markets in the modern era, two primary functions are mentioned, risk management and price discovery.

Agriculture markets are highly competitive on the supply side and output is subject to the whims of nature, so commodity prices, in general, have always been more volatile than prices of manufactured goods. The primary function of futures markets, then, is to provide a mechanism which allows producers to protect themselves from price movements once crops are planted or livestock is being raised. In most food commodity markets there are typically more producers than consumers, and therefore a greater number of producers who want to sell commodities in the future relative to consumers who want to buy commodities in the future. This imbalance, or "missing demand," explains the need for speculators: they provide additional liquidity to the markets allowing them to function more efficiently. Speculators close the supply and demand gap, and they willingly take on price risk that producers wish to discard.

The second important function of futures markets is price discovery. Since commodities vary in terms of quality, geography, and size, futures markets provide a formal institutional arrangement where the price of a standard commodity is "discovered" based on the fundamental market forces of supply and demand. Historically, grain market structure suggests there is *asymmetrical information*, which creates an information advantage to one side of the market. The supply side is a highly competitive market, composed of millions of farmers and ranchers who grow and raise output in different regions of the country; whereas, on the demand side, the market is highly concentrated, dominated by a handful of large grain merchants who are knowledgeable of national and international market conditions. Futures markets level the information playing field because *all* participants have access to the same price information.

Producers and consumers across the country and around the globe rely on prices established in futures markets to determine prices in the spot market, or what is known as the *cash market*. The cash market is the market for immediate delivery, which is typically facilitated by grain broker-dealers. This is an important point, and will be discussed in greater detail: there are two distinct markets where producers and consumers can sell and buy commodities, the futures and cash markets. While the futures contract specifies a certain grade of commodity, there are literally hundreds of variants, and real-world prices are adjusted for quality differences. For example, global futures exchanges trade various types of "sweet" crude oil with names associated with their geographical areas of production, like West Texas Intermediate (WTI) and Dubai Sour. The petroleum services firm Intertek provides a partial list of over 180 grades of oil which are graded on levels of viscosity and acidity.[3]

When they function properly, futures markets are truly amazing and important institutions that provide a relatively liquid market and mechanism for discovering the price of a commodity based on the fundamental market forces of supply and demand – when they function properly. It is this price discovery function that is used to justify restrictions on speculators, as prices should reflect the "true" underlying fundamentals of supply and demand, reflected by producers and consumers in a market. Historically, futures markets were not as broad (number of participants) and deep (liquid) as stock and bond markets, so price discovery could easily be overwhelmed if speculators dominated markets. The goal in futures markets, then, is to ensure the right balance of commercial and speculative trading: commercial traders should dominate trading for the price discovery function, and speculators should be prevalent enough to ensure market liquidity. I discuss the role and regulation of speculators in the final section of this chapter.

Mechanics of futures trading

Futures contracts are fixed in quality, quantity, and delivery dates. On the CBOT, for example, one quality of wheat traded is "No. 2 Soft Red Winter" (SRW), quantity of a contract is 5,000 bushels, and available contract months are March, May, July, September, and December.[4] Futures participants are required to put a minimum amount of collateral on margin with the exchange, between 5 and 10 percent of the contract's value depending on the commodity, and daily price changes are *marked-to-market*; that is, profits/losses are added/subtracted to/from accounts. For example (see Table 3.1), a trader contracts to buy (takes a long position) one July 2015 SRW wheat contract for $5.00 per bushel on May 5, 2015. The dollar value of the contract is $25,000 ($5 × 5,000 bu). If the contract price increases to $5.05/bushel on the fifth day of May 2015, then the value of the contract rises to $25,250 ($5.05 × 5,000 bu), and the margin account is credited $250. Note, when one trader contracts to buy wheat, there must be a second who has taken the "other side" of the trade, contracting to sell (a short position); therefore, while the long position gained $250, on the other side of the trade, the short position lost $250. If the price of the July contract continues to rise, the short position may get a *margin call*, requiring additional capital placed on account. In theory, the exchange, or more accurately the clearing house for the exchange, has a riskless position, and simply transfers funds between accounts; in practice, there is *counterparty risk*, the risk that one cannot make the payment. To reduce counterparty risk, the exchange requires a margin account, and it establishes a daily price limit move. For SRW wheat, the current maintenance margin is $1,300 and the contract's daily price limit is $0.35.[5]

When a contract expires, wheat and other grain contracts specify physical delivery to warehouse locations designated by the exchange. The trader contracting to sell is expected to sell at the price *settled* on the last trading day of the contract, and deliver grain to the warehouse no more than two business days after the contract has settled. The trader contracting to buy is expected to buy at the settled price and take delivery from the warehouse within the same two-day period. In practice, no more than 2–3 percent of contracts are physically settled. If all market participants were expected to deliver or take delivery, then very few speculators would participate, and futures markets would not have sufficient liquidity to function. Most traders, commercial hedgers included, *offset* positions by taking the other side of the contract prior to expiration, which for wheat is the last business day prior to the fifteenth calendar day of the contract month. In our example, the buyer of a July 2015 SWR wheat contract will offset her position through initiating a sell order for the same contract at any time up to the last trading day on July 14, 2015. When one holds contracts to both buy and sell July 2015 SRW wheat, the position is effectively closed.[6] Note, however, to close her position with a sell, there must be another trader on the other side willing to buy. Waiting until expiration to close a position can be a dangerous game.

Another concept that can muddle an understanding of futures trading is, in theory, there is no limit to the number of contracts offered for a given commodity and contract month. For stocks and bonds, at any point in time there exist a set number of outstanding tradable shares. The number of futures contracts offered is limited only by the willingness of traders to take the other side of new contracts offered. This gives rise to the concept of *open interest*. Market volume is the total number of trades on a given day; whereas, open interest is the total number of outstanding contracts which have not yet been cancelled by an offsetting transaction. Given there is a short for every long, one can measure open interest measured by summing up either the longs or the shorts.[7]

There are essentially three types of futures trades one can make, and for each trade, volume would change by one, but open interest may or may not change. One, a new buyer trades with a new seller, which creates one open interest position. Two, traders currently holding contracts offset each other's position. From trade one, the buyer sells and the seller buys, so each position is offset and effectively closed, decreasing open interest by one. Three, the buyer in trade one offers to sell a contract and a new trader agrees to buy. The first trader's position is offset and closed, but the new trader has an open position, so measured open interest is unchanged. As long as a new sell contract is purchased by a trader who is not taking an offsetting position, open interest increases. Therefore, the only thing that limits the number of contracts created (open interest) is the number of traders willing take on more positions. In today's financialized futures markets, open interest often reaches levels that are detached from underlying economic activity.

One of the most difficult concepts to understand in commodity markets is the relationship between contract prices. All markets offer multiple contracts per year, so there is a spectrum of futures prices, and the plot of these prices is known as the *term structure* or *futures price curve*. Most energy futures contracts are offered monthly, so there are twelve different contracts in each year, each with its own price. Energy commodities like crude oil also trade 7–8 years out (wheat trades about three years out), which means there may be over 80 contracts trading at any given time. The futures price (F) can be above or below the current spot price (S), and the difference between the futures and spot price is known as the *basis* ($S - F$). As time goes by, and the futures contract nears expiration, F and S should converge: that is, the basis is supposed to approach zero ($S = F$). At expiration, the futures transaction is essentially a spot transaction, and arbitrage profits can be made if the basis is not zero. Table 3.1 provides an example, with the simplifying assumption the spot price (S) is constant at \$5.20/bushel. On May 4, 2015, the price of the July 2015 SRW futures contract is \$5.00/bushel, and the basis is 20 cents. As time goes by, the futures price changes as market conditions change through supply and demand for the contract. For example, on June 15, the futures price is \$5.10, the basis is 10 cents, and there are 29 calendar days remaining on the contract. Recall, the long position gained \$250 when the price increased to \$5.05, and her gain is now \$500 at the price of \$5.10. The last day of trading on the July 2015 SRW wheat contract is July 14, 2015 (the business day prior to the fifteenth day of the calendar month), so the futures price should be equal to the spot or cash price, otherwise an arbitrage profit is possible.

A futures trader who wants to buy wheat has two options at expiration: hold the contract to maturity, and buy at the settled price from a designated exchange warehouse; or close the futures position through an offsetting transaction, and buy wheat in the cash market. For example, assume the futures price is \$5.10/bu on July 14, lower than the spot price of \$5.20. Those wanting to buy wheat would buy a futures contract for \$5.10 and take delivery from the warehouse, and those futures traders who intended to sell wheat, instead offset their sell positions with a buy, then sell wheat at the higher price in the cash market. These actions cause the spot and futures prices to converge, as the demand for futures contracts increases, increasing F, and the supply of wheat in the cash market increases, reducing S. The reader may be gaining an appreciation for why financial market participants in the US have to pass an additional exam to trade commodity futures and other derivative products.[8]

A final point from the example about hedging: the futures contract is supposed to lock-in a price for buyers and sellers. Our trader contracted to buy SRW wheat on May 4 at \$5/bu. Assume she offsets her position at expiration with a sell. The price

Table 3.1 Soft Red Winter (SRW) wheat July 2015 contract (example)

Date	Futures price, F (US\$)	Spot price, S (US\$)	Basis, S – F (US\$)	Contract value (US\$)	Calendar days to expiration
May 4	5.00	5.20	0.20	25,000	71
May 5	5.05	5.20	0.15	25,250	70
June 15	5.10	5.20	0.10	25,500	29
July 14	5.20	5.20	0	26,000	1

of the contract is $5.20/bushel, equal to the spot price, where she intends to buy. The profit on her futures contract of 20 cents per bushel offsets the higher price she pays in the cash market, guaranteeing her price of $5/bushel.

Given the number of contracts offered, the futures price curve can take many different shapes. If the spectrum of contract prices is rising, the market is said to be in *contango*; if the spectrum of prices is falling, the market is said to be in *backwardation*. There has been much debate about the "normal" shape of the futures curve. Figure 3.1 shows the futures price curve for WTI crude oil for three different dates: March 1, 2006; March 25, 2010; and March 25, 2015. Each one indicates different forms of contango markets, though the 2006 curve shows steep contango through the first year, then backwardation through the remainder of the price curve.

A key question to answer: what determines the shape of the futures curve? There is debate. On one side, Keynes (1930) suggested, under "normal conditions" which he defined as a balance of supply and demand in the spot market, the spot price should be above the future price ($F < S$); therefore, the normal shape of the futures price curve is backwardation. Keynes considered backwardation normal because, as he argued, sellers must pay a *risk premium* (*rp*) to buyers as an incentive to get them to take on the price risk. Speculators will only buy if they expect the price to rise over time, so the risk premium is reflected in the forward price lower than the spot price. Most discussions regarding Keynes and futures markets tend to focus only on his explanation for normal backwardation, but Keynes also

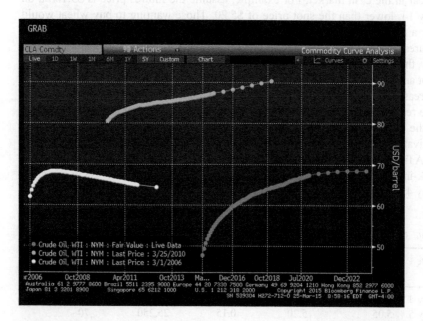

Figure 3.1 Term structure of oil futures prices.

Source: Bloomberg Finance LP.

explained the existence of contango. According to Keynes, contango is the result of a surfeit of goods in the spot market. The excess supply causes the spot price to fall below the forward price, and *S* must fall low enough for the basis to cover full storage costs, allowing firms to carry excess inventory until it is eliminated.[9] This is a very important point related to speculation, and we discuss it in more detail in the last section of the chapter.

Kaldor (1939) expanded upon Keynes and introduced two other factors that could influence commodity prices and the futures price curve, the *convenience yield* (*cy*) and the possibility markets are dominated by long hedgers. The convenience yield is the benefit derived from holding inventory, which is measured by *stock out costs*, the loss of sales and customers that occur when inventory is depleted. Working (1949) is the most oft-cited work related to the forward-spot relationship, and most of his research focused on commodity markets with surpluses, like grains, and he is associated with the argument "normal" markets are characterized by contango through the cost of storage model. While Working receives much of the attention and credit for developing the forward-spot model of storage, it is simply Keynes' cost of carry model combined with Kaldor's convenience yield.

For markets dominated by long hedgers, Kaldor suggested speculative sellers would need to be compensated to take on the price risk, so the risk premium would be reflected in a futures price higher than the spot ($F > S$), or contango. While this point received little attention, it has significant implications for today's financialized futures markets. For example, Frankel (2014) introduced the possibility the risk premium could be influenced by investors, if commodities offer diversification benefits. Essentially, if commodities in the form of futures contracts are a portfolio investment option, and they provide significant diversification gains, then investor demand for commodity futures contracts can reduce or eliminate the risk premium. *This is important:* if the investment demand for futures exceeds the hedging needs of commercial sellers, then the "normal" state of futures markets would be contango, regardless of the conditions in the spot markets.

Based on these discussions, we can establish a formal relationship between futures and spot prices from the perspective of commercial hedgers who are selling commodity futures:

$$F = S \times (1 + c) \tag{3.1}$$
$$c = cy - (sc + i) + rp \tag{3.2}$$

- c = the full cost of carry expressed as a percentage of the spot rate;
- cy = the convenience yield, the benefit derived from holding inventory;
- sc = explicit cost of storing a commodity, including warehouse rates, insurance, security, and spoilage;
- i = the interest rate on an instrument with a maturity equivalent to the futures contract maturity, so it represents the opportunity cost of capital invested in the physical commodity;
- rp = the risk premium, the cost of insuring against price movements.

To simplify the discussion, assume the marginal benefit of holding inventory equals the marginal full cost (including opportunity costs) of carrying inventory, $cy = sc + i$, and equation (3.2) becomes $c = rp$. In markets that are well balanced, backwardation occurs if markets are dominated by hedgers selling forward, which requires payment of a risk premium to speculators, and $c = -rp$; so $(1 + c) < 1$, and $F < S$. Contango occurs when investors seeking diversification benefits are willing to pay a premium to hedgers, $c = rp$; therefore, $(1 + c) > 1$, and $F > S$. The relationship is more complicated if we relax the assumption the convenience yield is equal to full carrying costs.

For surplus storable commodities like grains, the markets tend to exhibit contango to cover the cost of storage. If the basis $(S - F)$ does not cover the cost of storage, then warehouses would sell current output until the spot price falls low enough to cover the cost of carrying inventory. Contango is usually expressed in equation (3.2) by stating that the convenience yield exceeds storage costs. Assuming $rp = 0$, if $cy > (sc + i)$, then $c > 0$, and $F > S$. The basis increases, as Keynes explained, by grain merchants selling off surplus output until S falls low enough to cover the carrying cost.

For those with the ability to store commodities, strong contango markets generate risk-free arbitrage profit opportunities. In strong contango markets, the basis can exceed the carrying cost $(F/S > 1 + c)$. For example, assume the front-month wheat futures price, $F = \$5$/bushel, $S = \$4$/bushel, and $c = 10$ percent of the spot price $= 40$ cents. In this case, one would buy wheat spot at $4, sell a futures contract at $5, and store the commodity at a cost of 40 cents per bushel, making a profit of 60 cents per bushel. When the contract expires, the grain merchant can either deliver the wheat from storage, then continue the game if the new front-month basis again exceeds carrying costs. As more grain merchants take advantage of this storage arbitrage trade, inventories rise and prices adjust until $F/S = (1 + c)$; that is, buying grain spot increases S, and selling futures decreases F.

Two important points: first, storage arbitrage connects the spot price to the futures price; therefore, if demand for futures contracts causes higher futures prices, the spot price will rise as well; second, related to Frankel (2014), if investors desire to hold commodities for diversification benefits, then $rp > 0$, and grain warehouses receive a return over storage costs, which provides a financial incentive to hold inventory.

Futures markets and prices are certainly complicated. While the normal shape of the futures price curve is debatable, prior to 2000, storable surplus commodities like corn and wheat were mostly characterized by contango, whereas perishable commodities like feeder cattle and live hogs were characterized by backwardation. Extracted commodities like metals and crude oil, which can be "stored" in the ground, were also typically characterized by backwardation.

To summarize the discussion on the relationship between spot and futures prices, for storable surplus commodities like grains, they are typically characterized by contango markets to cover the cost of storage. Contango is caused because grain merchants have the surplus goods to sell grain spot, lowering S until the spread (or basis) covers carrying costs. For balanced markets dominated by sellers, markets are typically characterized by backwardation because sellers pay speculators a risk premium to absorb their price risk. However, if commodities provide diversification benefits for investors, then investors buying commodity futures willingly pay a premium to sellers, and markets will be characterized by contango. This gets at the crux of the financialization argument, and we dig deeper into these issues in Chapters 4 and 5, but the important point to be made is a market dominated by investors changes the nature of the price relationships.

The role of speculation in commodity futures markets

Given that commercial sellers historically outnumbered commercial buyers in most markets, speculators have always been welcomed as "necessary evils" because they increase market liquidity for thin markets. The most heated debate regarding futures markets concerns the role of speculators. Specifically, the central question is, what level of speculation is necessary to ensure market liquidity without creating market volatility? According to Hieronymus (1977), "The first fifty years of the history of futures trading in the US is the history of feverish speculative activity, of contests among giants, and of attempts to manipulate prices" (pp. 83–84). Certainly the CBOT attempted to restrain speculation for fear of losing its charter, and it passed several rules to prevent traders from *cornering markets*, the most common form of speculation. Despite these efforts, speculation reigned, and the public rightly perceived futures markets as dens of speculation, which of course led to government attempts to rein them in. The first bill to abolish futures trading was introduced in Congress in the 1880s, and some 200 bills would be introduced over the next forty years (CFTC, 2015).

In 1920 the USDA published a voluminous report on the grain trade, which included a recommendation to establish speculative position limits. In 1921 the Futures Trading Act was passed which created a regulatory body to oversee grain futures, and it taxed all options and off-exchange futures trades. The next year the act was struck down by the Supreme Court on grounds that this use of Congress' taxing power was unconstitutional. However, on September 21, 1922, the Grain Futures Act (GFA) was passed:

> Unlike the Future Trading Act, the Grain Futures Act is based on the interstate commerce clause and bans off-contract-market futures trading rather than taxing it. The Grain Futures Administration is formed as an agency of the U.S. Department of Agriculture (USDA) to administer the Grain Futures Act. The Grain Futures Act also creates the Grain Futures Commission, which consists of the Secretary of Agriculture, the Secretary of Commerce, and the Attorney General. The authority to suspend or revoke a contract market designation is vested in the Grain Futures Commission.
>
> (CFTC, 2015)

With respect to restricting market speculation, position limit rules on speculators was the most important regulation. In June 1923, the Grain Futures

Commission enacted a *large trader* reporting system to track the accounts of traders exceeding 500,000 bushels of grain.[10] The 1936 Commodity Exchange Act (CEA) granted authority to the Grain Futures Commission, formally named the Commodity Exchange Commission in the CEA, to set position limits. In 1938, position limits of two million bushels were established for grains, including wheat, corn, sorghum, oats, barley, flaxseed, and rye. According to Hieronymus (1977), the two million bushel limit was formed on the basis of three 1920s government-sponsored studies which found correlations between large trader positions and futures price movements. One study in particular found a strong correlation (0.71) between futures prices and the positions held by 42 large traders. Upon further evaluation, the correlation was almost entirely due to five very large positions, each holding over two million bushels of wheat, hence the two million limit established by the CEC (Hieronymus 1977, p. 335)

With the turbulence of commodity prices in the 1970s, Congress passed the Commodity Futures Trading Commission Act of 1974 which created the Commodity Futures Trading Commission, giving it powers to regulate *all* futures, since financial futures were expanding rapidly during this volatile period as well. Consistent with the rise of neoliberalism, a major change in the position limit rule was amended in 1982 to give the exchanges authority to determine contract limits for most, but not all, commodities; limits on some agricultural commodities were still set by the CEA, administered through the CFTC. During the 1980s and early 1990s, in markets that were not formally deregulated, exchanges were given power to self-regulate, as was the case for commodity markets. With self-regulation, what could go wrong?

According to Morgan (2000), with increases in commodity prices and volatility in the 1970s, the large grain merchants established commodity brokerage businesses to profit from the increased activity. With their operations on the physical side, the grain merchants had two significant advantages in futures market: first, they had superior knowledge of global supply and demand conditions; second, as commercial participants, the CFTC typically gave position limit exemptions to the large grain merchants. With inside knowledge of the forces influencing grain prices, the five global grain merchants ruled both the physical and financial side of the agricultural markets toward the end of the twentieth century.

Given their dominant position, and control of storage facilities, the grain merchants could certainly "game" the futures markets if they wanted; however, with the majority of profits derived from the commercial side, and they made profits regardless of price conditions, there was more to lose (like their exemptions) from gaming the markets than there was to gain. Given their monopoly positions, and the fact many were privately held companies, they tended to prefer calm and relative obscurity rather than pursue speculative profits that could cause a public backlash. When a speculative manipulation did occur, it was usually a non-commercial speculator trying to corner markets, not the grain merchants.[11]

Based on the power wielded by the grain merchants, Hieronymus argued that large speculator positions were needed to offset the trading power of grain merchants who could use their stored grain power to push spot prices lower, creating wider spreads and higher profits from storage arbitrage. Certainly large commercial traders attempted to manipulate prices in their favor just as speculators tried to move prices in their favor. For this reason, Hieronymus believed that speculators should not be subject to position limits; in fact, he believed large speculators created a stabilizing counterbalance to the big grain firms who dominated trading.

The discussion raises important questions. How do we define speculation? How does one determine if speculation impacts price? How much is too much speculation? To use Keynes' metaphor, when does speculation go from a stream of liquidity to a whirlpool of volatility? I address these questions in the final section of this chapter.

Measuring speculation

According to the Commodity Exchange Act of 1936, and updated by the 1974 Commodity Futures Trading Commission Act:

> Excessive speculation in any commodity under contracts of sale of such commodity for future delivery ... causing sudden or unreasonable fluctuations or unwarranted changes in the price of such commodity, is an undue and unnecessary burden on interstate commerce in such commodity.
>
> (US Commodity Exchange Act, 1936)

The CFTC was given authority to establish position limits to restrain *excessive* speculation if speculators cause unwarranted change in price which is an undue burden on interstate commerce. This begs the question, what is "excessive"? While attempts to manipulate prices by cornering markets and fraudulent trades are easier to identify and prosecute, influencing or manipulating prices through trading is significantly more difficult to detect. How can one measure or detect speculation? Is speculation solely caused by speculative traders? A difficult task indeed.

The USDA attempted to answer some of these questions in a 1960s study (USDA, 1967). Measures used to evaluate speculative influences on prices included:

$$\text{Working's } T\text{-index} = 1 + [SS/(HL + HS)] \text{ (for } HS > HL) \qquad (3.3)$$

Where SS = speculative short positions (SL = speculative long positions); HL = commercial long positions; and HS = commercial short positions.

The measure is somewhat counterintuitive. First, for every long there must be a short, so $HL + SL = HS + SS$. If $SS = 0$, then $T = 1$, and $SL = HS - HL$. The speculative long positions cover the net short positions assumed in the above relation. As SS increases, SL must increase, so $SL - SS = HS - HL$: the net long position of speculators covers the net short position of commercial hedgers. As SS increases, it indicates a greater presence of speculators in the market.[12]

$$\text{Hedge Ratio } (HR) = HL/HS \qquad (3.4)$$

HR is an indication of the hedging needs of commercial traders. A lower number indicates a greater need for *SL* positions to cover the hedging needs.

$$\text{Total Hedging Load} = (HL + HS)/OI, \text{ where } OI = \text{total open interest} \quad (3.5)$$

This measures the extent to which hedgers dominate markets.

The USDA study gives us a good example of the difficulty in finding evidence of speculation. Some of their general conclusions were: one, the hedge ratio was "possibly" more closely correlated with price changes than the *T*-index, though with a four-month lag; two, the total hedging load followed price changes closely; three, the *T*-index often moved in the opposite direction to prices; and, four, a higher *T*-index was associated with higher price volatility.

The total hedging load indicates the extent to which hedgers dominate markets, so if total hedging load is high, it means prices are being determined by hedgers, which is how the markets are supposed to function. The best one can conclude about Working's *T*-index, in isolation, is that it is positively related to price volatility. There is no magic bullet for finding evidence and measuring its impact, and the report concluded:

> If one assumes that the principal, measurable price effect of speculation is not caused by the holding of speculative positions over time, but, instead, by the immediate market reaction to the transaction (buying and selling) itself, then *no combination of measures which reflect merely the net change in 'ownership' of open contracts can adequately explain the real price effect of speculation* [emphasis mine].
>
> (USDA, 1967, p. 71)

To determine the impact from speculation, the report essentially concluded that one would need to know the volume flows by trader categories on a daily basis; that is, one would need to know which group was influencing the bids and offers, and "Appropriate examination of speculative activities and related price behavior over a wide sample of market situations would identify circumstances under which speculation quite likely was a measurable price-making factor" (USDA, 1967, p. 73).

Despite the difficulty of measuring speculation, the USDA report does provide a clue to when speculators influence prices, and they cited a suggestion from Working himself. Working stated the *T*-index could provide insight into explaining price volatility when combined with the hedging index. When the hedging load is high (indicating greater hedging activity) and the *T*-index is low, price volatility is higher because there is insufficient speculative liquidity. On the other hand, and pertinent to later arguments: "When moderate or light hedging is well balanced. *In such markets ... prices are determined mainly by speculative opinion* [emphasis mine]. Short-run price behavior in such markets has again confirmed his hypothesis" (USDA, 1967, p. 65)

To rephrase, Working suggested, first, prices are volatile when there is insufficient speculative liquidity to meet the needs of hedgers when their needs are high; and, second, *when hedging needs are low or balanced, and speculative positions dominate hedging positions, prices are (mainly) determined by speculative opinion.* The reason position limits were enacted was to ensure that producers and consumers of commodities determined prices, not speculators. As discussed in Chapter 5, in today's financialized commodity markets, financial traders dominate the price discovery process.

Modern statistical tests of speculation

There are two methods commonly used in the modern literature to test for speculative influence on prices: one, changes in trader positions or Working's *T*-index are used to test for *Granger causality*; second, vector autoregression (VAR) techniques are used in pricing models. According to Stock and Watson (2001):

A univariate autoregression is a single-equation, single-variable linear model in which the current value of a variable is explained by its own lagged values. A VAR is a n-equation, n-variable linear model in which each variable is in turn explained by its own lagged values, plus current and past values of the remaining n-1 variables.

(p.1)

The main issue underlying most debates about VAR models is the appropriate specification based on economic theory, "Structural VARs require 'identifying assumptions' that allow correlations to be interpreted causally" (Stock and Watson 2001, p. 4). Commodity price models incorporate market supply and demand variables, and additional variables are included to capture *shocks* from unexpected changes in market conditions or speculation.

Granger causality tests use *leads* and *lags* to establish which of two variables is "causing" the other to change. If the change in lagged variable *x* leads to a change in variable *y*, then variable *x* is said to "Granger-cause" variable *y*. As discussed in Chapter 5, most empirical tests of speculation use the open interest positions for different categories of traders to test the hypothesis "changes in open interest Granger cause changes in futures prices."

As we shall find, even with the use of modern sophisticated statistical methods, establishing if there has been a speculative influence on prices is difficult, and trying to estimate the extent of any price impact, more so. Now that we have set the proverbial table for the discussion of food and finance, the next chapter gets to the meat and potatoes, the financialization process in commodity futures markets.

Notes

1 I trust the reader understands that "corn" was the term used for wheat in Britain.
2 The $31 billion deal would not be exceeded until the 2000s.
3 http://www.intertek.com/petroleum/crude-oil-types/

4 Other qualities of wheat can be delivered. For example, the contract terms specify 5,000 bushels of No. 2 Soft Red Winter, No. 2 Hard Red Winter, No. 2 Dark Northern Spring, and No. 2 Northern Spring at par; and No. 1 Soft Red Winter, No. 1 Hard Red Winter, No. 1 Dark Northern Spring and No. 1 Northern Spring at 3 cents per bushel over contract price.

5 The daily price limit is reset every six months, and will be the higher of 7 percent of the average price over the six-month period or $0.30.

6 Most grains are physically settled, but some contracts are cash settled. Cash futures contracts are settled at expiration and traders are simply credited with any gains/losses on account relative to the spot price. Lean hogs and live cattle, for example, are cash settled contracts.

7 Technically, open interest includes the *spread positions* of speculators, where the same trader simultaneously buys and sells contracts of different maturity. For example, a trader might sell the July SRW wheat contract expecting prices to fall in the near term, and simultaneously buy the September contract expecting prices to rise a little further into the future.

8 For stock and bond trading, financial market participants have to pass the Series 7 exam, and for derivatives trading they have to pass the more difficult Series 3 exam.

9 Keynes used this discussion to explain how excess liquid stocks influenced the business cycle, and the lower spot price would eventually eliminate the excess through increased demand and decreased production; however, production would be idle over this excess inventory cycle.

10 The large trader reporting system is still in effect today under the auspices of the CFTC.

11 For example, after their somewhat successful attempt at manipulating the silver market, the Hunt brothers successfully cornered the soy bean market in 1976–77 (Morgan 1979, pp. 335–6).

12 Some examples: (1) If $HL = 50$, $HS = 150$, and $SS = 0$, SL (must) $=100$, and $T = 1$. Hedgers are net short $= 100$, covered by speculative longs. Also, total longs $=$ total shorts, $HL + SL = SS + HS = 150$. (2) If $SS = 75$, then $SL = 175$, so the speculative net long positions cover the net short positions of hedgers. However, $T = 1 + (75/(50 + 150)) = 1.375$. In example 1, total hedge positions are greater than total speculative positions; $HL + HS = 200 > SS + SL = 100$. In example 2, total speculative positions are greater than total hedge positions; $SS + SL = 250 > HL + HS = 200$. Speculators dominate the market. As SS increases, the number of speculative longs must increase, increasing the influence of speculators in the market.

Bibliography

Burch, D., and Lawrence, G. (2009). Towards a third food regime: behind the transformation. *Agriculture and human values, 26*(4), 267–279.

CFTC. (2015). History of the CFTC. Retrieved January 22, 2015, from http://www.cftc.gov/About/HistoryoftheCFTC/history_precftc

CMEGroup. (2015). Timeline of CME achievements. Retrieved March 14, 2015 from http://www.cmegroup.com/company/history/timeline-of-achievements.html

Current Population Survey. Living arrangements of children under 18 years old: 1960 to present. Retrieved May 18, 2015 from: https://www.census.gov/hhes/families/data/children.html

Dancs, A. and H. Scharber. (2015). Local food and the CASTE paradigm. Retrieved June 20, 2015 from http://triplecrisis.com/local-food-and-the-caste-paradigm/

Dimitri, C., Effland, A., and Conklin, N. (2005). The 20th century transformation of US agriculture and farm policy. *Electronic Information Bulletin* Number 3, June. Economic Research Service, US Department of Agriculture.

Frankel, J. A. (2014). Effects of speculation and interest rates in a "carry trade" model of commodity prices. *Journal of International Money and Finance, 42*, 88–112.

Grabel, I. (1997). Savings, investment and functional efficiency: a comparative examination of national financial complexes. In *The Macroeconomics of Saving, Finance, and Investment*. Ann Arbor: University of Michigan Press.

Gregory, O. K. (2005). Commodities markets. *Encyclopedia of Chicago*. Chicago Historical Society. Retrieved January 22, 2015 from http://www.encyclopedia.chicago-history.org/pages/317.html

Hendrickson, M., and Heffernan, W. (2007). Concentration of agricultural markets. Columbia, MO, Department of Rural Sociology, University of Missouri.

Hieronymus, T. A. (1977). *Economics of Futures Trading for Commercial and Personal Profit*. New York: Commodity Research Bureau.

Jensen, M. C. (1997). Eclipse of the public corporation. *Harvard Business Review* (Sept.-Oct. 1989), *67*(5), 61–74, revised.

Kaldor, N. (1939). Speculation and economic stability. *The Review of Economic Studies, 7*(1), 1–27.

Kaplan, S. N., and Strömberg, P. (2008). *Leveraged Buyouts and Private Equity*. National Bureau of Economic Research.

Kaufman, F. (2012). *Bet the Farm: How Food Stopped Being Food*. Hoboken, NJ: John Wiley & Sons.

Keynes, J. M. (1930). *A Treatise on Money*, Vol. II. London and New York: Macmillan & Co, 210.

Lewis, W. and Brendon, B.. (2003). *History of the Great Lakes*, ch. 28: Grain traffic. Retrieved January 23, 2015, from http://www.maritimehistoryofthegreatlakes.ca/GreatLakes/Documents/HGL/default.asp?ID=c028

Marx, K. (1977). *Capital, Volume 1: A Critique of Political Economy*. New York: International Publishers Co.

McMichael, P. (2009). A food regime analysis of the 'world food crisis'. *Agriculture and Human Values, 26*(4), 281–295.

Meerkatt, H., Rose, J., Brigi, M., Liechtenstein, H., Prats, M. J., and Herrera, A. (2008). The advantage of persistence: how the best private-equity firms "beat the fade". The Boston Consulting Group. Retrieved November 10, 2014 from https://www.bcgperspectives.com/content/articles/private_equity_growth_private_equity_engaging_for_growth/

Milken, M. (2014). Michael Milken on junk bonds as part of the 'prosperity formula'. *Bloomberg Business*. Retrieved January 10, 2015 from http://www.bloomberg.com/bw/articles/2014-12-04/junk-bonds-played-part-as-u-dot-s-dot-prosperity-grew-milken

Modigliani, F., and Miller, M. H. (1963). Corporate income taxes and the cost of capital: a correction. *The American Economic Review*, 433–443.

Morgan, D. (2000). *Merchants of Grain*. Lincoln, NE: iUniverse.

Nestle, M. (2013). *Food Politics: How the Food Industry Influences Nutrition and Health* (Vol. 3). Berkeley: University of California Press.

O'Donoghue, E. J., Hoppe, R. A., Banker, D. E., Ebel, R., Fuglie, K., Korb, P. *et al.* (2011). *The Changing Organization of US Farming*. US Department of Agriculture, Economic Research Service.

Palley, T. I. (2007). Financialization: what it is and why it matters. Political Economy Research Institute Amherst, Working Paper No. 153.

58   *Setting the table*

Patel, R., and McMichael, P. (2009). A political economy of the food riot. *Review (Fernand Braudel Center)*, *32*(1), 9–35.

Ricardo, D., and Hartwell, R. M. (1971). *On the Principles of Political Economy, and Taxation* (Vol. 165). Harmondsworth: Penguin Books.

Stock, J. H., and Watson, M. W. (2001). Vector autoregressions. *Journal of Economic Perspectives*, *15*(4), 101–115.

US Commodity Exchange Act, Legal Information Institute Cornell University Law School, Pub. L. No. 114–19 (1936).

USDA. (1967). *Margins Speculation and Prices in Grains Futures Markets*.

Veblen, T. (1978). *The Theory of Business Enterprise*. New Brunswick, NJ: Transaction Publishers.

Working, H. (1949). The theory of price of storage. *The American Economic Review*, 1254–1262.

4   The financialization process in commodity futures markets

Financialization of commodity futures markets allowed finance to transform and penetrate markets traditionally dominated by the corporations that produce and consume global commodities. From 2000 to 2008, the amount of money flowing into commodity markets increased from $6 billion to $270 billion, an indication that commodity markets were being financialized over this period (see Chapter 1, Figure 1.2).

The financialization process is driven by financial institutions' motivated by the need to maintain profits or the desire to enhance profits. The financialization process that took place in commodity futures markets is an example of the latter: the desire by finance to penetrate new markets. The process began with financial innovations which allowed the large global banks to offer commodity investment products to institutional and retail investors. The key barrier preventing expansion of these new products was contract limits placed on speculators. If commodity trading was going to be profitable for finance, then contract limits had to be circumvented.

While this chapter focuses on the financialization process that took place in commodity futures markets, there are other forms of financialization related to commodity trading, and those are discussed as well. The chapter is broken into four sections: the first describes the financial innovations; the second discusses the research on diversification benefits of commodity investments which encouraged large investors to purchase the products; the third discusses formal deregulation of the markets; and the fourth discusses the other aspects of financialization in commodity markets, including convergence of financial and commercial traders, and privatization of the futures exchanges.

Financial Innovations

The financial innovation that transformed commodity markets was the creation of a tradable commodity price index. The first commodity price index in the US was constructed by the Bureau of Labor Statistics (BLS) in the early 1940s, the BLS Spot Commodity Index, which was based on spot market data collected by the BLS. The Commodity Research Bureau (CRB), a private service provider, created its own index using commodity price information from the futures markets, and the CRB Index became the standard for measuring commodity prices in the 1950s. The BLS eventually ceased collecting data (Zoller, 2014). In 1986, the CRB became the first commodity index listed and traded on a futures exchange (listed on the New York Futures Exchange). The CRB is commonly known today as the Thomson Reuters/Jeffries CRB Index.

Sensing a profit opportunity in a market previously ignored, in 1991 Goldman Sachs created its own index, the Goldman Sachs Commodity Index (SP-GSCI).[1] According to Goldman Sachs Chief Operating Officer Gary Cohn, the index was created at the behest of producers to fill the missing demand in futures markets:

> Why you need the speculator in the market and why the commodity index was created many years ago is our industry, 20 years ago was a very difficult industry. We had only clients that wanted to sell future production forward. So we had many clients that wanted to go drill oil wells, but they needed some predictability of the price of oil they were going to receive out of the well to go borrow money. They tried to enter the market and sell the oil. There was no natural long in the market. The consumers are so fragmented that they don't amalgamate to a big enough position.
>
> So we actually, as a firm, came up with the idea in the early 1990s to create a long only, static investor in the commodity markets. We created the commodity index where we could allow people that were willing to commit large pools of capital into the market for a very long period of time to facilitate the actual producers and allow them to be able to hedge their production forward to increase their production.
>
> (Cited in Masters 2009, p. 11)

The index was initially composed of twenty-four commodities weighted by their importance in world commerce, with energy commodities having the largest weights.[2] The SP-GSCI was constructed using prices of futures contracts in the nearest dated months to the delivery month, so as to approximate spot prices. As contracts neared expiration, funds would need to be *rolled* into the next month's contracts; that is, expiring contracts had to be offset with corresponding sells (so as not to take delivery), and new contracts were purchased in the next contract month.

The SP-GSCI created a mechanism that allowed investors to bet on commodities without having to participate in formal futures markets with their position limit restrictions. Investors could simply buy a *swap* contract on the index from Goldman Sachs, and the swap was an agreement to pay investors increases in value as futures prices increased. To hedge its swaps exposure, Goldman Sachs needed to purchase the underlying futures contracts that made up the index. Commodity swaps were hugely profitable innovations and risk-free for the issuer as long as they were hedged. After a customer, typically a pension fund, deposited 100 percent of the value of the swap investment, the bank would take a 2 percent fee and use 8 percent to cover the margin on the futures contracts, with the remainder invested in risk-free US treasury bills. Any losses were incurred by the swaps buyer, and profits were split with the bank (Berg, 2011). The only issue of concern for Goldman Sachs was too much demand for SP-GSCI swaps would increase their hedging needs and push them up against the speculative contract limits.

One year after its creation, the Chicago Mercantile Exchange began trading futures on the SP-GSCI, which created an easier mechanism to invest in commodities. That is, rather than buying futures contracts on each commodity, investors could simply buy contracts on the SP-GSCI. Given significant profits with minimal risk, it did not take long for other large global banks to jump into the commodity index construction business. JPMorgan created an index in 1994, followed by AIG, Bear Stearns, and PIMCO over the next two years.

The second major innovation in commodity markets was the creation of Exchange Traded Funds (ETFs). An ETF is conceptually equivalent to a closed-end mutual fund. First, an open-ended mutual fund purchases assets (usually stocks and bonds) then sells shares of the fund to investors, the value of which is based on the values of the underlying assets. As more money flows in, the fund purchases more assets. For a closed-end mutual fund, the amount of money and the assets purchased are fixed, and shares are traded on exchanges like individual shares of stock. In theory, arbitrage is supposed to ensure that the shares of the fund traded on an exchange reflect the value of the underlying assets that make up the fund; in practice, the market price typically diverges from the underlying net asset value (Byrley, 1991). ETFs, then, purchase a fixed set of assets, then sell shares that are traded on a stock exchange.

The genesis of ETFs dates back to 1989 with the creation of *index participation shares* by the American Stock Exchange (AMEX). Index participation shares created a mechanism for investors to buy shares of the S&P 500 index that were tradable on stock exchanges. However, since the underlying value of the shares was based on buying S&P 500 futures contracts, the CME filed a lawsuit barring the use of a futures-based product to be traded on an equity exchange, and it was able to initially block their issuance. Subsequently, similar instruments were created and traded on foreign exchanges, and with their rising popularity, the AMEX created a product that would meet SEC approval. The Standard & Poor's Depository Receipts with the trading symbol SPY (colloquially known as "spider"), debuted in 1993. The SPY created a way for investors to purchase a share of the market index in a single tradable instrument. The ETF market never looked back.

The first commodity ETFs were created through buying physical precious metals, and gold and silver ETFs were offered as early as 2002–03.[3] Shell Oil created the first oil ETF a year later using swap agreements related to its futures contracts (Robison). As the demand for commodity investments grew, Wall Street jumped into the game and started developing futures-based ETFs for any and all commodities.

There was still one more problem to overcome related to the licensing of commodity trading professionals. Anyone who traded in traditional financial instruments like stocks and bonds had to pass the *Series 7 exam*; however, in order to trade commodities, one also had to pass the more difficult *Series 3 exam*.

The second exam was required in order to recognize that commodity investments are more sophisticated and riskier than other financial assets. The value of stocks and bonds are easier to understand and analyze because their value is related to the earnings they generate. Commodities, on the other hand, have no associated cash flow; price changes are the source of returns, and prices are subject to the vagaries of nature or new discoveries. Typically, investors who wanted to trade commodities had to sign a statement with their broker stating they understood the risks (as informed by their broker) of commodity investments. Now that any individual could trade commodities through ETFs, how would this hurdle be remedied?

> The U.S. Commodity Futures Trading Commission ... required buyers of certain commodity investments to sign a statement saying they understood the risks. The banks argued that it would be impossible to collect many thousands of signatures for a product designed to trade like a stock. In 2005, Deutsche Bank lawyer Greg Collett, who worked at the CFTC from 1998 to 1999, helped persuade the commission to waive the rule and let funds replace it with their prospectus. That would provide adequate warning the CFTC concluded.
>
> (Bjerga, 2010)

With the rule change, commodity ETFs sprouted in 2005–06, and as commodity investments gained in popularity, issuance of ETFs based on individual commodities increased. One could now bet on commodities like oil (USO or OIL), corn (CORN), cotton (BAL), Wheat (WEAT), and sugar (SGG), trading them on stock exchanges like traditional equity shares.[4] No longer constrained by the requirement of physical commodities to back ETFs, the only constraint on the creation of futures-based ETFs was the demand for commodity investments. If the demand for a commodity ETF drove the price above net asset value, the *authorized participants*, the large broker-dealers and banks that created and issued ETFs, had an incentive to create more shares, which could be done through the purchase of more futures contacts. Conversely, as the demand for an ETF waned, and the price fell below the underlying value of the contracts, the authorized participants could "destroy" shares by liquidating the underlying futures contracts and buying back the shares.

As a stock-like product, ETFs allowed retail investors to play the commodity betting game; however, there is a major difference between the return on a futures-based commodity ETF versus the return on a share of stock. Stock returns are generated from dividend payments and price changes, whereas the return on a futures-based ETF is generated by price changes and the *roll yield*. As the underlying futures contracts move into the delivery month, managers of ETFs (as well as commodity indexed funds) need to sell the soon-to-expire contracts and buy the next dated futures contract. This sell-and-buy requirement creates the roll yield, which can be positive or negative depending on the term structure of futures prices. If the term structure is in backwardation, the roll yield is positive because fund managers are selling expiring contracts at a higher price and buying at a lower price. On the other hand, if the market is in contango, fund managers are selling low and buying high, and the ETF loses value on the roll.

As the demand for ETFs by investors increased, the demand for futures contracts needed as the basis for creating more shares increased, and ETFs that purchased agricultural futures from listed exchanges bumped up against position limits. As the demand for swaps and ETFs increased, there was a growing constituency of financial interests pressing for a change in position limit regulations.

Swaps and ETFs served two purposes. First, they created a new source of fee and trading revenue; second, they created mechanisms for large institutional and retail investors to add commodities to portfolios – commodities became an asset class. Second, swaps and ETFs helped create another profit opportunity as these passive, long-only investments significantly increased the demand for futures contracts and pushed many commodity markets into contango, which created risk-free profit opportunities for those who can store commodities.[5] The stronger the demand for commodities, the more profits there were to be had. Wall Street needed a cheerleader to promote the investments.

Commodity investments and diversification

The third major factor influencing commodity investments was a 2004 research paper by Gorton and Rouwenhorst (2004) that showed:

> Fully-collateralized commodity futures have historically offered the same return and Sharpe ratio as equities. While the risk premium on commodity futures is essentially the same as equities, commodity futures returns are negatively correlated with equity returns and bond returns. The negative correlation between commodity futures and the other asset classes is due, in significant part, to different behavior over the business cycle. In addition, commodity futures are positively correlated with inflation, unexpected inflation, and changes in expected inflation.
>
> (Abstract)

Diversification is a risk-averse portfolio manager's dream. Given the negative correlation with stocks and bonds, by adding commodity investments into a portfolio, one could reduce the variability (risk) of returns. Gorton and Rouwenhorst were certainly not the first to show the benefits from long-only commodity investments, but they received notoriety because of their timing. Their paper coincided with creation of the new instruments which allowed investors to bet on commodities outside of regulated futures exchanges, not simply professional money managers of hedge funds and pension funds, but ETFs provided a mechanism for *anyone* to bet on commodities. Their paper was also timely in that investors were eager to find alternative investments in the wake of the *Enron scandal* and disappointing stock returns in the early 2000s.

Up to this point the flow of funds into commodity investments had been rising at a steady pace, and publication of the Gorton and Rouwenhorst paper was the catalyst for moving the herd (see Figure 1.2). The financial innovations of commodity index swaps and ETFs provided the mechanism for investing, and the research created the incentive for investors, but there was still one more issue to overcome, the regulatory hurdle of position limits.

Deregulation

The process of financialization of commodity markets began with the creation of the SP-GSCI in 1991, and a decade later financial and energy interests helped formalize the various rule changes needed to financialize the markets through the Commodity Futures Modernization Act (CFMA) of 2000. The CFMA was the final push by financial interests to legitimize the swaps markets which were trillions of dollars in magnitude. The issue concerned whether commodity swaps were considered a type of futures contract; if so, then they needed to be regulated by the CFTC under the 1936 Commodity Exchange Act. To the point, if commodity swaps were forced onto exchanges, banks would lose a huge unregulated market and their risk-free profits. Relatedly, even if the swaps were allowed to remain off exchange and unregulated, the growth of commodity swaps would be constrained by position limits, as banks hedged their swaps with futures contracts purchased on exchanges. The 2000 CFMA would identify the types of derivative instruments that could be traded in over-the-counter (OTC) markets, and therefore exempt from CFTC oversight.

The foundation for the CFMA was established in a 1999 report by the *President's Workgroup on Financial Markets* which concluded: (1) OTC swaps were made by "sophisticated parties" aware of all risks, so formal regulation was unnecessary; (2) activities of the OTC derivative dealers, since they were mostly Wall Street banks and investment banks, were already under the purview of the Federal Reserve and SEC; (3) there had been no manipulation of financial markets to date from OTC swaps; and (4) OTC derivatives performed no *price discovery* function (Summers *et al.*, 1999).[6]

The CFMA established three categories of commodities subject to varying degrees of regulation:

> Financial commodities (such as interest rates, currency prices, or stock indexes) were defined as *excluded commodities*. Excluded commodities can be traded in the OTC market with minimal CFTC oversight, provided that small public investors are not allowed to trade. A second category is *agricultural commodities*; here, because of concerns about price manipulation, the law specifies that all derivatives based on farm commodities must be traded on a CFTC-regulated exchange, **unless the CFTC issues a specific exemption** [emphasis mine] after finding that a proposed OTC agricultural contract would be consistent with the public interest. Finally, there is a third "all-other" category – *exempt commodities* – which includes whatever is neither financial nor agricultural. In today's markets, this means primarily metals and energy commodities. The statutory exemption from regulation

provided by the CFMA for exempt commodities is commonly known as the "Enron loophole."

(Jickling, 2008)

The *Enron loophole* unleashed OTC trading in energy commodities, with the only restriction they had to be traded on an electronic exchange in order to provide transparency. In fact, the Intercontinental Exchange (ICE) was created as a result of the CFMA, and some of its founding partners included BP Amoco, Deutsche Bank AG, Goldman Sachs, Dean Witter, Royal Dutch /Shell Group, SG Investment Bank, and Totalfina Elf Group.

The CFMA provided the leeway for commodity swap index investments and ETFs to purchase energy and metals futures from unregulated exchanges like ICE, but what about agriculture futures which had to be traded on regulated exchanges? After the creation of the SP-GSCI in 1991, the demand for commodity investments slowly increased, and Goldman Sachs (and other commodity swaps issuers) found themselves constrained by position limits on the regulated exchanges. J. Aron, Goldman Sach's commodity trading subsidiary, petitioned the CFTC for waivers, claiming they were simply hedging the OTC swap contracts they sold to hedge and pension funds. This was the same argument used to support the creation and trading of the SPY in 1986 which resulted in the CFTC classifying financial swap dealers as commercial hedgers, and therefore exempt from position limits. The CFTC agreed, and granted position limit exemptions, thus classifying financial swap dealers as *bona fide* hedgers. The CFTC's action provided an opening, and over the next few years other Wall Street commodity index swap dealers would petition and be given exemptions (US Senate, 2009).

The 2000 CFMA required that all agricultural futures be traded on regulated exchanges, "unless an exemption would be consistent with the public interest," so the futures exchanges still had the ability to apply position limits on agricultural products. However, the CFTC decided to allow the position limit exemptions for Goldman Sachs and other index trading banks to be carried over or grandfathered. This meant there were no effective constraints on the Wall Street bank/swap dealers other than the demand for commodity investments, which, as described earlier, had accelerated after the publication of the Gorton and Rouwenhorst paper. Wall Street "commodity analysts" were also pumping commodities. Erb and Harvey (2006) noted in their paper that a 2004 Goldman Sachs presentation ("The Case for Commodities as an Asset Class") only highlighted the commodities that historically experienced backwardation more often, as these would generate positive gains from the roll yield.

While the commodity swap dealers were given exemptions, how did the CFTC handle ETFs? As commodity ETFs increased in popularity, some of the larger funds also bumped up against position limits on agricultural futures. In 2006, rather than provide exemptions, the CFTC issued *no action* letters which allowed two large ETFs to exceed contract limits as long as they did not carry their positions into the spot month (US Senate, 2009). In the CFTC's view, as long as financial investments did not influence spot prices as futures contract converged in the delivery month, then they believed ETFs would not influence the underlying physical prices, and therefore the price discovery process.

The combination of the CFMA, exemptions, innovations, and belief that commodity investments were (almost) a free lunch, caused an influx of funds into these new products and commodity prices increased with the increased investment flows (Figure 1.2). The tremendous flow of funds into commodities and rising prices led to the final act in the financialization of commodity markets, the convergence of financial and physical commodity trading firms.

Convergence of finance and food

The new commodity instruments were generating significant revenues for Wall Street and, as some of the banks discovered, there were risk-free profits available for those with the ability to store commodities. This was the final push; not content with profits from financial trades, finance moved into the commodity storage business.

For many commodities, the futures price curves historically exhibited backwardation. In fact, in their analysis of commodity returns, Erb and Harvey (2006) showed the roll yield from backwardation was responsible for 90 percent of the returns from passive long investment in commodities. On the other hand, as Working (1949) and Keynes (1930) argued, contango markets were necessary for surplus commodities like grains because higher futures prices cover the cost of storage for grain elevators and warehouses. In strong contango markets, the profits generated in the storage grain trade were risk-free. This was the reason Hieronymous (1977) argued that speculators were a necessary countervailing force to commercial hedgers who had the wherewithal (storage) to broaden contango and generate risk-free profits.

While the term structure of grain futures prices typically exhibited contango, energy and mineral commodities typically experienced backwardation. Once discovered, crude oil is not produced and stored; it can be pulled out of natural ground storage to meet demand. As more money flowed into commodity investments, oil and mineral commodities began to experience contango more often, and storable commodities were experiencing steeper episodes of contango (Figure 4.1). Until now, contango profit opportunities were the domain of big grain, mineral, and oil firms as they had the storage facilities and position limit exemptions that allowed them to take advantage of storage arbitrage when markets experienced contango.

The lucrative business of physical commodity trading did not escape Wall Street investment houses, and investment banks like Morgan Stanley and Goldman Sachs had been pushing the limits on physical trading restrictions since the early 1990s. According to Omarova (2013), Morgan Stanley was the earliest entrant into physical commodity trading:

> In the early 1990s, Morgan Stanley's oil trader Olav Refvik, struck deals to buy and deliver oil and oil products to large commercial users around

the globe .... During the same period, Morgan Stanley constructed power plants in Georgia, Alabama and Nevada, which allowed it to become a major electricity seller.

(p. 314)

Though most of Morgan Stanley's activities focused on energy, agriculture products were listed among its commodity trading activities in their 2012 SEC filings.

With the passage of the Gramm–Leach–Bliley Act in 1999, bank holding companies (BHC) were at first slow to push the limits on expanding into nonfinancial sectors like commodities, and for good reason, as the Federal Reserve still held sway over banks' activities that mixed their insured deposits with other areas of business. The GLBA allowed commercial and investment banks to affiliate under a Financial Holding Company (FHC) umbrella as long as they were well-capitalized and well-managed; further, the act allowed FHCs to engage in any activity that the Federal Reserve determined to be financial in nature, or *complementary to a financial activity* without creating undue risk to the financial system. To invest in physical commodities, the Wall Street FHCs pushed the envelope on what was deemed "complementary activities," arguing that physical commodity

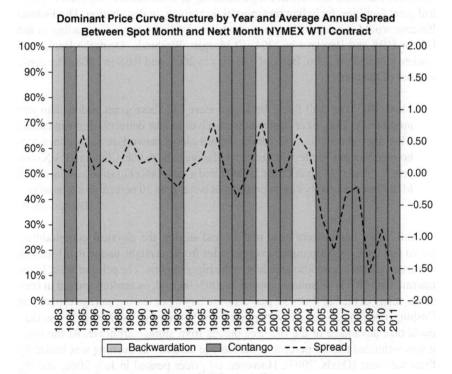

Figure 4.1 Dominant price structure of oil futures prices.

Source: Better Markets, 2011. Reproduced with permission.

trading was "complementary" to their financial swaps business. The GLBA also included a very specific grandfather clause for banks that were already engaged in physical commodity trades prior to September 30, 1997: any BHC that became an FHC after November 12, 1999 could continue to conduct their physical trading as long as, one, the commodity related activity did not exceed 5 percent of its consolidated assets; two, it did not cross-market its commodity products with any of its affiliated depository institutions. For all other FHCs, commodity trading was restricted to 5 percent of *Tier 1 capital* (Omarova, 2013).

It is surprising it took so long for Wall Street banks to learn about this game, but learn it they did. Starting in the mid-2000s, other Wall Street banks began investing in companies that transport and store commodities. Citigroup was the first FHC to be given Federal Reserve approval:

> Citigroup was allowed to purchase and sell oil, natural gas, agriculture products, and other non-financial commodities in the spot market and to take and make physical delivery of commodities to settle permissible commodity derivatives transactions.
>
> (Omarova 2013, p. 301)

However, the banks did not have legal authority to own, operate, or invest in physical asset facilities, including transportation, storage, or distribution. The Federal Reserve would subsequently approve similar physical commodity trading in the US for UBS and Barclays in 2004, JP Morgan, Wachovia, Deutsche Banks and Societe Generale in 2006, Bank of America in 2007, and RBS in 2008. The genie was out of the bottle:

> These days, the Wall Street banks are more like those grain traders than you might think. They have equipped themselves to take delivery of raw materials when they choose to ... Goldman owns a global network of aluminum warehouses. Morgan Stanley (MS) chartered more tankers than Chevron (CVX) last year .... And JPMorgan Chase (JPM) hired a supertanker to store heating oil off Malta last year, likely earning returns of better than 50 percent in six months.
>
> (Bjerga, 2010)

Wall Street banks were now trading and storing the physical commodities. Given that the CFMA exempted energy trades from oversight, and with oil such an important global commodity, crude was the biggest game. The price of West Texas Intermediate (WTI) oil spiked upward in 2005–06, and, as markets moved in contango, many of the big financial players were buying or leasing storage capacity in Cushing, Oklahoma – the delivery point for WTI traded on the NYMEX – so they could take advantage of the risk-free profits from storage arbitrage. At the time, it was estimated that 35 percent of the storage capacity in Cushing was leased by financial firms (Davis, 2007). However, oil prices peaked in July 2006, and the market reverted to backwardation. The experience gave Wall Street banks a taste for the game, and it acted as a prelude for things to come in 2008.

The 2008 financial crisis put Wall Street banks and the Federal Reserve in a sticky situation related to regulations over physical commodity trading by banks. First, JPMorgan was strong-armed by the Federal Reserve into purchasing Bear Stearns, an investment bank that also had physical energy commodity trading assets; second, after Lehman Brothers filed for bankruptcy on September 15, 2008, Goldman Sachs and Morgan Stanley were forced to become BHCs, subjecting them to the same physical commodity rules that applied to all BHCs. The issues surrounding the physical trading of commodities by Wall Street banks came to a head through a US Senate investigation into their activities, which is discussed in greater detail in Chapter 7.

For oil and minerals, at least, finance could now play all sides of the commodity game. They earned fees selling swaps and ETFs to investors, the demand for which created contango markets, and they could now profit from the physical side with the ability to store commodities. On the other side of the trading floor, the significant profit opportunities from financial commodity investments created an incentive for commodity producers like Cargill and ADM to ramp up their own financial trading arms, becoming a more important source of their own profits. Prior to financialization of the commodity markets, the big grain firms tried to keep a low profile, as the last thing they wanted was to create any public perception of profiteering in the futures markets off of food commodities. As the markets became financialized, with financial interests dominating most aspects of the market, the big grain merchants increased their financial trading and investment offerings, as they now had a cover in the form of the banks.

The grain merchants have always played the futures game, and their physical trading gives them knowledge of the global supply and demand conditions for commodities; however, in the era of financialization, they have ramped up their financial trading and investments. For example, Cargill Risk Management was created in 1994 to expand on its expertise in commodity trading, hedging, and investing. According to their website, Cargill's "Investor Products has been providing commodity exposure to a select group of the world's largest and most respected pension plans, endowments and foundations" (Cargill, 2015). Products offered include a passive commodity index, global commodity index, customized indexes, volatility trading strategies, and futures strategies to name a few. Cargill creates OTC hedging instruments that can be tailored to meet the needs of their customers, and they claim to offer their investments at lower costs than the Wall Street banks.

While Cargill had operated a proprietary commodities trading arm from 1984 to 2003, it created Black River Asset Management in 2003 as an independent subsidiary to manage investors' money and operate as a private equity fund. According to their website, Black River Asset Management's "global presence and worldwide connectivity with Cargill provide us with broad perspectives that help us identify opportunities and manage risk. We apply these insights to our highly focused strategies built on our core capabilities" (Management, 2015). According to a June 3, 2011 *Financial Times* article, "the company manages more than $5bn in assets, investing in commodities, fixed income, currencies and private equity style projects in areas such as agriculture, food, clean energy and mining" (Blas, 2011).

Another Cargill financial subsidiary is Cargill Trade & Structured Finance, which focuses on trade financing; this includes trade receivable discounting, letters of credit, supplier finance, collateralized lending, warehouse financing, and trade and supply chain financing. Last, CarVal Investors was created in 1987 as a management investing company focused on corporate securities, liquidations, loan portfolios, structured credit and commercial real estate (Cargill, 2015).

During the 2007–08 commodity bubble Louis Dreyfus launched a commodities hedge fund, the LDC Alpha fund, and by the end of 2012 it was managing over $2.4 billion in assets. A December 2012 Reuter's article pointed out the "unique" position of the commodity giants, as both the LDC Alpha fund and Cargill's Black River fund were up 7 percent and 9.2 percent respectively, while the average commodity fund had declined by 3.02 percent through November 2012 (Wilkes, 2012).

ADM (Archer–Daniels–Midland) expanded its trading arm through an acquisition in 1985, and according to its website:

> ADMIS roots reach back to the 1930's with the founding of Tabor Grain and Feed Company, an independently owned grain merchandising operation in Central Illinois. In 1956, the firm expanded to provide customers with investment banking and stock trading services. In 1966, the company changed its name to Tabor Commodities, became a clearing member of the Chicago Board of Trade, and began executing and clearing futures trades. In 1975, the Archer Daniels Midland Company of Decatur, Illinois acquired the firm and in 1985, we adopted the name we continue to use today.
>
> (ADMIS, 2015)

Not to be outdone, Continental Grain established Arlon Group, a private equity subsidiary that invests across the entire food supply chain. According to their website, Arlon has $815 million in assets under management, and

> invests in private companies across the global food and agriculture supply chain in North America and Latin America, with a focus on the middle-market. In Asia, Arlon's affiliate, Continental Capital Limited, invests in private food and agriculture companies, with a focus on China.
>
> (Continental Grain, 2015)

A final institutional change which has helped promote financialization of commodity markets concerns the exchanges themselves. Most stock and commodity exchanges were member-owned organizations, and one had to buy a "seat" on the exchange in order to trade. The desire to expand and adapt to twenty-first century trading motivated the exchanges to become for-profit entities. The CME *demutualized* in November 2000, becoming the first US exchange to go public, issuing an IPO in December 2002, listing on the NYSE. The CBOT followed suit in 2005,

Table 4.1 CME Group revenues and trading volume

Year	Revenue (Million US$)	Change (%)	Volume (Millions)	Change (%)
2002	446	NA	549	NA
2004	722	61.9	787	43.4
2006	1,090	51.0	1,341	70.4
2008	2,561	135	2,988	122.8
2010	3,004	17.3	3,078	3
2011	3,281	9.2	3,387	10
2012	2,915	−11.2	2,890	−14.7

Source: CME Group Annual Reports.

demutualizing and going public as well, and the two would merge a year later to become the CME Group.

As for-profit entities, with profits generated by trading volume, futures exchanges have an incentive to drive trading higher, and this conflict of interest suggests the exchanges have an incentive to support policies that increase trading; for example, by reducing position limit barriers for financial traders. Table 4.1 shows revenues and volume reported by the CME Group, and commodity derivatives trading certainly was a significant part of their growth. From 2002 to 2008, the peak of the commodity bubble, revenue increased by 475 percent and volume by almost 450 percent. The commodity bubble was profitable for the exchange.

Over the past ten years global equity and futures exchanges have been merging, so they are larger and fewer in number. For example, in 2008 the CME Group acquired NYMEX; and, in 2013, ICE acquired NYSE Euronext, which owned several derivative exchanges as well, including the London International Financial Futures and Options Exchange (LIFFE). It is interesting to note that ICE, which has been in existence for less than 15 years, acquired the NYSE, which has been trading for about 150 years, an indication that derivative markets may be more important than equity markets now. Equity markets are experiencing declining volumes as more firms are taken private through PE deals, and big institutional traders like hedge and pension funds more often engage in large block trades done off-exchange, known as *dark pools of liquidity*.

Conclusion

The financialization process has resulted in "flipping" of the commodity futures markets. Speculators were historically constrained by position limits, which limited their open interest to 20–30 percent of the market; and now, financial interests dominate trading, accounting for 70–80 percent of open interest in many markets.[7] Position limits on financial traders were circumvented through innovations, and the 2000 CFMA formally deregulated the markets. The innovations of commodity index swaps and ETFs has turned commodities into an asset, and, like the price of any liquid financial asset, prices are more volatile and prone to bubbles. However, there is a vigorous debate regarding whether or not these new investment flows did indeed influence the price of commodities, especially during the 2008 bubble. There is a vocal group of economists who argue that financial flows do not impact prices. Regardless, if one accepts the argument that financial flows influence commodity prices, to what extent did speculators cause prices to rise? There are alternative villains behind the 2008 food price bubble and riots, and we dig into this debate in the next chapter.

Notes

1 In 2008, the GSCI was taken over by Standard & Poor's and is now known as the S&P-GSCI.
2 The index weights by commodity groups for 2012 were 67.5 percent energy-related, 11.4 percent metals, and 21.1 percent agriculture and livestock.
3 Typically the generic term used for commodity-based exchange traded funds is "exchange traded products" or ETPs.
4 The acronyms in parentheses are their exchange trading symbols.
5 The ability of these investments to increase prices is a contentious issue which is addressed in Chapter 5.
6 As head of the CFTC at the time, Brooksley Born was a member of the Working Group and supported regulating derivatives. The remaining members of the group, which included Alan Greenspan, Larry Summers, and Arthur Levitt, were opposed to regulating derivatives. As it became clear her position was lost, Born resigned before the report was finalized.
7 In summer of 2011, U.S. Senator Bernie Sanders (D. VT.) released confidential CFTC data from the 2008 bubble that showed financial interests held 80 percent of outstanding oil futures contracts.

Bibliography

ADMIS. (2015). About us. Retrieved January 15, 2015 from http://www.admis.com/who-we-are/who-we-are.

Berg, A. (2011). The rise of commodity speculation: from villainous to venerable. In A. Prakash (ed.) *Safeguarding Food Security in Volatile Global Markets*. FAO. Retrieved October 27, 2015 from https://www.nefiactioncenter.com/PDF/theriseofcommodityspeculation.pdf

Better Markets. (2011). Position limits for derivatives. Comments. Retrieved October 21, 2014 from https://www.bettermarkets.com/sites/default/files/CFTC%20Position%20Limits%20CL%20As%20Submitted%20Hi%20Res.pdf

Bjerga, A., Loder, A., and Robison, P. (July 22, 2010). Amber waves of pain. *Bloomberg BusinessWeek*. Retrieved February 12, 2015 from http://www.bloomberg.com/bw/magazine/content/10_31/b4189050970461.html

Black River Asset Management (2015). Homepage. Retrieved January 15, 2015 from https://www.black-river.com/

Blas, J. (2011, June 3). Big traders emerge from the shadows as demand grows. *Financial Times*.

Byrley, T. F. (1991). Transaction costs and market efficiency for closed-end mutual funds. *Akron Business and Economic Review, 22*(1), 107.

Cargill. (2015). Investor products. Retrieved January 15, 2015 from http://www.cargill. com/company/businesses/cargill-risk-management/investor-risk/index.jsp

Continental Grain. (2015). Arlon. Retrieved January 15, 2015 from http://www.continental grain.com/arlon/Default.aspx

Davis, A. (2007, October 6). Where has all the oil gone? *Wall Street Journal.* Retrieved April 21, 2012 from http://www.wsj.com/articles/SB119162309507450611.

Erb, C. B., and Harvey, C. R. (2006). The strategic and tactical value of commodity futures. *Financial Analysts Journal, 62*(2), 69–97.

Gorton, G., and KG Rouwenhorst (2004), Facts and fantasies about commodity futures. NBER Working Paper, 10595.

Hieronymus, T. A. (1977). *Economics of Futures Trading for Commercial and Personal Profit.* New York: Commodity Research Bureau.

Jickling, M. (2008). *The Enron Loophole*. Washington, DC: Congressional Research Service, Library of Congress.

Keynes, J. M. (1930). *Treatise on Money, Vol. 2: Applied Theory of Money*. London: Macmillan.

Masters, M. (2009). Testimony of Michael W. Masters Managing Member. Portfolio Manager Masters Capital Management LLC before the Commodity Future Trading Commission. http://www. cftc. gov/ucm/groups/public/@newsroom/documents/file/ hearing080509_masters. pdf.

Omarova, S. T. (2013). The merchants of Wall Street: banking, commerce, and commodities. *Minnesota Law Review, 98*(1), 266–355.

Summers, L., Greenspan, A., Levitt, A., and Ranier, W. (1999). *Over-the-Counter Derivatives Markets and the Commodity Exchange Act: Report of The President's Working Group on Financial Markets*. Washington, DC, November.

US Senate (2009). Excessive speculation in the wheat market. *Majority and Minority Staff Report. Permanent Subcommittee on Investigations, 24,* 107–108.

Wilkes, T., and Onstad, E.. (2012, Dec 19, 2012). Commodity trader hedge funds outsmart standalone rivals. Retrieved April 15, 2015 from http://uk.reuters.com/article/2012/12/19/ commodity-hedgefunds-idUKL5E8NE7VE20121219

Working, H. (1949). The theory of price of storage. *The American Economic Review,* 1254–1262.

Zoller, J. H. (2014). History of Commodity Research Bureau (CRB). Retrieved October 21, 2015 from http://www.crbtrader.com/history.asp

5 The speculation debate

The most controversial change in commodity futures markets has been the massive flood of investment dollars from pension funds and endowments into passive Commodity Index Funds (CIF), and these investors are motivated by the diversification gains from holding commodities long term. Traditional speculators, on the other hand, make bets on the direction of prices, up or down. One of the most contentious debates regarding financialization of commodities concerns the growth and influence from these long-only positions. Questions surrounding the impact from the rapid growth of CIFs were brought to a head when, on May 20, 2008, portfolio manager Michael Masters (2008) stated in testimony to a Senate panel investigating speculation in the wheat market that long-only CIFs, a new form of speculation, were the cause of higher commodity prices. Masters' testimony put a target on Wall Street swaps dealers and reignited a longstanding speculation debate. Hundreds of academic papers and testimonies to government bodies were presented (and the literature is growing), with heated arguments made from both sides, yet seemingly no conclusive evidence has been sufficient to cause one side to back down.[1]

In this chapter we address the "simple" question which has engendered such vigorous debate: has financialization of commodity markets increased the influence of speculators on prices? Given the tone of this book, it may seem strange that this is a question in need of an answer, but there is a vocal group of economists who argue that speculators cannot influence prices, and I will attempt to separate the wheat from the chaff to shed light on this contentious issue.[2] The academic debate is suggestive of a scene from Ridley Scott's film *Kingdom of Heaven*, where, in the attempt to retake Jerusalem, the Muslims have breached a portion of the city's wall and are met by Balian and his defenders. After hours of bloodshed, the mass of bodies goes nowhere. And there is a reasonable explanation for this stand-off in the speculation debate: both fundamental factors and financial forces influenced prices, so disentangling the effects of speculation from fundamentals is no easy task. Finally, to be clear about the academic arguments, at issue is whether or not investment flows impact prices. Unfortunately, much of the debate has focused on a subset of investors, the CIFs, and this has distracted from the broader question.

Before dipping into the murky waters of the speculation debate, some qualifications are needed. First, given the extant literature related to the debate, the discussion here is focused mainly on the markets for oil and wheat. There are several reasons for this: first, the US Senate investigated speculation in both markets; second, the 2008 oil price bubble received significant attention in the academic literature; third, and most important, financialization has created a new mechanism in the way energy prices influence food prices.

Second, it is important to make a distinction between speculators and investors. Traditional speculators bet on price changes in either direction, and until recently, the CFTC specified two categories of traders in its Commitment of Traders (COT) report: commercial, those with commodity-related businesses; and noncommercial, those with no business interest in commodities. CIFs muddle the concept of speculation. Should we define CIFs as speculators if they only take long positions? I think not. However, like investors in any asset, CIFs influence prices by portfolio allocation decisions. For this reason, we define a speculator as a trader who bets on short-term price movements (up or down), and investors as traders who hold long positions for the diversification benefits of commodities. From these definitions, financialization of commodity markets is defined as the dominance of financial over commercial trading, and financialization's impact on prices arises from the combined positions of financial traders, both speculators and investors.

Third, for brevity's sake, those researchers who consistently indicate no influence on prices from financial traders, "the fundamentals did it" group, we label as the "No" group. Those researchers who find evidence that financial traders have influenced prices we label as the "Yes" group. We begin the discussion with a brief summary of the original skirmish between Masters and Irwin and Sanders (2010), as this was the spark that ignited the speculation debate, and it provides a starting point for the main issues underlying many of the academic studies that followed. Once the main issues have been presented, we turn to the oil speculation debate, where much of the academic heat was initially generated. Next, we summarize the food speculation debate focusing on the wheat market, and conclude the chapter with a look at the evidence in support of the financialization thesis.

The Masters hypothesis

During the commodity price bubble from 2007 to 2008, commercial wheat traders were complaining about the impact on prices from a new set of financial investors. Rapidly rising prices caused *margin calls* on their (traditionally) short positions, and many commercial traders were being driven out of markets because they could not raise the capital necessary to fund the increased margin costs. This was not the first time market participants had complained about these new speculative influences. The US Senate's Permanent Subcommittee on Investigations published reports on speculation in the oil and gas markets in 2006 and 2007 respectively. On May 20, 2008, near the peak of the bubble, Michael Masters gave his testimony to the Senate thus setting off the "great speculation debate."

Masters provided data (see Chapter 1, Figure 1.2) which showed the dramatic increase in assets allocated to CIFs mirrored the increase in commodity prices. As he stated,

Assets allocated to commodity index trading strategies have risen from $13 billion at the end of 2003 to $260 billion as of March 2008, and the prices of the 25 commodities that compose these indices have risen by an average of 183 percent in those five years!

(Masters, 2008, p. 2)

In what was dubbed the *Masters hypothesis* by Irwin and Sanders (2010), Masters argued that the significant inflows of funds by passive index investors purchasing long-only futures contracts was the driving force of dramatically higher futures prices and, therefore, higher spot prices through the price discovery function of futures markets.

The Masters testimony created an equal and opposite reaction among a group of academics, which is best illustrated by the Irwin and Sanders paper published for the OECD. Part literature review and part analysis, Irwin and Sanders responded with a host of criticisms of the Masters hypothesis:

* There is no formal explanation by Masters for how increases in futures prices cause increases in physical spot prices.
* In order to impact spot or cash prices, speculators would have to withhold inventory or "corner" the spot market; however, inventories did not increase for most commodities over the 2006–08 price rise.
* Correlation does not prove causation.
* If index funds caused prices to deviate from equilibrium, arbitrage traders would take advantage of these opportunities.
* Markets without index fund investing and/or futures markets also experienced price increases.
* Analyses of trading data show no evidence of systematic impact on prices or measured volatility from changes in index and/or swap positions.
* Speculation was not excessive based on Working's *T*-index.

In their formal analysis of the Masters hypothesis, Irwin and Sanders used relatively new data provided by the CFTC which was created in response to trader complaints about the growing influence of CIFs in the markets. The CFTC created the *Supplemental Commodity Index Trader* (SCIT) report in 2007 which provided CIF position data for twelve agriculture commodities. In addition, the CFTC created a new *Disaggregated Commitment of Trader*s (DCOT) report which provided greater detail on trading groups.[3] Under the old Commitment of Traders report pension funds and swap dealers were included in the commercial category, because they were "hedging" OTC financial trades. The new weekly DCOT report, which included energy and metals along with the twelve food commodities, was released in September 2009 and classified large traders into four categories: swaps dealers; managed money traders (MMT); processors and merchants (commercials); and *other reportables*. Though it was released in September 2009, the CFTC was able to provide data going back to June 2006.

Irwin and Sanders used the DCOT and SCIT datasets to test the Masters hypothesis: did the influx of funds generated by CIFs and swaps increase commodity prices and volatility?[4] Based on the new position data, they used Granger causality tests to determine if changes in CIF or swap open interest positions *Granger-caused* price changes. For oil, gas, and the twelve agriculture commodities included in the SCIT reports, they found "there is no convincing evidence that positions held by index traders or swap dealers impact market returns" (Irwin and Sanders 2010, p. 17). They also found no evidence that changes in swaps or CIF positions lead to increases in measured volatility; in fact, their results indicated that increases in swaps and CIF positions actually lead to lower volatility, contrary to what critics claimed.

Finding no evidence that CIFs and swaps influence prices, Irwin and Sanders looked for broader evidence of speculation using Working's Speculative *T*-index. Focusing on the twelve food commodities, they found that higher *T*-index values Granger-caused increased volatility for corn, cocoa, feeder cattle, and lean hogs at the 95 percent confidence level. *This is an important distinction:* they found no increase in volatility when analyzing CIF or swaps position independently, but there were at least four food markets (oil and natural gas were not included in this part of the analysis) in which high levels of speculation measured by the *T*-index increased volatility. We return to this issue in the data section of this chapter.

A rejoinder to the Irwin and Sanders paper came from *Better Markets, Inc.* (Frenk, 2010), a non-profit organization founded by Masters. The main criticisms directed at Irwin and Sanders related to the CFTC data and use of Granger causality tests. Specifically, Frenk criticized Irwin and Sanders for using the swap dealer category as a proxy for index investors in energy markets. While there is a closer relationship between swaps and CIF positions for most of the food commodities, the swaps category is a poor proxy for CIF positions in the energy categories. This issue was acknowledged by Irwin and Sanders, but they used the swaps category as a proxy for CIF positions anyway.

Frenk's rejoinder was most critical of the Granger causality tests. He cited research (Phillips and Loretan, 1990) that Granger tests were not reliable when dependent variables are highly volatile, stating that researchers found, during a period with less volatility than the 2000s, that commodity prices were indeed too volatile for Granger tests to be reliable. Second, Frenk suggested that the use of a one-week time lag to estimate the impact from CIF flows on commodity prices was insufficient to capture the impact from investments built up over longer time horizons.

The debate created a torrent of research from both sides, and before reviewing the academic debate, let me enumerate some of the important issues and criticisms raised from this opening salvo:

1   There is no formal economic model to explain how speculators impact spot prices consistent with observed outcomes in some physical markets (for example, there was no observed inventory accumulation in oil during the 2007–08 bubble).
2   The data are inconclusive regarding the hypothesis that index funds *caused* price increases – correlation does not prove causation.

3   If index funds caused prices to deviate from equilibrium, then arbitrage traders would take advantage of the price discrepancies.
4   Commodities without CIF investments or futures markets also experienced price increases, indicating other (fundamental) forces must have caused prices to rise.
5   Speculation was not excessive based on Working's *T*-index.

The skirmish between Masters and Irwin and Sanders was the catalyst for a broader speculation debate, and we take a glimpse of the academic kerfuffle over speculation in the oil market in the next section.

The academic debate (oil)

An answer for point 1 above was provided by Hamilton (2009). Hamilton constructed an inventory/profit-maximization model which showed that the condition necessary to explain the speculation story is the short-run price elasticity of demand for oil must be equal to or near zero. With a low price elasticity of demand, increases in the price of oil driven by speculators would have minimal impact on demand, and therefore minimal impact on inventory changes. As Hamilton stated:

> If the price elasticity is small but not zero, this feedback will be subtle, and it might conceivably take some time before the mispricing arising from the futures markets would be recognized and corrected. It is interesting to note, however, that the same conditions needed to rationalize a speculation-based interpretation of the oil shock of 2007–08 – a very low price elasticity of oil demand – is exactly the same condition that allows the event to be attributed to fundamentals alone.
>
> (Hamilton 2009, pp. 21–22)

Hamilton is actually a member of the "No" group and argued that the fundamentals were behind the price rise, but, as he acknowledged, *both* the fundamentals and speculation stories require a low price elasticity of demand. Based on the supply-and-demand model, Hamilton showed the observed price rise from $55/barrel in 2005 to $142 in 2008 can be generated if the price elasticity of demand (ε) is equal to 0.06; however, the results are sensitive to the elasticity value. He provided a second example using a value of $\varepsilon = 0.1$, which generated a predicted price increase of $97. Hamilton provided evidence from a literature survey on estimates of oil price elasticities, and the short-run estimates ranged from 0.05 to 0.07, which certainly meets the criteria necessary to support either side in the debate.

Hamilton's discussion is informative regarding the difficulty in proving which view is correct, and he has also addressed the first point raised by Irwin and Sanders: one can construct a formal price model of speculation consistent with no observed inventory buildup during the 2007–08 price rise.

In fact, in his discussion on speculation, Hamilton suggested a second possible explanation: if the current supply of oil is influenced by the future price of oil, then suppliers might forgo current production in order to sell reserves at higher prices in the distant future, and "One might then hypothesize that oil-producing countries *were misled* by the speculative purchases of oil futures contracts into reducing current production [emphasis mine]" (Hamilton 2009, p. 22). It is possible that futures prices, driven higher by speculation, were sending false signals to producers, who reacted by postponing production.

Juvenal and Petrella (2011) constructed an oil price model that formalized Hamilton's supply-side speculation possibility, though they correctly attributed the idea to Davidson, Falk, and Lee (1974). Davidson *et al.* argued that producers of a non-renewable resource like oil, when producing a barrel today, must consider the discounted future revenues given up. If the present value of profits generated by a barrel of oil produced in the future is greater than the profits produced by a barrel of oil today, then the profit-maximizing decision is to keep reserves in the ground. Up to this point, most oil price models incorporated demand-side speculative shocks or supply disruptions. Juvenal and Petrella tweaked the traditional model to add this possibility of a speculative supply-side shock from the futures market. That is, if speculators caused higher oil futures prices, then producers could be induced by this false signal to forgo production today, and sell output in the future when prices are expected to be higher.

Juvenal and Petrella used a structural price model which included numerous macroeconomic variables, shock variables related to unexpected changes in global demand and supply, and a financial shock variable related to futures prices. They used a variation of VAR which allowed them to estimate the impact of each variable on the price of oil. Based on their original October 2011 working paper, they concluded:

> While global demand shocks account for the largest share of oil price fluctuations, speculative shocks are the second most driver. The comovement between oil prices and the prices of other commodities is explained by global demand and speculative shocks. The increase in oil prices over the last decade is mainly driven by the strength of global demand. However, speculation played a significant role in the oil price increases between 2004 and 2008 and its subsequent collapse. Our results support the view that the financialization process of commodity markets explains part of the recent increase in oil prices.
> (Juvenal and Petrella 2011, Abstract)

Juvenal and Petrella found the speculative supply shock variable was responsible for 15 percent of the price spike during the 2008 bubble, with global demand accounting for almost 60 percent. Their results are consistent with most studies from the "Yes" group; increased global demand was the primary factor influencing prices and speculation a secondary factor.

A notable study from the "Yes" group is Singleton (2013). Singleton used CFTC position data to Granger test for a speculative impact on prices, but there are three significant differences between his approach and "No" group studies: an assumption of imperfect information; the use of imputed data from the SCIT; and the use of a longer investment period. Singleton assumed that *informational frictions* cause prices to drift away from fundamental values, leading to a boom and bust in oil prices, and criticized researchers who failed to use this more realistic approach:

> The prototypical dynamic models referenced in discussions of the oil boom (e.g., Hamilton (2009a), Pirrong (2009)) have representative agent-types (producer, storage operator, commercial consumer, etc.) and simplified forms of demand/supply uncertainty. Moreover, these models, as well as the price-setting environment underlying Irwin and Sanders' (2010) case against a role for speculative trading, do not allow for learning under imperfect information, heterogeneity of beliefs, and capital market and agency-related frictions that limit arbitrage activity. As such, they abstract entirely from the consequent rational motives for many categories of market participants to speculate in commodity markets based on their individual circumstances and views about fundamental economic factors.
>
> (Singleton 2013, p. 1)

Singleton noted that several empirical studies found forecasts for demand and estimates of supply from official sources were weakly reliable and highly variable, so public information is not perfect. In an earlier paper, Singleton (1987) constructed a formal model of Keynes' beauty contest analogy, showing when agents hold different views about the future, the optimal investment strategy was to forecast the forecast of others.[5]

The second important difference was the use of SCIT position data to impute estimates of oil contract positions held by CIFs. Since the SCIT reports do not include energy commodity position data, energy CIF positions must be imputed from the agriculture data. This was also the approach used by Masters, a key reason for the different findings, because the imputed data does not precisely match the trend for swaps position data.[6]

A third major difference is the time period of analysis. Most of the "No" group's studies evaluated price impacts from CIF trader position changes over a week or less. Singleton used the prior three months' CIF position flows to test the impact on excess returns in futures contracts ranging in maturities from one to twenty-four months, and found, "increases in flows into index funds over the preceding three months predict higher subsequent futures prices. These effects are significant for contracts of all maturities" (Singleton, 2013, p. 23). Singleton tested the relationships using one-week flow data, the time period used in many of the studies rejecting speculation, and found, similar to those results, no predictive content. The time period matters, as Frenk's (Frenk, 2010) criticism of Irwin and Sanders suggested.

Representative of the "No" group is Fattouh *et al.* (2012). They provided a fairly comprehensive survey of the issues raised in the oil speculation debate, and their review included criticisms of the Singleton and Juvenal and Petrella papers. Regarding Singleton, Fattouh *et al.* first stated that he focused on a limited time period, the 2008 run-up and subsequent crash. They cited a paper by Hamilton and Wu (2014) that found Singleton's predictive correlation breaks down when the sample is extended by two years. Second, they cited an Irwin and Sanders (2012) paper critical of the method used to impute CIF positions from the SCIT reports, arguing that the estimates can be exaggerated.

Regarding the Juvenal and Petrella study, Fattouh *et al.* stated that the speculative financial supply shock postulated cannot be separately identified from other forms of supply shocks which also explain a buildup of producers' inventory; therefore "the analysis of Juvenal and Petrella is not informative about the role of financial speculation" (Fattouh *et al.*, 2012, p. 20). It appears the argument is one of correctly specifying the shocks consistent with the data.

One aim of the paper by Fattouh *et al.* was to outline the set of common factors where both sides were in agreement. First, there is clear evidence that commodity markets have been financialized, and this is reflected in the increased co-movements of prices across commodities and other asset classes. Second, according to them, there is no "compelling" evidence that financial traders' positions predict changes in oil futures prices. A final point of agreement noted recent evidence that the risk premium became more volatile and the mean declined after 2004, which implies that CIF long positions have reduced the risk premium commercial traders historically paid to speculators (Hamilton and Wu, 2014).

Frankel (2014) addressed some of the major criticisms leveled at the "No" group. Frankel evaluated speculation through an interest rate channel and argued that commodity prices are negatively related to real interest rates through the cost of storage relationship. High real interest rates increase the cost of storage, reducing the demand for inventories, and thus commodities in general; whereas, low real interest rates reduce the cost of carrying inventory, increasing demand for commodities. Frankel adapted Dornbusch's (1976) foreign exchange overshooting model to commodity prices. Dornbusch argued that overshooting occurred because asset prices (the exchange rate) react faster than goods' prices (trade balances). Frankel argued that a decline in the real interest rate increased demand for commodities (by both commercial and financial interests), causing prices to rise above the long-term trend; however, prices eventually revert to trend as market participants adjust to the long-run disequilibrium.

There are two important points to highlight from Frankel's paper. First, he used a unique dataset on price expectations, a survey of price forecasts by market participants. Previous researchers used either a proxy (e.g. inventory changes) or ex post predicted values derived from their models. As discussed, a major criticism of the speculation story is the lack of observed accumulation of inventory during the 2007–08 price spike. Frankel's model does find a positive, statistically significant relation between speculation and inventory, stating, "it [the speculation measure] furnishes what some have considered a missing link (via inventories) in the theories that either easy monetary policy or speculation are responsible for some of the price variation over the last decade" (Frankel, 2014, p. 18).

Frankel's analysis also confirmed that the risk premium "disappeared" after 2005, which is consistent with the findings of Hamilton and Wu (2014) that "the entry of financial investors into the futures market, via the intermediation of commodity funds, has provided a counterparty for producers wishing to hedge" (cited in Frankel 2014, p. 23, note 18). These results are consistent with evidence from the "No" group that CIFs have increased liquidity in markets, reducing the risk premium traditionally paid by commercial interests.

Summing up the academic speculation debate for oil, the main differences between the sides relate to the data used and model specifications. For studies using CFTC data, the "No" group uses the DCOT and SCIT reports to test if CIF or swaps positions Granger-cause price changes over periods of a week or less, whereas the "Yes" group uses imputed investment flows derived from SCIT reports to perform similar tests, but over longer time horizons. For structural price models, the debate appears to rest on the proper specification of speculative shocks. Essentially, the modeler's definition of a speculative shock determines whether or not one finds evidence of financial speculation. Given this standoff in the academic debate, the next section evaluates evidence from market participants, the Senate's 2007 oil investigation, and other public testimonies.

Senate oil speculation investigation and testimony

The steady rise in energy prices from 2002 to 2006 prompted the US Senate to investigate speculation in the oil futures market, and a final report (US Senate, 2006) was published in June 2006. At the time, the narrative of higher energy prices was driven by supply disruptions from events like the second Iraq War, Hurricane Katrina, and rising demand from emerging market economies. However, the investigation was instigated by industry complaints about the growing influence from financial players in the unregulated OTC energy markets, specifically on ICE. The Senate Oil Report (SOR) relied less on rigorous academic studies and more on the testimonies from market participants, as well as the most basic indication of speculation, high prices accompanied by rising inventories:

> As a result, over the past 2 years, crude oil inventories have been steadily growing, resulting in U.S. crude oil inventories that are now higher than at any time in the previous 8 years. The last time crude oil inventories were this high ... the price of crude oil was about $15 per barrel. By contrast, the price of crude oil today is about $70 per barrel. The large influx of speculative investment into oil futures has led to a situation where we have both high supplies of crude oil and high crude oil prices.
>
> (US Senate, 2006, p. 12)

Not only were US oil inventories rising, but the SOR noted OECD oil inventories also reached a 20-year high. Recall, Wall Street banks like Morgan Stanley and Goldman Sachs had leased or bought significant storage facilities to take advantage of rising prices and contango markets and generate risk-free profits from the oil storage trade.

Even Federal Reserve Chairman Alan Greenspan acknowledged the speculative impact: "There has been a major upsurge in over-the-counter trading of oil futures and other commodity derivatives … with the demand from the investment community, oil prices have moved up sooner than they would have otherwise" (US Senate, 2006, p. 3). Greenspan essentially describes the Frankel model: investment flows into OTC swaps caused oil prices to overshoot on the high side, simultaneously leading to higher production and reduced demand, resulting in higher inventories, the conventional indication of speculation.

Toward the end of this first bubble, oil producers began to recognize the false signals. For example, CEOs from ExxonMobil and British Petroleum stated that the fundamentals were not driving prices, and the president of OPEC attributed rising prices to "refinery tightness, geopolitical developments and speculative activity" (US Senate, 2006, p. 19). And they were correct. The price of oil peaked in July 2006 at $74.40/barrel, and subsequently declined by 25 percent over the next six months.

Market experts and participants also blamed financial traders. "What you have on the financial side is a bunch of money being thrown at the energy futures market. It's just pulling more and more cash. That's the side of the market where we have runaway demand, not on the physical side" (US Senate 2006, p. 18). And, as all bubbles need, the hype:

> There's [sic] a few hedge fund managers out there who are masters at knowing how to exploit the peak theories … and hot buttons of supply and demand, [and] by making bold predictions of shocking price advancements to come [they] only add more fuel to the bullish fire in a sort of self-fulfilling prophecy.
> (US Senate, 2006, p. 19)

Several Wall Street banks had published reports that speculators were driving up oil prices. A May 5, 2006 Citigroup report concluded, "We believe the hike in speculative positions has been a key driver of the latest surge in commodity prices" (US Senate, 2006, p. 20), and Goldman Sachs issued a report in late 2004 which suggested that speculators had boosted prices by 20 percent, and "shifts in speculative positions could affect crude oil to the same degree as actual changes in the supply of or demand for crude oil" (US Senate, 2006, p. 21).

The main culprit named in the SOR was the non-regulated ICE. ICE was the wild west of energy commodity trading, and there was very little if any oversight by the CFTC because it designated ICE as an exempt commercial market under the Enron Loophole. However, this parallel, unregulated futures market could very well allow speculators to game regulation of the formal exchanges (NYMEX) by offsetting positions on the unregulated ICE. As a result of the Senate's investigation, Senator Carl Levin introduced legislation to close the Enron Loophole and rein-in the OTC and ICE markets, subjecting them to CFTC oversight. Unfortunately, the bill languished under the republican congress, but Senator Levin would eventually kill the Enron Loophole in legislation passed during the financial crisis, ironically included in the 2008 Farm Bill.

The second oil price spike began in early 2007, and this bubble would lead to the global food riots of 2008. Michael Masters gave his first testimony to the Senate just two months before the bubble popped.[7] As the financial crisis receded in 2009, the CFTC began taking testimony on the role of CIFs, and speculation in general, in order to determine if stronger position limit rules were necessary. The testimonies would also be used to inform the Dodd–Frank bill, which would be passed in summer 2010. One of the most illuminating testimonies was given by Todd Petzel (2009) who was chief investment officer of an investment firm at the time, but he had previously served as chief economist for the CME from 1988 to 1995. Petzel first laid out three arguments claimed by those who believe index investors are only liquidity providers and have no impact on the underlying prices of commodities:

- Commodity index owners are always buying and then selling, never taking delivery. Therefore it is not "real demand." The act of selling the soon to expire futures contract when the more deferred contract is purchased is a neutral act.
- Commodity index owners rebalance these exposures to maintain target portfolio weights, just as they do their bond and stock exposures. Rebalancing involves selling after markets appreciate and buying after declines, so commodity index owners add stability to the market.
- Commodity index buyers had no impact on the markets as evidenced by the fact that prices for commodities that had futures and those that did not both went up in 2007 and early 2008. If index buyers had an impact, then futures-based commodities would have gone up while those without futures would not have.

(Petzel 2009, p. 6–7)

In response to point one, Petzel stated that the act of rolling is neutral only after the initial positions have been established. As new money flows in from CIFs, additional demand is created for long futures contracts, and higher prices are required to induce shorts (typically commercial traders) to become counterparties to those contracts. In addition, Petzel explained that the need to roll the contracts might not cause the price level of commodities to rise, but it does put pressure on the spread, and the fixed roll dates of CIFs created opportunities for experienced traders to take advantage of these known trades.

On rebalancing, Petzel stated, similar to the first response, when there is a significant inflow of dollars each month, "the net effect was still a major net addition to the long side as prices rallied" (Petzel 2009, p. 7). Last, on price increases for off-exchange commodities (issue number four raised by Irwin and Sanders):

The correlation argument is made only by those people who fail to understand or acknowledge that physical commodity markets are linked in many ways. Coal and rice are two commodities for which futures markets have never achieved serious liquidity. And yet, their prices rose in 2007 and 20008 without futures buyers. Unfortunately for this assertion, many end users of natural gas and heating oil on the energy side and wheat and corn on the food side have the ability and incentive to shift to coal and rice when the prices of the futures commodities go up. In economics this is called a cross elasticity of demand.

(Petzel, 2009, p. 7)

Petzel's overall conclusion was somewhat prescient. He predicted that the steeper contango markets caused by increased investment demand for commodities would eventually lead to a decline in their popularity and put downward pressure on prices. This would occur because, one, the negative roll yield from contango markets would reduce the demand for commodity investments, and two, steep contango created risk-free profits from the storage trade, which would cause inventories to build, leading to an eventual pull-back in prices.

How did OPEC react during the 2008 bubble? OPEC learned from the last bubble that futures prices were no longer indicative of future demand, and they stated speculation was one of the factors underlying the price increase. In early 2008 Qatar's oil minister had stated, "OPEC will not increase production of crude oil because what is happening now is not an increase in oil demand, but heavy speculation on oil futures .... That's what's making oil prices so high" (as cited in Davidson, 2008).

While academics were tussling over the proper specification of models and data, traders were well aware that financial interests had significantly changed the futures markets. The world's major oil producers, OPEC especially, had learned during the 2002–06 price rise that oil prices in the futures markets were no longer a reliable gauge of the fundamentals. Toward the latter part of the 2007–08 bubble, OPEC indicated that some members were having difficulty finding buyers, so there was no reason to increase supply. As Davidson (2008) argued, even if producers were paying attention to the price signals from the futures market, the profit-maximizing decision suggested that they should save reserves, and sell when prices were higher in the future. In 2008, commentators like Paul Krugman (2008) claimed that speculators were not the cause of the price spike because there was no buildup of inventory; however, as OPEC's comments indicate, there was no buildup in *above ground* inventory because OPEC refused to react to higher prices driven by the futures markets.

The food speculation debate

Irwin and Sanders' OECD paper evaluated both energy and food commodities. Recall, their conclusions were that CIF positions did not Granger-cause changes in commodity prices, and swap positions did not lead realized volatility; in fact, they found that larger CIF and swap positions reduced measured volatility. However, when they used the broader measure of speculation, Working's *T*-index, they found a positive relationship between the *T*-index and volatility for corn, lean hogs, feeder cattle, and cocoa. Despite these findings, they stated "the maximums [*T*-index values] are not beyond those recorded by prior researchers, the average values are near historic norms, and the minimums could be considered inadequate" (Irwin and Sanders 2010, p. 19). Their conclusion ignores the most important impact CIFs have on futures markets, which will be addressed in the data section of the chapter.

In the "Yes" group, Gilbert (2010) tested the impact from CIF activity on a set of commodity prices, including oil, metals, wheat, corn, and soybeans. To measure CIF activity, he used an index of position data created from the SCIT report similar to the method used by Masters and Singleton. Gilbert tested the impact from changes in index positions on futures prices, controlling for other macroeconomic variables, including the dollar and equity returns. He found that changes in CIF positions impacted the prices of each commodity, with oil and minerals experiencing the largest increases. Based on his regression estimates, Gilbert calculated the annualized impact from changes in CIF positions, and a partial list of his results is provided in Table 5.1. The largest price increases occurred for oil and minerals (not shown), which is consistent with the fact oil and minerals have larger weights than grains in the SP-GSCI and DJ-UBS indices, so one would expect changes in CIF positions to have a greater impact on the prices of commodities with larger index weights.[8]

Gilbert's estimates indicated a substantial impact on prices from CIF investors in the first half of 2008: 14.8 percent for wheat, 13.0 percent for corn, 12.3 percent for soybeans, and 23.7 percent for oil. He concluded: "According to these estimates, it would be incorrect to argue that high oil, metal and grains prices were driven by index-based investment but index investors do appear to have amplified fundamentally-driven price movements" (Gilbert 2010, p 28). Gilbert does not suggest that CIF investments are the *cause* of higher food prices, rather that they *amplify* price movements driven by underlying fundamentals.

Lagi *et al.* (2011) constructed a theoretical model of food prices that incorporates speculators and ethanol production into a fundamental supply and demand model. Their analysis differs from most presented so far in that they construct a model that "best fits" changes in spot food prices measured by the FAO Food Price Index. Lagi *et al.* assume that speculators are trend chasers or momentum traders, motivated to allocate funds toward the highest return in competition with other assets. Like Gilbert (2010), they do not view investors as causing price

Table 5.1 Estimated annualized price impact from CIF investments (percent)

Commodity	2006	2007	2008/first half
Oil	8.2	4.9	23.7
Wheat	5.2	3.1	14.8
Corn	4.6	2.7	13.0
Soybeans	4.3	2.5	12.3

Source: Gilbert (2010).

movements rather they amplify price changes. Ethanol production is incorporated using a trend parameter of ethanol production, with the price impact related to less land available for production of grains and other food commodities. Like most structural price models, they assumed inventory changes signal disequilibrium, and, since most market participants hedge their activities with derivatives, they assumed a lagged inventory response.

A speculation parameter is incorporated into a Cobweb price model which will either converge or diverge based on its value; "a small amount of speculation may help prices to converge to their equilibrium value, but if the market power of speculators is too great they will have a destabilizing effect on the price dynamics" (Lagi *et al.*, 2011, pp. 36–37). Based on observed outcomes, they posited that the speculation parameter is in a range where prices are amplified over a period of time by trend following, then prices return to equilibrium through the actions of fundamental traders. As can be seen in Figure 5.1, their price model closely fits the price movements measured by the FAO Index.

They concluded that falling house and stock prices provided the impetus for investors to shift into commodities, and these speculative forces combined with biofuels mandates are the dominant forces underlying the increase in food prices: "We can attribute the sharp peaks in 2007/08 and 2010/2011 to speculation, and the underlying upward trend to biofuels. The impact of changes in all other factors is small enough to be neglected in comparison to these effects" (Lagi *et al.*, 2011, p. 18). Similar to Singleton (2013), they argued that the speculative cycle will continue if traders operate under the *greater fool* theory; that is, if investors believe they can time markets better than others, then they will persist in their investment strategies and the boom–bust cycle will continue.

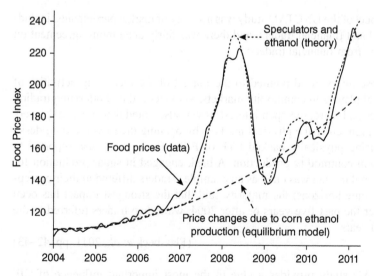

Figure 5.1 Food price model with speculators and ethanol. (Source: Lagi *et al.*, 2011.

Source: Reproduced with permission from the New England Complex Systems Institute.)

The 2008 food price bubble, and the food riots it triggered, prompted significant efforts by many organizations to determine its causes. In 2011, the United Nations Conference on Trade and Development (UNCTAD) published a broad-based study (Flassbeck *et al.*, 2011) on financialization of commodity markets. Their basic argument, consistent with the main thrust of this book, was financialization changed the behavior of commodity prices, with prices now influenced to a greater degree by financial motivations. Like most of the literature from the "Yes" group, they assumed that financial markets are not efficient and that investors tend to engage in herd-like behavior, chasing after returns.

The UNCTAD study expanded the debate beyond a focus on CIFs, evaluating all financial traders. In fact, they found that the influence from CIF investors had diminished after the 2008 bubble, with MMT positions having a greater influence on price movements in the post-crisis period. During the commodity price increase from July 2009 to February 2011, they estimated the following correlations between futures prices and CIF/MMT positions: 0.18/0.81 for oil; 0.09/0.56 for wheat; −0.08/0.52 for corn; and −0.12/0.54 for sugar. In addition, commodity prices became increasingly correlated with other assets:

> More recently, cross-market linkages have appeared with a large variety of currencies, stocks and commodity derivatives, thus reinforcing the evidence of investor herding in multiple assets. Hedge funds are widely believed to contribute significantly to cross-market correlation through the sharing of investment ideas and by using the same macroeconomic indicators to formulate their trades.
>
> (Flassbeck *et al.*, 2011, p. 32)

Another aspect of the UNCTAD study was a survey of market participants, including physical and financial traders, and there was fairly unanimous agreement on the influence from financial traders:

> All those interviewed pointed to the impact of the increasing activities of financial players in commodity markets, as evidenced by both rising trading volumes and increased open interest. It was also noted that financial players increasingly enter the physical markets by opening their own trading desks or devising physically backed ETF or ETN. Banks were also reported to engage in commodity production. A bank engaged in sugar production for the ethanol market was cited as an example. Traders differed in their perception of time horizons: the majority said that the strongest impact has been felt over the past five years or after 2004, while two traders referred to the past 10 years.
>
> (Flassbeck *et al.*, 2011, pp. 42–43)

The UNCTAD study provides a clue to the most important influence of CIF positions: *if CIF long positions cover the short positions of commercial hedgers –* hedging needs are balanced, *prices will be determined by the opinions of speculators* – MMTs and other reportable positions. This is essentially what Working suggested, and we discuss this influence in greater detail in the next section.

The US Senate investigated speculative activities in the wheat market during the 2007–08 price bubble (US Senate, 2009). Like the oil market investigation, market participants were complaining about the rising costs of hedging from persistent and rapidly rising prices; additionally, there was a systemic lack of convergence between futures and spot markets – the basis failed to move to zero, an indication of market failure. The lack of convergence between futures and physical prices was the main focus of the SWR. If the basis does not approach zero at expiration, then the ability to hedge is compromised.[9] Lack of convergence is uncommon in futures markets, and suggests a market failure. According to the SWR, virtually all of the grain traders and many of the market analysts said that the most significant factor underlying the lack of convergence was the dramatic growth and presence of index traders on the Chicago Board of Trade. The subcommittee noted that in previous investigations of speculation activity there were typically a range of views on the causes of price movements, not this time.

The SWR focused its investigation on the exchanges with the highest level of index traders, the CBOT and Kansas City Board of Trade (KCBOT), as index trading constituted as much as 50 percent of the long open interest on the CBOT, and 30 percent on the KCBOT. Table 5.2 compiles some of basis data from the SWR. From 2000 to 2005, the delivery basis averaged 21 cents on the CBOT and 26 cents on the KCBOT. From 2006 to 2007, the delivery basis widened to an average of 56 cents and 37 cents on the CBOT and KCBOT respectively; and the 2008 maximums in each market were $1.53 and 50 cents. The growth of the basis at expiration created a puzzling situation: why weren't grain warehouses taking advantage of price differences between the cash and futures markets which would force the basis back to average delivery cost? The arbitrage play in this case would be for grain warehouses to sell a futures contract and deliver wheat at the higher price offered in the futures market, thus driving the futures price down toward the spot price.

One of the more vocal "No" group critics is Professor Craig Pirrong from the University of Houston. Pirrong criticized the SWR (Pirrong, 2009) for exactly this issue. He questioned why the operators of delivery warehouse facilities (he listed ADM, Cargill, and The Andersons) did not pursue the risk-free arbitrage profit

Table 5.2 Average daily delivery and front-month basis (US$)

Basis at delivery	2000–05	2006–07	2008 maximum
Chicago	0.21	0.56	1.53
KC	0.26	0.37	0.50
Front-month basis			
Chicago	0.25	1.10	2.25
KC	0.25	0.51	0.90

Source: US Senate (2009).

opportunities, and he suggested it was a "flagrant failure" of the report that they did not ask the grain merchants this question. In fact, the report did provide an explanation. Grain warehouses have the ability to profit from an alternative, the storage arbitrage trade. As more investment funds flowed into wheat futures, the front-month basis increased sharply, and the storage arbitrage profits generated from the steep contango were greater than delivery arbitrage profits.

Table 5.2 includes the average front-month and delivery basis values from 2000 to 2008 presented in the SWR. The average daily basis for the front-month contract was about 25 cents per bushel in both markets; however, from 2006 to 2007, the front-month basis increased to $1.10 per bushel on the CBOT, and 51 cents on the KCBOT. In 2008, the maximum basis peaked at $2.25 on the CBOT and 90 cents on the KCBOT. Comparing the two arbitrage opportunities during the 2006–07 period, the front-month basis (storage arbitrage) exceeded the delivery basis (delivery arbitrage) by 54 cents on the CBOT, and the 2008 maximum for the front month exceeded the delivery month by 72 cents. For those with the capacity to store wheat, the storage arbitrage play was optimal, even after consideration of storage and opportunity costs.[10] As the SWR noted,

> Elevator operators and other grain market participants told the Subcommittee that, in recent years, because the futures and cash price difference has been so great, this approach [the storage trade] … was more profitable than any other type of prudent investment strategy.
>
> (US Senate, 2009, p. 138)

The only way grain warehouses would pursue arbitrage profits from delivery is if they had unlimited space, capital, and wheat. Warehouse space and wheat are finite, and research has shown there are limits to arbitrage as well, related to the amount of capital investors are willing to allocate to alternative profit opportunities (De Long *et al.*, 1990).

Irwin *et al.* (2009) were critical of the findings in the SWR. They analyzed basis issues in the wheat, corn, and soybean markets because there were convergence problems there as well. Irwin *et al.* agreed with the SWR, the main reason for lack of convergence was steep contango on the front-month contract making storage arbitrage more profitable than delivery arbitrage, and possible explanations included: one, CBOT's storage rates were a few cents lower than commercial rates, which made the carry trade a little more profitable for delivery warehouses; and, two, the presence of long-only CIFs. As one might expect, Irwin *et al.* claimed that CIFs were not the cause, and their arguments in this earlier paper included: (1) there is an increase in the spread during the roll, but it recedes over the next few days, so rolling does not permanently increase the spread; (2) the spike in the spread began several years before convergence became an issue; and (3) index fund positions did not change much after 2006, yet the variability of the spread increased over time.

There is, however, compelling evidence that CIF traders impact the spread through the required rolling of contracts. Mou (2010) showed that there were large arbitrage opportunities created by the *Goldman roll*. Investors could earn profits by front-running the roll of the passive CIFs which occurred on specified trading days of the month.[11] Mou focused his analysis on the SP-GSCI because it is the largest CIF, and the contracts are rolled over a five-day period prior to moving into the delivery month. Mou estimated returns for two strategies, one that front-runs the roll by 10 days, and one that front-runs by 5 days. From 1980 to 1999, the pre-CFMA era, estimated returns were low or negative for both strategies; however, from 2000 to 2010, the estimated annualized, unlevered excess returns ranged from 7.8 percent to 10.5 percent for strategy 1, and 5.2 percent to 10.8 percent for strategy 2. The only way one could generate excess returns from these strategies is if rolling impacts the spread. As a control, Mou estimated returns for non-indexed commodities and found: "When the same strategies are applied to 18 commodities not included in the SP-GSCI, there were no abnormal returns earned in either period" (Mou, 2010, p. 5). This is certainly compelling evidence that CIF positions affected the spread through the roll.

Mou tried to gauge when arbitrage investors began taking advantage of front-running strategies, and noted that speculative spread positions take a five-fold jump starting in 2004, peaking in 2008. The returns from his strategies had been declining since 2006, "and the average excess returns dropped to levels close to 0. The livestock portfolio even experienced negative average excess returns since 2008, which suggests a possibility of overexploiting by arbitrageurs" (Mou, 2010, p. 21). Mou suggested that many ETF and ETN funds changed their roll strategies (so-called *second generation* funds) beginning in 2006 in order to reduce the negative roll yields from contango markets.

It is clear from Mou's research that CIFs were affecting the spread and distorting prices in the futures markets, and their actions created profit opportunities for arbitrage investors. While CIF positions may not have increased after 2006, arbitrage funds did increase spread positions to front-run the roll, and this explained the observation by Irwin *et al.* that the variability of the spread was changing after 2006 even though index fund positions were relatively unchanged.

What have we learned? Has the mass of bodies moved? The academic debate may never be resolved because, as the USDA report (1967) suggested, it is difficult to find the smoking gun of speculation if one relies solely on position data; rather, a wide sample of market situations is necessary to identify the periods when speculation has a measurable impact on prices. Reflecting back on the questions raised from the original Masters–Irwin and Sanders skirmish: (1) one can construct formal models (Hamilton, 2008; Frankel, 2014) to explain how speculation impacts prices; (2) the data on CIFs influencing prices are inconclusive; (3) arbitrage traders have taken advantage of price discrepancies caused by CIFs (Mou, 2010); (4) substitution effects and cross-elasticities of demand explain price increases for off-exchange commodities (Petzel, 2009); and (5) as will be discussed in the next section, financialization of commodity markets implies that it is inappropriate to compare Working's *T*-index values pre versus post CFMA. It is the contention in this work, as the UNCTAD report (2011) suggested, that the influence from CIF positions arises from the fact that, in many markets, they balance the hedging needs of commercial traders, thus increasing the influence from other speculative positions during the price discovery process of futures markets.

Despite the disagreement among academics, market participants, including Wall Street banks, acknowledge that financial flows impacted prices. The next section summarizes the data in support of the financialization thesis, providing a broad spectrum of evidence. We also address the relevance of Working's Speculative *T*-index in today's financialized markets.

Financialization of commodities: The evidence

We begin with data on the "known knowns," the points on which both sides are in agreement: the composition of traders in many markets has changed significantly, with financial traders dominating most markets; commodity markets have increased in size; comovements between individual commodities have increased, more so for indexed commodities; and correlations between commodity returns and other assets have increased.

Changing structure of the markets

Historically commercial traders had accounted for two-thirds to three-quarters of open interest in most markets; however, since the 2000 CFMA, the combination of CIFs, swaps, managed money, and other financial traders now dominates trading activity in most markets. For CBOT corn, commercials held 75.0 percent of open interest pre-CFMA (Figure 5.2) and 50 percent post-CFMA (Figure 5.3). CBOT wheat is an example of a market that has literally flipped. Pre-CFMA, commercial traders averaged about 70.0 percent of open interest (Figure 5.4), and they currently account for about 30.0 percent (Figure 5.5). Crude oil is another market that has flipped, as commercials previously held about 80 percent of open interest (Figure 5.6), and now account for about 20 percent (Figure 5.7).

Better Markets (2011) calculated Workings' *T*-index values for several commodities, both pre and post CFMA, and those values are also included in Figures 5.2–5.7. Pre-CFMA values for wheat, corn, and oil averaged about 1.2, 1.1, and 1.05 respectively; post-CFMA values were about 1.8, 1.5, and 1.3. In comparison, *T*-index estimates from Irwin and Sanders (2010) for wheat and corn were 1.44 (maximum value of 1.87) and 1.15 (maximum of 1.34) respectively, though their sampling period was shorter. While Irwin and Sanders (2010) did not calculate *T*-indexes for energy categories, they did provide open interest held by commercial traders based on DCOT data for oil and natural gas. For crude oil, only 18.0 percent of open interest was held by commercials and 12.0 percent for natural gas.

Market size

Prior to the CFMA, commodity markets were regarded as relatively thin, smaller in size than other financial markets, hence the need for the double-edged sword of speculators. As Masters' data showed (Figure 1.2), the amount of money flowing

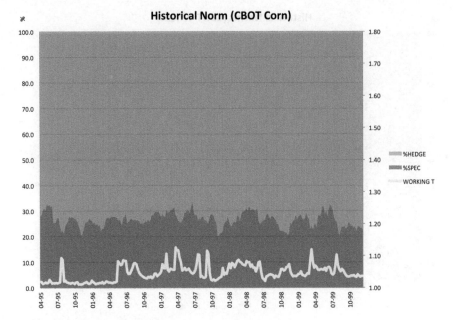

Figure 5.2 Market structure CBOT corn – historical norm.

Source: Better Markets, 2011.

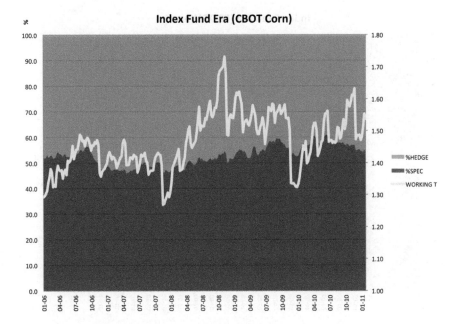

Figure 5.3 Market structure CBOT corn – index fund era.

Source: Better Markets, 2011.

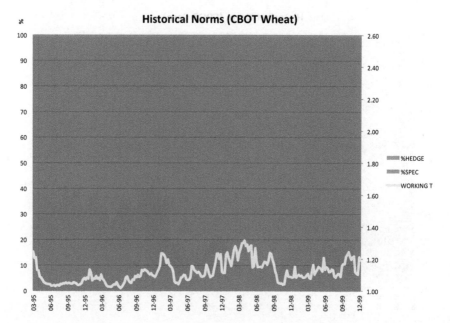

Figure 5.4 Market structure CBOT wheat – historical norm.

Source: Better Markets, 2011.

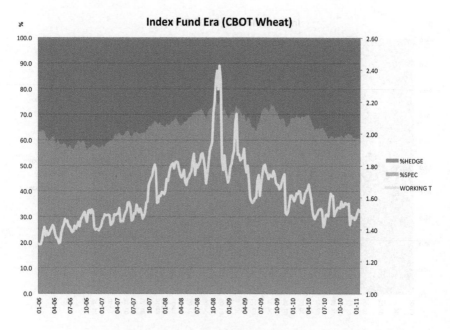

Figure 5.5 Market structure CBOT wheat – index fund era.

Source: Better Markets, 2011.

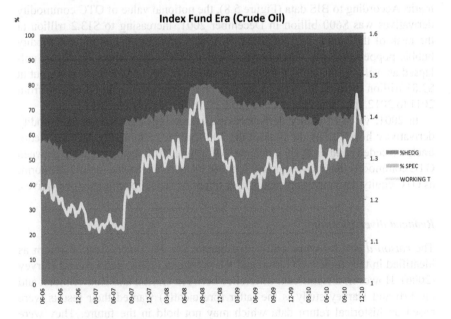

Figure 5.6 Market structure WTI oil – historical norm.

Source: Better Markets, 2011.

Figure 5.7 Market structure WTI oil – index fund era.

Source: Better Markets, 2011.

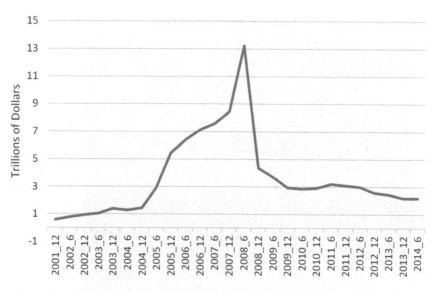

Figure 5.8 Notional value of commodity derivatives.

Source: Bank for International Settlement OTC Derivative Statistics.

into major commodity indexes increased from $13 billion in 2000 to $270 billion in 2008. The investment flows into OTC commodity derivatives were just as dramatic. According to BIS data (Figure 5.8), the notional value of OTC commodity derivatives was $600 billion in December 2001, increasing to $13.2 trillion at the peak of the bubble in June 2008, a 22-fold increase. When the commodity bubble popped in 2008, the notional value of OTC commodity derivatives collapsed as well, falling to $4.4 trillion by the end of 2008. After bottoming out at $2.85 trillion in June 2010, the notional value remained around $3 trillion from 2011 to 2012, and has since declined to $2.2 trillion as of June 2014.

In 2001, value of equity derivatives was three times the size of commodity derivatives; however, by the peak of the 2008 bubble, commodity derivative contracts exceeded equities by 30.0 percent. As of June 2014, the relationship between OTC commodity derivatives and equities seems to have returned to the 2001 norm, as OTC equity derivatives are again three times the size of commodity derivatives.

Reduced diversification

The *raison d'etre* for commodity investments was the diversification return as identified in the studies of Gorton and Rouwenhorst (2006) and Erb and Harvey (2006). However, a significant difference between Gorton and Rouwenhorst and the Erb and Harvey study is the latter (presciently) warned their results were based on historical return data which may not hold in the future. They were right. Financialization of commodity markets has all but eliminated the perceived diversification benefits. Erb and Harvey estimated that the return correlations between individual commodities were near zero for their period of analysis, 1982 to 2004, and these results suggested one could view returns on individual commodities as a collection of independent assets. Therefore, adding individual (or indexed) commodities into a portfolio could generate a diversification gain. As investors herded into commodities, the historical return relationship changed.

Tang and Xiong (2012) is one of the most comprehensive studies on changes in comovements between individual commodities, and comovements between commodities and other assets, and their data sample covered 1980 to 2011, which allowed them to evaluate the most important period for financialization. Consistent with Erb and Campbell, Tang and Xiong found the average rolling correlations between individual commodities stayed below 0.1 from the 1980s through the early 2000s; however, by 2009, the correlations among indexed commodities had increased to 0.5, while off-indexed commodities increased to 0.2. Individual commodities included in indexes were losing their diversification return because, as part of an indexed portfolio, they were no longer independent assets.

Increased correlations between oil and indexed commodities

One of the main issues addressed in the Tang and Xiong paper was the comovement between oil and other commodities. Their straightforward hypothesis was that more money flowing into CIFs increases the correlation between oil and indexed commodities, since oil carries the largest weight in commodity indexes. They found that correlations between oil and individual commodity returns displayed little or no trends through 2004, then significant positive correlations thereafter, consistent with the significant rise of funds flowing into commodity index investments. In contrast, they note the correlations of returns among non-indexed commodities and oil increased at a lesser rate. Specifically, the correlations of non-indexed commodities with oil increased by a rate of 0.04 from 2004 to 2011, for a total change of 0.28; and correlations of indexed commodities with oil increased by 0.06 per year (50 percent higher per year), for a cumulative change of 0.42.

Tang and Xiong's results provide strong evidence that changes in oil prices influence prices of all indexed commodities through a portfolio channel. Regardless of whether one believes that speculators caused the price of oil to rise, as the largest component of commodity indices, changes in the price of oil cause changes in the prices of *all* indexed commodities. The direct mechanism is the rebalancing effect. In a fixed-weight portfolio, as oil prices increase, portfolio managers need to purchase more contracts of all other components to maintain the index weights. The creation of CIFs, and the significant amount of money invested in them, has created a financial transmission from oil prices to other commodities.

Another connection between oil and non-energy commodities was identified in recent research on herding behavior in commodity markets. Demirer *et al.* (2013) found evidence that herding behavior in energy and metals influenced herding behavior in grains:

Our findings suggest the presence of herd behavior in the market for grains only with no evidence of herding in other commodity sectors. Herd behavior in grains is observed during the high market volatility state only .... On the other hand, a significant cross-market herding effect on grains is observed from the energy and metals markets, suggesting that large price movements in energy and metals tend to contribute to herding among investors in grains futures.

(p. 4)

Digging a little deeper into the oil–wheat relationship, Figure 5.9 displays oil and wheat prices from 1995 through 2014. Prior to enactment of the 2000 CFMA, the simple correlation between oil and wheat prices was –0.12, and post-CFMA the correlation increased to 0.815. Adding SRW wheat (and other commodities) into commodity indexes like the SP-GSCI has created a financial mechanism that allows oil prices to influence wheat prices.

Baffes and Haniotis (2010) evaluated the 2006–08 commodity price boom and noted, when considering the impact of energy prices on non-energy commodities, "the effect of energy prices on the prices of all commodities has increased considerably when the recent boom is taken into consideration – suggesting that the energy/non-energy price link has strengthened" (p. 17). The pass-through from energy prices to non-energy prices (which included a food price index) is measured using price elasticities. Baffes and Haniotis noted their previous estimate, based on data ending in 2005, of the long-run price elasticity relation was 0.18 – a 10 percent increase in energy prices was associated with a 1.8 percent increase in food prices. This paper updated the data, extending through 2008, and they found the long-run price elasticity increased from 0.18 to 0.27, a 50 percent increase. Adding three more years of data, which coincided with the financialization of

Figure 5.9 Wheat and oil prices (November 2006 = 100).

Source: www.Indexmundi.com

commodity markets, caused a significant jump in the elasticity estimate. There was no clear-cut explanation offered for the change, though they mentioned corn ethanol as a possibility. The most logical explanation for the change in the price elasticity is the increased comovements between the price of oil and the prices of all other indexed commodities, including food.

Commodity and equity correlations

Tang and Xiong (2010) found that financialization of commodities from rising inflows of CIF investors also changed the relationship between commodity and equity investments. For the SP-GSCI and S&P 500 stock index, the rolling correlations ranged between −0.2 and 0.1 from the mid-1990s to 2006, and by 2008 it increased to 0.6. Tang and Xiong's (2010) conclusion succinctly sums up financialization's impact:

> As a result of the financialization process, the price of an individual commodity is no longer determined by its supply and demand. Instead, prices are also determined by the aggregate risk appetite for financial assets and the investment behavior of diversified commodity index investors. This fundamental change is likely to persist as long as commodity index investment remains popular among financial investors and has profound implications for a wide range of issues such as commodity producers' hedging strategies, investors' investment strategies, and countries' energy and food policies.
>
> (p. 27)

Demand for commodities from China

Tang and Xiong (2012) evaluated the claim that increased global demand from emerging market economies, especially China, was the main cause of commodity price increases in the 2000s. First, they analyzed front-month futures prices for six commodities (heating oil, copper, soybeans, wheat, corn, and cotton) traded on both US and Chinese futures exchanges. The first three displayed similar price trends in both markets, but the latter three showed no pronounced price spikes in the Chinese futures market during the 2007–08 bubble. As they explained, China was not a net importer of wheat, corn, and cotton, so the "demand from China" story is irrelevant for explaining the price spikes in these commodities on US futures markets. An alternative explanation is required.

In an earlier version of their paper, Tang and Xiong (2010) provided data on individual return correlations between eight commodities (heating oil, corn, wheat, soybeans, cotton, sugar, copper, and gold) traded on both futures exchanges. From 1980 through 2005–06, return correlations averaged about 0.1 on both exchanges, then correlations on US exchanges increased to 0.5, while correlations on Chinese markets stayed below 0.2. They concluded, "This contrast again refutes commodity demands from China as the driver of the large increases in commodity price comovements in the US" (Tang and Xiong, 2010, p. 12). Other researchers have argued that the China story is lacking, especially during the peak of the 2008 bubble, at a time when the global economy (China included) was slowing down (Baffes and Haniotis, 2010).

Increased volatility

Tang and Xiong (2012) examined changes in volatility of returns (measured as the annualized daily return volatility) for oil, the non-energy (food commodities) excess return index of the SP-GSCI, and Morgan Stanley's world equity index. They found oil price volatility increased significantly from 30 percent to 60 percent in 2008, a number matched in their sample only by the volatility caused by the 1991 Gulf War. More important, the return volatility of the non-energy commodity index was relatively stable at 10 percent over most of the period but increased to 27 percent in 2008 and 2009.

Oil and the dollar

There has been a significant amount of research on the increased correlation between the US dollar and oil. While indexed commodities have become more correlated with the dollar, oil has experienced the most significant change. The most common explanation for the relationship is that a decline in the dollar reduces revenues of producers when converted into domestic currency, so they must increase the dollar price of oil to maintain expected revenues. A second explanation is that commodities are used to hedge against inflation and depreciating currencies, so a falling dollar stimulates increased investment in commodities. Oil is an asset used by investors to hedge against price changes. One issue with these explanations is that the negative correlation between oil and the dollar can only be found *after* the 2000 CFMA was enacted: the correlation between oil and the dollar prior to 2000 is non-existent. Therefore, the likely explanation is that the financialization process in commodity markets expanded the ability of investors to buy *paper oil*, and trends following macro hedge funds have turned a fad into what is perceived as a permanent historical relationship.

Figure 5.10 shows the rolling correlations between the US dollar and WTI crude oil pre and post CFMA. There is no discernible trend prior to 2002, but the correlation turns decidedly negative beginning in 2003, and strengthening over time. Table 5.3 confirms these changes with simple correlation coefficients between the Broad Dollar Index and WTI Oil. Prior to the CFMA, the dollar–oil relation is non-existent, and it turns significantly negative after 2000. Oil price volatility also increased as measured by both the standard deviation and coefficient of variation.[12]

Measuring speculation and its impact

Irwin and Sanders (2010) found a relationship between high levels of Working's Speculative *T*-index and volatility for some commodities in their study, but they argued that "the maximums are not beyond those recorded by prior researchers,

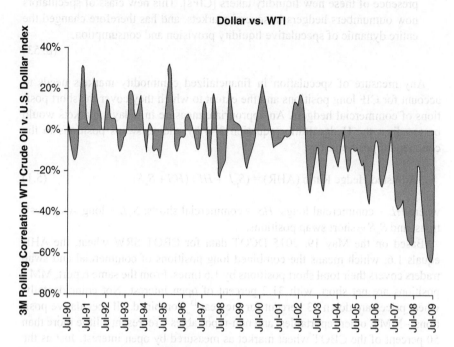

Figure 5.10 WTI oil and US dollar correlations.

Source: Better Markets, 2011. Reproduced with permission.

the average values are near historic norms, and the minimums could be considered inadequate" (p. 19). Given the dramatic change in the structure of futures markets brought about by financialization, comparing historical speculative measures with post-CFMA measures is essentially a meaningless comparison. In a comment letter to the CFTC, *Better Markets* (2011) summarized the issue:

> The point is that today's commodity futures markets are structurally different from those that Holbrook Working originally studied .... While Working's methodology is sound, its use must appropriately take into account the

Table 5.3 WTI oil and the major currency dollar index

Time period	Dollar–oil correlation	Oil standard deviation	Coefficient of variation
January 1986 to December 1999	−0.05	3.7	0.19
January 2000 to December 2004	−0.74	6.7	0.22
January 2005 to May 2015	−0.84	20.4	0.25

Source: Federal Reserve Economic Data (Author's calculations).

presence of these new liquidity takers [CIFs]. This new class of speculators now outnumbers hedgers in several markets, and has therefore changed the entire dynamic of speculative liquidity provision and consumption.

(p. 53)

Any measure of speculation in financialized commodity markets needs to account for CIF long positions and the extent to which they cover the short positions of commercial hedgers. An appropriate measure in today's markets would be to adjust the Hedge Ratio (equation 3.4) by adding swaps positions to the commercial positions:

$$\text{Adjusted Hedge Ratio (AHR)} = (S_w L + HL)/(HS + S_w S) \qquad (5.1)$$

where HL = commercial longs; HS = commercial shorts; $S_w L$ = long swap positions; and $S_w S$ = short swap positions.

Based on the May 19, 2015 DCOT data for CBOT SRW wheat, the AHR equals 1.6, which means the combined long positions of commercial and swap traders covers their total short positions by 1.6 times. From the same report, MMT positions are net short, with 31.2 percent of open interest. Not coincidentally, wheat prices are down 13 percent for the year.[13] Combined, all speculative positions – MMT, other reportables, and non-reportables – represent a little more than 50 percent of the CBOT wheat market as measured by open interest. Just as the marginal investor determines prices in equity valuation models, true speculators now significantly influence futures prices in the short run. Again, this is not to say they determine prices, rather they amplify and cause overshooting.

As the UNCTAD (2011) study found, MMT positions and commodity prices were highly correlated from July 2009 to February 2011, with oil equal to 0.81. A 2015 *Financial Times* article stated as much:

> Forget the interplay between supply and demand. When it comes to oil prices, hedge funds and speculators are exerting an uncommonly large influence, say many in one of the world's most important market .... Traders say funds have bought oil futures not just as a bet on an eventual oil price recovery, but as a hedge against a weaker dollar, rising government bond yields and shifting inflation expectations, which have roiled the bigger part of their portfolios.
>
> (Sheppard and Hume, 2015)

As the Adjusted Hedge Ratio indicates, CIF positions dominate wheat and corn markets as well, and the correlations measured by UNCTAD for wheat and corn prices and MMT positions were both over 0.5.

In today's financialized markets, commercial traders are also more than likely engaged in speculative or financial activity. Financialization has increased the prevalence of contango, and commercial traders have reacted to CIF traders by "selling into the demand" as Petzel (2009) stated:

Seasoned observers of commodity markets know that as noncommercial participants enter a market, the opposite side is usually taken by a short-term liquidity provider, but the ultimate counterparty is likely to be a commercial. In the case of commodity index buyers, evidence suggests that the sellers are not typically other investors or leveraged speculators. Instead, *they are owners of the physical commodity who are willing to sell into futures market and either deliver at expiration or roll their hedge forward if the spread allows them to profit from continued storage* [emphasis mine]. This activity is effectively creating synthetic long positions in the commodity for the index investor, matched against real inventories held by the shorts. We have seen high spot prices along with large inventories and strong positive carry relationships as a result of the expanded index activity over the last few years.

(pp. 8–9)

Contango has encouraged commercial traders to engage in financial activity through the storage arbitrage trade. It is more profitable to hold inventory and sell wheat to investors who will never take delivery. Figure 5.11 shows annual wheat production and weekly average short contracts held by commercial traders in CBOT wheat from 1997 to 2013. While wheat production declined somewhat from 2001 through 2008, the number of short contracts held by commercial traders increased dramatically beginning in 2003. From 1997 to 2002, weekly short contracts held by commercial interests averaged about 61,000, and from 2003 to 2008, the average number of weekly short contracts increased to 151,000, a 147 percent increase. If hedging is the dominant motive of commercial wheat traders, then one would expect to find the number of short contracts positively related

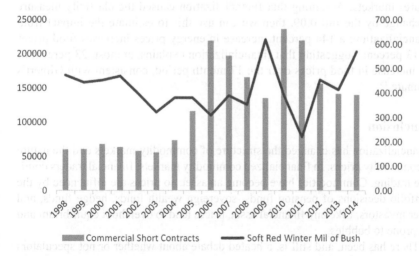

Figure 5.11 Wheat production and commercial short futures positions.

Source: USDA Economic Research Service; and CFTC Commitment of Traders Reports (Author's calculations).

to wheat production. For the period from 1997 to 2002, the correlation between wheat production and the number of short contracts was +0.7; since 2002, the correlation has been negative, equal to −0.44. These data are consistent with the Senate Wheat Report (US Senate, 2009) which showed the average front-month basis increased sharply after 2005, rising from an average of 25 cents per bushel to $1.10 over the 2006–07 period. Commercial traders took advantage of contango markets, "selling into demand" created by CIF positions, just as Petzel stated.

To the most important question: to what extent did financialization influence food prices during the 2008 bubble? The three main factors blamed for the rise in prices are global demand, bio-fuel mandates, and financialization. Gilbert (2010) provided estimates of the impact from CIF investments on wheat, corn, and soybeans for the first half of 2008. His estimates range from 12 percent to 15 percent annualized, or approximately 6–7 percent over the six-month period. Based on the FAO Food Price Index, prices increased about 25 percent in the first six months of 2008, so Gilbert's estimates suggest that financialization could be responsible for about one-quarter of the increase.

An alternative estimate can be inferred from Baffes and Haniotis' (2010) energy–food elasticity measure. The trough to peak for energy prices during the 2007–08 bubble was January 2007 to July 2008 (17 months).[14] Over this period, the Energy Commodity Index increased 144 percent, and the Food Commodity Index increased 57 percent (The FAO Food Price Index increased by 58 percent over a similar period). Assuming that financialization of commodities is the dominant factor that changed the long-run elasticity relationship between food and energy prices, then we can use the measured change (from 0.18 to 0.27) to estimate the impact from speculation. The price elasticity estimate increased by 0.09 over the 2005–08 period, which coincides with financialization of futures markets. Assuming that financialization caused the elasticity measure to change by the full 0.09, then we can use this to estimate the impact from financialization: a 144 percent increase in energy prices increases food prices by 13 percent, suggesting that financialization explains, at most, 23 percent of the increase in food prices over the 17 month period, consistent with Gilbert's estimate.[15]

Conclusion

Financialization has changed the structure of commodity markets and the nature of commodity prices. In financialized commodity markets, financial traders dominate trading. Commodities have become an asset, so prices are influenced by the portfolio decisions of pension funds, sovereign wealth funds, hedge funds, and other investors. Like any financial asset, prices tend to overshoot equilibrium and are prone to bubbles.

There has been, and still is, a heated debate about whether or not speculators influence prices. Much of the academic research has focused on the influence from CIFs, which misses the key change in commodity markets: when net long positions of CIFs cover the majority of net short positions of commercial hedgers, prices will be influenced by the remaining positions, traditional speculators. While a group of researchers dismisses the possibility that speculators influence prices, market participants do not.

The commodity market super-cycle of the 2000s was an unprecedented era of volatility and price peaks. While the 1970s was a similar if not more volatile period, prices were influenced by oil embargos and there was double-digit inflation; neither of these was evident in the 2000s. Certainly speculation cannot increase commodity prices alone, and global demand growth was a necessary condition for enterprise to be driven by a whirlpool of speculation. Given the low price elasticity of demand for oil and other commodities, speculative bubbles can endure for months at a time. Demand or supply shocks are necessary ingredients that "give legs" to speculative bubbles, but this time was different.

Financialization and higher commodity prices had other consequences. Higher commodity prices increased the value of farmland, and in the New Normal post-financial crisis world of low returns on traditional assets, rising farmland values created an appetite by hedge funds, pension funds, and other investors. Low returns on traditional investments were expressed in other ways, as merger and acquisition activity went into hyper mode driven by the resurgence of private equity. In the next chapter we discuss changes in the food industry under the financialization food regime.

Notes

1 For evidence in support of speculators influencing commodity prices, a list of over 130 papers and links has been compiled by Markus Henn of World Economy, Ecology & Development at http://www2.weed-online.org/uploads/evidence_on_impact_of_com modity_speculation.pdf. For evidence speculators do not influence prices, one can find another long list of citations on a website created by the International Swaps and Derivatives Association at http://www.commodityfact.org/what-the-experts-say/.

2 Let me begin with a warning: there appear to be preconceived biases on both sides of the debate, even among the "rigorous" academic studies, and I hold no illusions that the arguments made in this chapter will settle the issue. If the data are unable to convince one of a particular view, then most researchers tend toward confirmation bias, and I certainly am not immune.

3 The two new reports are somewhat related. The SCIT provides detailed position data on CIFs while the DCOT report incorporates CIF positions into the swaps category, with some differences. For example, pension (and other investment) funds that place index investment directly into the futures markets are classified as *managed money* or *other reportables* in the DCOT. More detailed information can be found in the DCOT's *explanatory notes* at http://www.cftc.gov/ucm/groups/public/@commitmentsoftraders/documents/file/disaggregatedcotexplanatorynot.pdf

4 It should be noted that the majority of studies focus on returns measured as the change in prices over a holding period.

5 Keynes described picking stocks as like a newspaper contest where contestants were asked to identify the prettiest six faces out of one hundred, and the person who selects the most in the top six wins. The optimal strategy is to pick the six faces that you believe the majority will select, not who you actually believe are the six prettiest.

6 The imputation method is the same approach was used by Masters to generate the data in Figure 1.2. Estimates of total dollars invested by CIFs are found by taking the product of the number of contracts held by CIFs in a specific agriculture commodity (provided in the SCIT report) times the dollar value of the contract divided by the weight of the commodity. Based on estimates of the total dollars invested, one can then find the dollars invested or number of contracts held for any other non-agriculture commodity in the index. A formal example can be found in Masters (2008).

7 Masters provided additional testimony to the CFTC in 2009 and 2010.

8 The DJ-UBS index was known as the DJ-AIG index until 2008, when AIG was nationalized.

9 It should be noted that the basis does not actually move to zero at expiration due to transportation costs to delivery points. In addition, it is more accurate to state that hedging becomes more difficult when the basis is volatile and unpredictable.

10 Average monthly storage costs at CBOT warehouses were about 5 cents per bushel, and interest rates were low as well.

11 One simply sells a contract before the roll, then offsets with a buy as the roll drives the price lower. On the front-month end, one buys before the index buys, and sells after the index buying drives prices higher.

12 The coefficient of variation is the standard deviation divided by the mean, creating a normalized measure, or variability per unit.

13 The data are similar for corn and soybeans. The AHR for corn is 1.3, and for soybeans it is 1.45, while MMT positions are net short in both commodities.

14 The data are from Indexmundi.com, which is originally sourced from IMF data.

15 Certainly, other factors may have caused a change in the price elasticity relationship, so this estimate represents an upper bound.

Bibliography

Baffes, J., and Haniotis, T. (2010). Placing the 2006/08 commodity price boom into perspective. *World Bank Policy Research Working Paper Series* (No. 5371).

BetterMarkets. (2011). Comments on position limits for derivatives. http://www.better markets.com/sites/default/files/documents/CFTC%20Position%20Limits%20CL%20As%20Submitted%20Hi%20Res.pdf. Retrieved October 21, 2014

Davidson, P. (2008). Crude oil prices:" market fundamentals" or speculation? *Challenge, 51*(4), 110–118.

Davidson, P., Falk, L. H., and Lee, H. (1974). Oil: its time allocation and project independence. *Brookings Papers on Economic Activity*, 411–448.

De Long, J. B., Shleifer, A., Summers, L. H., and Waldmann, R. J. (1990). Noise trader risk in financial markets. *Journal of political Economy*, 703–738.

Demirer, R., Lee, H.-T., and Lien, D. D. (2013). Commodity financialization and herd behavior in commodity futures markets. Available at SSRN: http://papers.ssrn.com/sol3/papers.cfm?abstract_id=2265506

Dornbusch, R. (1976). Expectations and exchange rate dynamics. *The Journal of Political Economy, 84*(6), 1161–1176.

Erb, C. B., and Harvey, C. R. (2006). The strategic and tactical value of commodity futures. *Financial Analysts Journal, 62*(2), 69–97.

Fattouh, B., Kilian, L., and Mahadeva, L. (2012). The role of speculation in oil markets: What have we learned so far? CEPR Discussion Paper No. DP8916. Available at SSRN: http://papers.ssrn.com/sol3/papers.cfm?abstract_id=2034134

Flassbeck, H., Bicchetti, D., Mayer, J., and Rietzler, K. (2011). Price formation in finan-cialized commodity markets: the role of information. Paper presented at the United Nations Conference on Trade and Development (UNCTAD).

Frankel, J. A. (2014). Effects of speculation and interest rates in a "carry trade" model of commodity prices. *Journal of International Money and Finance, 42*, 88–112.

Frenk, D. (2010). *Review of Irwin and Sanders 2010 OECD Reports.* Better Markets, Inc.

Gilbert, C. (2010). Speculative influences on commodity futures prices, 2006–2008. UNCTAD Discussion Papers 197.

Gorton, G., and Rouwenhorst, K. G. (2006). Facts and fantasies about commodity futures. *Financial Analysts Journal, 62*(2), 47–68.

Hamilton, J. D. (2009). *Causes and Consequences of the Oil Shock of 2007–08.* National Bureau of Economic Research.

Hamilton, J. D., and Wu, J. C. (2014). Risk premia in crude oil futures prices. *Journal of International Money and Finance, 42*, 9–37.

Irwin, S. H., and Sanders, D. R. (2010). The impact of index and swap funds on commod-ity futures markets. OECD Food, Agriculture and Fisheries Papers, No. 27, OECD Publishing. http://dx.doi.org/10.1787/5kmd40wl1t5f-en

Irwin, S. H., and Sanders, D. R. (2012). Testing the Masters Hypothesis in commodity futures markets. *Energy economics, 34*(1), 256–269.

Irwin, S. H., Garcia, P., Good, D. L., and Kunda, E. (2009). Poor convergence performance of CBOT corn, soybean and wheat futures contracts: Causes and solutions. *Marketing and Outlook Research Report, 2.*

Juvenal, L., and Petrella, I. (2011). Speculation in the oil market. Working Paper, Federal Reserve Bank of St Louis.

Krugman, P. (2008). More on oil speculation. [Web log message.] Retrieved April 10, 2015 from http://krugman.blogs.nytimes.com/2008/05/13/more-on-oil-and-speculation/?_r=1

Lagi, M., Bar-Yam, Y., Bertrand, K. Z., and Bar-Yam, Y. (2011). The food crises: A quan-titative model of food prices including speculators and ethanol conversion. Available at SSRN: http://papers.ssrn.com/sol3/papers.cfm?abstract_id=1932247

Masters, M. W. (2008). Testimony of Michael W. Masters before the Committee on Homeland Security and Governmental Affairs United States Senate. May 20.

Mou, Y. (2010). Limits to arbitrage and commodity index investment: front-running the Goldman roll. Available at SSRN: http://papers.ssrn.com/sol3/papers.cfm?abstract_id=1716841

Petzel, T. (2009). Testimony before the CFTC. July. Retrieved December 18, 2014 from http://www.cftc.gov/ucm/groups/public/@newsroom/documents/file/hearing072809_petzel2.pdf

Phillips, P. C., and Loretan, M. (1990). *Testing Covariance Stationarity Under Moment Condition Failure with an Application to Common Stock Returns.* Cowles Foundation for Research in Economics, Yale University.

Pirrong, C. (2009). More of the same. [Web log message.] Retrieved January 12, 2015 from http://streetwiseprofessor.com/index.php?s=wheat+speculation&paged=2

Sheppard, D. and N. Hume. (2015, May 16–17). Oil's future is transformed by hedge funds. *Financial Times*, p. 11.

Singleton, K. J. (1987). Asset prices in a time series model with disparately informed, competitive traders. In W. A. Burnett and K. J. Singleton (eds), *New Approaches to Monetary Economics.* New York: Cambridge University Press.

Singleton, K. J. (2013). Investor flows and the 2008 boom/bust in oil prices. *Management Science, 60*(2), 300–318.

Tang, K., and Xiong, W. (2010). Index investment and financialization of commodities. NBER Working Paper, w16385.

Tang, K., and Xiong, W. (2012). Index investment and the financialization of commodities. *Financial Analysts Journal, 68*(5), 54–74.

USDA. (1967). *Margins Speculation and Prices in Grains Futures Markets.*

US Senate. (2006). The role of market speculation in rising oil and gas prices: a need to put the cop back on the beat. *United States Senate Permanent Subcommittee on Investigations of the Committee on Homeland Security and Governmental Affairs, 27*, 2006.

US Senate. (2009). Excessive speculation in the wheat market. *Majority and Minority Staff Report. Permanent Subcommittee on Investigations, 24*, 107–108.

6 Private equity bought the farm
The impact of financialization

Financialization has been one of the dominant forces shaping the US and global economies since the emergence of neoliberalism in 1980. It has been *the* dominant force since 2000. In the real world this is evidenced by financialization of commodity markets, the dramatic growth in private equity, the explosion in derivatives, and the implosion of the global economy. More and more evidence suggests finance in the US has expanded beyond a point where it is harmful to growth, and the evidence comes from both heterodox and mainstream sources (Cecchetti and Kharroubi, 2012; Palley, 2007). Evidence from Cecchetti and Kharroubi suggests that reining in and reducing the size of the financial sector could raise productivity and economic growth. A recent high-profile economic debate suggests otherwise; any policy suggestion may prove fruitless in an era of *secular stagnation*.

Ben Bernanke and Larry Summers sparked a blogosphere debate over the possible causes of a long-term decline in US economic growth (Krugman, 2015). Bernanke blamed a global savings glut generated by emerging market economies, and those savings were funneled into the US, increasing the value of the dollar, causing large US trade deficits and slower growth. Summers, on the other hand, suggested that the slowdown in growth and investment was due to insufficient demand from a decline in population growth and innovation. A report by the IMF (2015) supported the Summers' hypothesis: the main explanations for declining expenditures in capital investment were slower population growth and overall weakness of economic activity.

The stagnation debate is also borne out in the real world through financial activity of corporations and private equity. The lack of investment opportunities is expressed through increased financial activities, as suggested in the financialization literature. During the neoliberal period (1980–2000), annual growth in real GDP averaged 3.4 percent; under the financialization regime, from 2001 to 2014, annual real GDP growth has averaged 1.8 percent. As investment manager Bill Gross (2009) described, "we are heading into what we call the New Normal, which is a period of time in which economies grow very slowly" (para. 5). When productive investment opportunities disappear, then the financial sector becomes the mechanism for profit generation, as Veblen suggested (1904).

The mid-2000s have been described as the golden age of private equity, and despite a slowdown in post-crisis activity, M&A activity has accelerated, with the

PE industry leading the way. The current wave of M&A activity, share buybacks, and dividend payouts are the consequence of a lack of investment opportunities and low interest rates. As a *Financial Times* article noted:

> Nick Lawson, head of event driven strategies at Deutsche Bank, says the fear in corporate boardrooms has shifted from concerns over a company's cost base to its strategy and outlook. "Following the crisis, revenue was a swear word and now M&A masks a multitude of sins. There's a real lack of capital expenditure ambition and it was first hidden by the idea of buybacks and now by M&A," he says.
>
> (Massoudi, 2015)

Have we reached a hyper-financialization stage signaling the end of the American empire as Arrighi (1994) suggested? The food industry certainly represents a test case. As merger activity accelerates, food industry firms have the qualities that Jensen suggested were ripe for private equity's pickings, slow, steady growth, which explains why food mergers have been some of the biggest dating back to the RJR-Nabisco hostile takeover in 1989. We begin this chapter with a look at private equity under the current financialization regime, focusing on recent M&A activity in the food sector in section one. While there have been recent announcements of mega-deals in 2014 and 2015, these are just the tip of the iceberg (lettuce), as there have been hundreds of mergers and takeovers over the past few years.

One of the consequences of financialization of commodity markets and increased agriculture commodity prices is an increase in farmland values, and low returns from traditional investments have whet the appetite of private equity, pension funds, and sovereign wealth funds, all of which have piled into alternative assets like farmland. We look at this financialization of farmland in section two. As investors struggle for yield, they literally are scouring the globe in search of new sources of returns, and the global chase for suitable farmland investments has been dubbed the "global land grab." First, we look at investment flows and their impact to US farmland, then we discuss the global farmland rush.

Private equity and the food industry

Private equity has been one of the dominant forces of change under the financialization regime. In the post-crisis years, market observers believed the golden age of private equity had passed, as the number of deals peaked in 2007; however, PE activity is back with a vengeance. Perhaps we are witnessing the start of its second golden age (Drean, 2014)? Several food industry mega-deals were announced in 2015. Private equity firm 3G Capital, in partnership with Warren Buffett, announced a $46 billion merger between Heinz and Kraft Foods, creating the third largest food conglomerate in the US, and fifth largest in the world. Monsanto made a $45 billion bid for Syngenta, which would create the world's largest seed and fertilizer company. And Kraft is not the first food industry takeover for 3G capital, as it has been gobbling up firms in the food and beverage industry over the past few years, including Anheuser-Busch in 2008 ($52 billion), and Burger King's acquisition of Tim Horton in 2014 ($11.4 billion). These recent takeovers suggest that the PE industry has recovered from the crisis years, and is moving full speed ahead.

The period from 2005 to mid-2007 was viewed as the so-called golden age because the number of private equity deals exploded. In the first quarter of 2005, there were close to 500 PE deals valued at $70 billion (PEGCC, 2015), and at the peak of the golden age, the third quarter of 2007, the number of deals exceeded 800, with a market value of almost $300 billion. In the first quarter of 2009, the number of deals and capital invested had collapsed along with the economy, bottoming out at roughly 400 deals valued at $30 billion. It did not take long for PE to make a comeback in the New Normal world with hundreds of billions of dollars seeking yield. The industry recovered with a bang. From 2012 to 2014, the number of deals averaged about 800 per quarter and about $140 billion in capital invested per quarter. In terms of impact, as of August 2014, there were 3,300 PE firms headquartered in the US, with 11,130 US companies and 7.5 million employees under PE fund management (PEGCC, 2015).

As discussed in Chapter 3, the source of returns from PE deals arise from the debt tax shield, market timing, and operational efficiencies. Takeovers focused on operational efficiencies tend to occur in mature industries with stable cash flows, which explains why the food industry has always been a prime target in takeovers. However, M&A activity is also driven from within, as firms use mergers to expand into new markets or increase market control through increasing market share – the inexorable march toward concentration in the capitalist system.

FoodProcessing.com, a website for the Food & Beverage industry, maintains data on industry M&A activity. Table 6.1 presents some of the M&A data provided on their website. There were 281 deals in 2013, and, of these, investment firms and banks were involved in 47, or 15 percent of all activity. One of the largest deals in 2013 was the takeover of H.J. Heinz by 3G and Berkshire Hathaway, valued at $28 billion. Other notable deals in 2013 included Shuanghui International Holdings purchase of Smithfield Foods for $7.1 billion; Sysco's $8.2 billion merger with US Foods, giving it 25 percent of the $235 billion food service market; and Kroger's purchase of Harris Teeter, the fourth largest acquisition in the supermarket industry in the past ten years.

Table 6.1 Food and beverage industry mergers

Category	2013	2012	2011	2009	2006
Diversified firms	12	18	20	5	0
Total food processors (multiproduct processors)	96 (36)	76 (28)	79 (34)	58 (16)	110 (43)
Total	281	287	381	264	392

Source: FoodProcessing.com.

Food industry M&A activity was just getting warmed up in 2013, as there were 503 deals in 2014, an increase of 80 percent. Some of the largest deals were Burger King's $11 billion acquisition of Tim Horton, the purchase of Safeway supermarkets by private equity firm AB Acquisitions LLC, and Tyson Food's $8.5 billion purchase of Hillshire Brands.

Private equity is the prime mover, the agent of change, under the food financialization regime. As returns from market timing and leverage have become more difficult to generate, only operational efficiencies remain. One has to question how new PE deals will generate returns when firms are already disciplined through high levels of debt. What is left is intensification. Without extensive productive opportunities, without outlets for billions in capital formed, there is only one option left, "squeeze blood from the turnip." A March 26, 2015 *Fortune* article described how 3G increases profits out of highly leveraged, slow-growth firms: "[3G] is known for swift layoffs, cost-cutting – and profit" (Roberts, 2015). After 3G's takeover of Anheuser-Busch, 1,400 people lost their jobs, and 350 jobs were lost one month after their Tim Horton's deal was announced. 3G's management model also uses "the concept of 'zero-based budgeting,' wherein every expense must be newly justified every year, not just new ones, and the goal is to bring it lower than the year prior" (Roberts, 2015). Finance, through PE firms, is paring the carcass to the bone. Since operational efficiencies are most likely the main source of returns going forward, some PE firms are seeking outside help by hiring executives from the industries they target (Banerjee, 2015).

If PE firms like 3G are pushing efficiencies to the limit, one has to question the efficacy of the model. Not simply testing whether PE generates superior returns over time, but what the impact has been on the economy as a whole. Jensen (1997) believed that the private equity revolution would have a positive influence on growth and shareholder value through compensating managers with stock options and commitment of investment funds for longer periods of time. Once a firm is taken private, it no longer faces the pressure from external shareholders, but it is driven to improve medium-term value to ensure a gain when the firm exits the PE fund. Evidence suggests that the US economy has been harmed by the focus on short-term profitability:

> We all pay the price for short termism. Researchers at Stanford University have concluded that pressure to meet quarterly earnings targets may be reducing research and development spending, and cutting US growth by 0.1 percentage points a year. Others have found that privately held companies, free to take a longer-term approach, invest at almost 2.5 times the rate of publicly held counterparts in the same industries. The persistent lower investment rate among America's biggest 350 listed companies may be reducing US growth by an additional 0.2 percentage points a year .... The best-run funds tie managers' compensation to performance over much longer spells – 25 years in one case.
>
> (Barton and Wiseman, 2015, para. 3)

Blame is placed on public corporations and their boards, who emphasize short-termism, but their conclusion raises similar questions about PE funds with investment horizons of five years on average. If returns from future PE deals will mainly focus on operational efficiencies, then, as 3G's previous deals indicate, labor will bear the brunt of the returns generated. How much more profit can be squeezed through efficiencies in industries that have already been forced to be efficient by high leverage ratios as a result of past deals or the threat of new ones? In the next section we evaluate capital structure across the food industry and attempt to assess where future M&A activity will come from.

Food industry capital structure

The threat of PE takeovers creates pressure on all industries and all firms, and that is expressed in an increased leverage ratio. While most food industry takeovers are driven from within the industry, PE firms have been involved in some of the largest deals. In this section we evaluate the capital structure of the food industry. Jensen's prediction of the demise of the public corporation focused on industries where long-term growth was slow and funds generated internally could not find suitable investment outlets. He might as well have described the current state of the US food industry. If, as Jensen suggested, the mature industries with slow growth are prime targets, then we would expect to find higher average leverage ratios in the food industry than the general economy. Based on this cursory look at capital structures of industries along the food supply chain, will we be able to discern any trends? Are some food industries ripe for the pickings?

The 1980s LBO phase caused a permanent increase in overall corporate leverage. Figure 6.1 shows the ratio of nonfinancial corporate liabilities to assets (L/A) from 1965 to 2014. From 1965 to 1980, total corporate leverage, with assets measured at market value, averaged 35.2 percent. During the LBO phase of the 1980s through the peak in 1993, average leverage increased to 43.8 percent. The leverage ratio has remained above the pre-1980 period, as total leverage has averaged 46.0 percent since 1993. While PE leveraged takeovers are one reason behind the overall rise in leverage, the threat of takeovers forces all firms to increase leverage in defense.

It should be noted that financial statement data on assets presented in this section are valued at historical cost, not market, and financial data are sourced from Yahoo finance.com using their last annual financial statements. First, for comparative purposes, the aggregate historical L/A ratio, since the global crisis in 2008, is 53.2 percent.

Starting at the bottom of the food chain, the historically dominant grain companies represent an interesting case, as the industry is dominated by privately held corporations Cargill, Louis Dreyfus, and Continental, while ADM and Bunge are publicly held corporations. Given more than half of the largest global grain traders are privately held, the industry may be less affected by the pressure of private equity, and more focused on long-term profitability. While it would be interesting to evaluate the capital structure of these firms, we unfortunately cannot obtain the

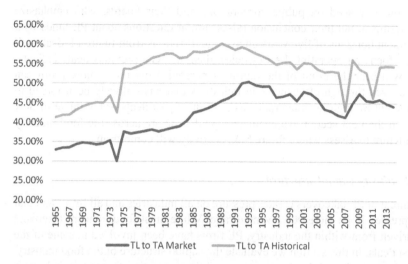

Figure 6.1 Aggregate corporate liability-to-asset ratio.
Source: Flow of Funds Data, Federal Reserve.

financial statements for privately held firms. The L/A ratios for ADM and Bunge were 55.4 and 60.4 percent respectively, not much different than the economy-wide average. It would not be surprising to see ADM merged in the near future.

The leverage structures are very similar for firms that dominate the biochemical seed market. DuPont, Monsanto and Syngenta have L/A ratios of 73.3, 64.2, and 55.4 percent respectively. Syngenta's leverage ratio certainly did not prohibit Monsanto's recent bid for Syngenta.

Moving up the food chain, the largest food corporations in the US are mainly publicly traded firms, Kraft (Heinz), Pepsico, Conagra, General Mills, and Campbell's. Their L/A ratios are 81, 75.3, 72.8, 67.5, and 80 percent respectively, an average of 75.3 percent. One would think the high leverage ratio and the size of the deals would make mergers difficult, but not under the financialization food regime.

At the supermarket chain level, the top firms in the US have mixed ownership structures. Kroger, the largest chain, is publicly held; the second largest firm is the recently merged duo of Safeway and Albertson's owned by PE firm Cerberus Capital Management; the third largest is Publix and is worker owned; fourth is H.E. Butt, which is privately owned; and fifth is Whole Foods, which is publicly owned. Kroger's L/A ratio is 81.6 percent, whereas Whole Foods is 33.6 percent, which would seem to make it a prime target.[1]

Hypermarket stores are those with a significant amount of food sales, but it is not their primary business. Stores in this category include Wal-Mart, Costco, and Target. Their L/A ratios are 62.7 percent, 62.7 percent, and 66.2 percent respectively. A fourth firm, BJs Wholesale, was purchased by private equity firms Leonard Green and Partners and CVC Partners in 2011. Prior to their takeover,

BJ's L/A ratio was 50.2 percent, which may have motivated other firms in this group to raise their L/A ratios, as Wal-Mart's ratio was 58.5 percent in 2010 and Costco's 54.6 percent.

Most of the activity among food firms is being driven by the changing demands of consumers, as the large companies are targeting acquisitions of "good for you" food companies. Some examples of takeovers from 2014 include General Mills' purchase of Annie's Inc., an organic foods company, for $840 million; Hormel bought protein drink maker Muscle Milk for $450 million; Pinnacle Foods purchased Garden Protein International, a company that makes meat-like products from vegetables, for $155 million; and Peet's Coffee & Tea bought specialty tea company Mighty Leaf. Some recent deals announced with unknown size include ConAgra's purchase of Blake's All Natural Foods; DrPepper Snapple Group acquired BAI, which produces antioxidant infusion drinks; and Mondelez International acquired Enjoy Life Foods, which makes snacks that are free from allergens.

Financialization and the emergence of the private equity company has changed corporate financial structure and behavior. The aggregate level of corporate liabilities for publicly traded firms has experienced a permanent shift as a result of leveraged takeovers and in defense of takeovers. Higher leverage forces firms to be more "efficient" in order to meet debt obligations. The 2000s witnessed what some have called the golden age of private equity, which peaked in 2007, and the global crisis temporarily reduced the number of takeovers. However, we are witnessing a new era of takeovers in the age of secular stagnation. With fewer real opportunities for productive investment, takeovers are the outlet for the billions of dollars searching for returns, and the food industry in advanced countries is a central figure in this movement, since food-related firms have relatively stable cash flows and little growth opportunities. The future of the food industry appears to be a continuance of M&A activity, which means greater industry concentration, which means higher prices and fewer choices for consumers.

The global farmland grab

The secular rise in commodity prices in the 2000s made farmland more valuable. As returns from traditional asset markets languished, investors sought new outlets for funds, farmland being one. In addition, after the food riots of 2008, food deficit nations were concerned about food security, as ensuring access to food supplies was necessary to prevent an "Arab Spring." There are multiple actors in the global farms race, and certainly the global grain merchants are one. In this section we discuss these trends that are leading to financialization of farmland.

A 2011 World Bank report (Deininger and Byerlee, 2011) stated that demand for global farmland is being driven by three factors: to meet the needs of increasing populations and incomes in developing economies; biofuel mandates; and cheaper access to land for the production of bulk commodities. These broad factors are also motivating the financialization of global farmland, as financial interests now view farmland as an asset to incorporate into portfolios. There are a number of factors influencing investors' desire to purchase farmland. First, equity markets have been highly volatile since the 2008 global financial crisis. Second, loose monetary policy has created an extended environment of low interest rates, stoking the flames of inflationary expectations. Third, global demand for commodities and financialization of commodity futures markets helped create an extended period of higher commodity prices from 2002 to 2012, making farmland more valuable. A 2011 Bloomberg article (Lubove, 2011) provided a snapshot of the various actors involved: first, well-known investor Jim Rogers was touting farmland investments: "I have frequently told people that one of the best investments in the world will be farmland." In addition, it noted that an investment fund controlled by George Soros owned 23.4 percent of South American farmland venture Adecoagro SA, and TIAA-CREF, the US pension fund for college professors, began investing in farmland in Australia, Brazil, and North America in 2007.

Certainly there are different motivations for investing in farmland, especially globally. Sovereign Wealth Funds are more concerned about food security than returns, and corporations, especially large agribusiness firms, are concerned about securing their supply chains. In the next section, we begin with a look at the actors involved in acquisition of US farmland.

US farmland investments

According to the USDA (Nickerson *et al.*, 2012), almost one-third of US farmers are 65 or older, which has investors salivating at the prospect of a fairly large turnover in US farmland. While the value of farmland real estate has steadily increased since the late 1980s, returns experienced more rapid growth since 2004, consistent with the financialization of commodity markets and the rise in commodity prices. Nickerson *et al.* estimated average farm real-estate values increased from 2 to 4 percent annually from 1994 to 2004 in real terms, and values took a significant spike-up beginning in 2005, increasing by 16 percent in 2005, 11 percent in 2006, and 6–7 percent during 2007 and 2008.

The National Council of Real Estate Investment Fiduciaries collects data on US farmland investments owned or controlled by tax-exempt institutional investors, most of which are pension funds. Figure 6.2 shows the returns to farmland investments, with returns measures including net operating income plus land appreciation. From 1992 to 2003, returns to investors remained relatively stable, averaging 7.7 percent with a standard deviation of 2.2 percent; however, during the commodity bubble(s), returns and variability increased significantly, with an average return of 17.2 percent from 2004 to 2014, and standard deviation of 7.34 percent. Contrast this with the S&P 500, which has averaged just under 8 percent during the same period.

The leading actors in the financialization of US farmland are PE funds, investment management firms, and institutional investors. Many of the PE firms focused on farmland have been started by former Wall Street traders and investors. Ceres Partners LLC is typical of the private equity funds moving into farmland.

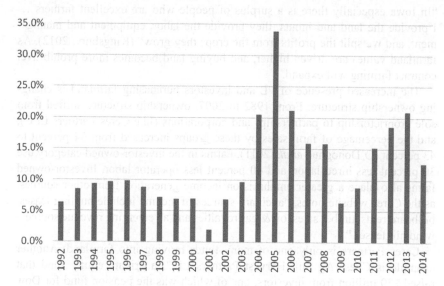

Figure 6.2 Returns on farmland investments.

Source: National Council of Real Estate Investment Fiduciaries.

Ceres Partners was founded in 2006 by a former investment fund manager with a focus on investing in US farms and farmland. According to their website, Ceres has 244 investors and currently manages 161 farms with over 50,000 acres of farmland valued at $323 million (Ceres Partners, 2014). The fund requires a minimum $250,000 investment with a one-year lock up period. Ceres provided a list of reasons for investing in farmland, and they should look familiar: global demographics increased demand for food; growing Asian middle-class demand for protein; alternative energy demands for ethanol, biodiesel, and wind; declining global supply of arable land; the US has a comparative advantage in agriculture; a declining dollar stimulates agricultural exports; and farmland is uncorrelated with stocks and bonds.

Ceres personifies a growing trend in farm ownership and management. Investment management companies like Ceres purchase farmland then lease it to farmer-operators in the form of either cash rent or crop share. Cash rent is assessed based on the farm's tillable acres and is generally paid in full before any crops are planted, and all risks associated with planting, growing and harvesting the crop are assumed by the tenant farmer. In a crop share lease, the investor-landowner is paid a percentage of the crop's revenue. In crop share arrangements the landowner also shares the risk of crop failure, but crop insurance can be purchased to lessen this risk. Since there is more risk in a crop share lease, the return is designed to exceed what a cash rent would provide. As investor-owned farms increase, more "farmers" are becoming contract workers. As an Iowa State agribusiness professor, who has invested in farmland, stated in a Reuters article,

"In Iowa especially there is a surplus of people who are excellent farmers ... I provide the land and inputs, they provide the labor, equipment and management, and we split the profits from the crops they grow" (Kingsbury, 2012). As farmland values are driven higher, and buying land becomes more prohibitive, contract farming will expand.

The increased presence of PE and investors purchasing farmland is changing ownership structure. From 1982 to 2007, ownership structure shifted from sole proprietorship to partnerships and corporations (like Ceres Partners LLC), and the percentage of farm sales by these groups increased from 34 percent to 43 percent (O'Donoghue *et al.*, 2011). Farms in the investor-owned category use 30 percent less hired labor, and 40 percent less operator labor. Investor-owned farms also place a greater emphasis on income generation from other sources, as the Ceres website notes, "ancillary sources of income include hunting leases, billboard rents, timber sales, oil & gas royalties and an emerging revenue source – windmill leases."

Ceres Partners is only one of many funds moving into farmland. Another example is Chess Ag Full Harvest Partners LLC, a private equity fund that raised $30 million from investors, one of which was the pension fund for Dow Chemical. The fund is structured as a typical PE fund where investors agree to stay invested for seven years; management earns a 2 percent fee and takes 20 percent of the profits. The fund hopes to generate 13–16 percent annual returns, generated from crop yields (4–6 percent) and land appreciation (8 percent) (AGProfessional, 2011).

The most direct way to financialize farmland is through a Real Estate Investment Trust (REIT). REITs are closed-end funds, similar to ETFs, and their shares are traded on equity exchanges. To date, there are two US REITs focused on US farmland, Farmland Partners Inc. (FPI) and Gladstone Land Corporation (GLC). As of March 2015, Farmland Partners Inc. owned 93 farms with almost 50,000 acres in Arkansas, Colorado, Illinois, Louisiana, Mississippi, Nebraska, and South Carolina (Farmland Partners, 2015). REITs like FPI rely on a buy-lease strategy, locking into relatively long-term leases with farmers in order to generate steady income:

> Farmland Partners has sought to insulate itself against volatility in the farming business by structuring the vast majority of its leases so that annual rental payments are fixed and due in cash before the start of each spring planting season.
>
> (Robaton, 2015)

The lease agreements are usually structured as a percentage of the farm's gross proceeds, and if crop prices decline, most farmers protect themselves with crop insurance. FPI is traded on the NYSE, and its 52-week trading range as of April 2015 was $9.10 to $14.

Gladstone Land Corporation (NYSE symbol *Land*) was the first farmland REIT created. According to its website, GLC owns farmland in Arizona, California,

Florida, Oregon, and Michigan with an appraised value of $213 million. According to its profile on Yahoo Finance.com, the fund invests in farms that grow row crops, lettuce, tomatoes, and berries. As of April 2015, the stock price was trading around $12, with a 52-week range of $8.89 to $13.87, and market analysts had it as a recommended buy. Between Gladstone and FPI, one can truly "bet the farm."

At the other end of the investment spectrum are pension funds and college endowments, and they have been a major force in both commodity and farmland investments since 2004, the year Gorton and Rouwenhorst published their paper promoting the virtues of commodity diversification. TIAA-CREF (my own pension fund) started investing in farmland in 2007. TIAA-CREF is more than a passive investor, as they have also acquired management companies to oversee their global investments: the Westchester Group Investment Management Inc. located in Illinois, and Radar Propriedades Agricolas, located in Brazil.

At the beginning of 2013, TIAA-CREF managed over 1.2 million acres of global farmland in Brazil (43.5 percent), Australia (35.6 percent), the US (14 percent), and Europe (7 percent) valued at over $4.5 billion. The majority of the crops are focused on grains and oilseeds (74.4 percent) and sugarcane (21.4 percent) (TIAA-CREF, 2014). As of June 30, 2013, TIAA-CREF owned over 170,000 acres of US farmland in California, Washington, Oregon, Illinois, Wisconsin, Indiana, Arkansas, Louisiana, Mississippi, Florida, and Ohio, running the gamut of foods from oilseeds, fruits and nuts, grains, and vineyards.

In the New Normal era of searching for yield, TIAA-CREF is expanding its reach beyond farmland, and they are moving up the production and distribution supply chain:

> In addition to exposure to the underlying almond orchards, we recognized that controlling some of the stages of production, marketing, and delivery – the vertical integration that exists at the intersection of agriculture and infrastructure – would help derive additional value. Not only do we own the farms, we also have a financial interest in the production, marketing, storage, and transportation of almonds. Investing in the different stages of production and delivery has enabled us to adjust products and supply based on changing market needs, providing a value-added strategy that can increase potential income from this attractive sector.
>
> (Davis, 2013)

Given their clientele (college professors like myself), pension funds and college endowments are more easily influenced by external pressures and tend to invest more responsibly than private investors. After the food riots of 2008, various organizations put pressure on pension funds, including TIAA-CREF, which motivated them to become an original signatory to the "Principles for Responsible Investment in Farmland," known as the *Farmland Principles*, which were designed to guide institutional investors and ensure their investments are managed in a responsible manner. The five principles are: (1) promoting environmental sustainability; (2) respecting labor and human rights; (3) respecting existing land and resource rights; (4) upholding high business and ethical standards; and (5) reporting on activities and progress towards implementing and promoting the principles (TIAA-CREF, 2014).

Despite their attempt to be good stewards of the land, investing in food and farmland is inherent with conflict. As noted, TIAA-CREF has major farmland investment in almonds, mainly in California, which is currently experiencing a serious drought. Urban areas have been mandated to reduce water consumption by 25 percent, with no similar requirement for farms, though the drought is severe enough that federal allocations of water have been reduced:

> For the second year in a row, Central Valley growers without senior water rights are likely to get no supplies from the valley's big federal irrigation project. Last year farmers idled about 500,000 acres for lack of water, and this year they may be forced to leave even more cropland unplanted.
>
> (Megerian, 2015)

Almonds are a water-intensive crop, requiring a gallon of water to produce a single almond. Even though pension funds like TIAA-CREF can be influenced through pressure from its clients, the California drought puts (we) investors squarely at odds with the needs of ordinary citizens.

Food commodity prices have been decreasing since March 2014, leading to a decline on farmland investment returns. Many investors have dug in for the long term, and they are spreading their investment seed across the globe. However, investors are not the only group interested in global farmland, and the next section provides a sketch of the important actors motivated to eat up what remains of the world's fertile farmlands.

Global farmland investments

Investments in global farmland were rising prior to 2008, and the global food riots and financial crisis helped set off a global land rush, with nations, corporations, and investors rushing in. The amount of land changing hands is significant:

> By early 2012, the ILC's [International Land Coalition] estimates had soared to a whopping 203 million hectares' worth of land deals 'approved or under negotiation' between 2000 and 2010. Some projections have gone even further; a September 2011 Oxfam study contends that nearly 230 million hectares – an area equivalent to the size of Western Europe – have been sold or leased since 2001, with most of this land acquired since 2008.
>
> (Kugelman 2012, p. 1)

The need to feed a growing population was highlighted in a 2009 report by the FAO which estimated that global population will rise by 34 percent by 2050 (9.1 billion), which would require additional investments in agriculture equal to

$83 billion annually (FAO). There is a need for increased land devoted to production and to increase farm productivity. The numbers suggest an inherent conflict. Much of the prime farmland available for expansion is in the hands of small farmers in developing countries, so how can countries balance the need to feed their populations and the desire for farmland by SWF, corporations, and investors? The increased demand for global farmland will, and has, come at the expense of peasant farmers.

The World Bank (Deininger and Byerlee, 2011) attempted to quantify potential land for agriculture expansion: "The currently noncultivated area suitable for cropping that is nonforested, nonprotected, and populated with less than 25 persons/km^2 (or 20 ha/household) amounts to 446 million ha" (p. xxxiv). The majority of land, almost three-quarters, is in Sub-Sahara Africa (45 percent), Latin America (28 percent), and Eastern Europe–Central Asia (12 percent), and most of the "farms race" is taking place in these regions. Expansion of cultivated area seems unlikely to slow:

> Population growth, rising incomes, and urbanization will continue to drive demand growth for some food products, especially oilseed and livestock, and related demands for feed and industrial products. A conservative estimate is that, in developing countries, 6 million ha of additional land will be brought into production each year to 2030. Two-thirds of this expansion will be in Sub-Saharan Africa and Latin America, where potential farmland is most plentiful. At the same time, in many countries that are of interest to investors productivity on currently cultivated land is only a fraction of what could be achieved. Concerted efforts to allow existing cultivators to close yield gaps and make more effective use of the resources at their disposal could thus slow land expansion sharply while creating huge benefits for existing farmers.
>
> (Deininger and Byerlee, 2011, p. xxviii)

While it sounds good on paper, too often land sales are made without consulting local populations, and peasant farmers have been forced off the land. There have been hundreds of land deals over the past several years, so who have been the main the players in the global farmland grab? The NGO GRAIN maintained a database of farmland acquisitions covering the period from 2007 through 2011, which lists over 400 deals in 66 countries, amounting to almost 35 million hectares of farmland. Deals are categorized by various characteristics, including industry, size, and country. The largest number of deals, and largest in terms of land acquired, are those by agribusiness firms, with deals amounting to almost 15 million hectares. The other two major players in land deals are financial firms and governments. The financial firm category includes private equity funds, and these deals accounted for almost 10 million hectares of land. Deals involving governments accounted for 6.4 million hectares of land.

China has received much publicity in terms of global land acquisition, but many other countries are involved, with food security as the goal:

Saudi Arabia, Japan, China, India, Korea, Libya and Egypt all fall into this basket. High-level officials from many of these nations have been on the road since March 2008 in a diplomatic treasure hunt for fertile farmland in places like Uganda, Brazil, Cambodia, Sudan and Pakistan. Given the continuing Darfur crisis, where the World Food Programme is trying to feed 5.6 million refugees, it might seem crazy that foreign governments are buying up farmland in Sudan to produce and export food for their own citizens. Ditto in Cambodia, where 100,000 families, or half a million people, currently lack food. Yet this is what is happening today. Convinced that farming opportunities are limited and the market can't be relied upon, "food insecure" governments are shopping for land elsewhere to produce their own food. At the other end, those governments being courted for the use of their countries' farmland are generally welcoming these offers of fresh foreign investment.[2]

(GRAIN, 2008, p. 2)

China's drive for overseas farmland is motivated by issues related to urbanization, migration, climate change, among other factors. From 1996 to 2006, China lost almost 9 million hectares of farmland, and has tried to protect further encroachments, safeguarding some 120 million hectares of farmland (Ping, 2008). In its effort to meet the needs of its population and conserve domestic farmland, China continues to strike deals with countries considered to be on good terms, and entices nations into deals by offering to trade training and technology for land.

China is not alone. Saudi Arabia and other Gulf States reacted to 2008 food crisis with efforts to enhance their own food security. Given the lack of arable land and large migrant populations, the Gulf States require stable food sources and prices, and they offer similar enticements to establish deals:

Their idea is to secure deals, particularly in sister Islamic countries, by which they will supply capital and oil contracts in exchange for guarantees that their corporations will have access to farmland and be able to export the produce back home. The most heavily targeted states are, by far, Sudan and Pakistan, followed by quite a number in south-east Asia (Burma, Cambodia, Indonesia, Laos, Philippines, Thailand and Vietnam), Turkey, Kazakhstan, Uganda, Ukraine, Georgia, Brazil … the list goes on.

(GRAIN, 2008, p. 4)

Based on GRAIN's database, the large grain corporations are the most active players behind the acceleration of global farmland acquisitions. The pursuit of food security by nations and the search for yield by investors has raised the bar for the global grain merchants. Louis Dreyfus established Calyx Agro in 2007 to invest in Latin American farmland. Cargill has purchased farmland in South America, Australia, and Bulgaria, and its Black River Asset Management company has invested in farmland through its PE fund (GRAIN, 2012). However, the historically dominant grain corporations are being challenged by emerging market players. Olam International, headquartered in Singapore, has grown from a small firm trading cashews in 1989, to a global agribusiness firm with over $19 billion in revenues operating in 65 countries (Olamgroup, 2015). Olam was one of the largest dealmakers among the big grain-trading firms during the 2007–2011 period covered in GRAIN's database, purchasing over 400,000 ha of land in Argentina, Gabon, Mozambique, Russia, and the Ukraine.

Financial firms were the second largest group acquiring farmland. Adecoagro is a publicly traded company, and some of its largest shareholders are Soros Fund Management (21.5 percent), PE firm Ospraie Management LLC (8.84 percent), and PGGM (3.73 percent), a private management company that manages pension fund assets in the Netherlands. Pension funds are active players in the global farmland grab, and TIAA-CREF was one of the most active investors in the GRAIN database. TIAA-CREF purchased over 500,000 ha of farmland in Australia and Brazil during this period. Despite a fairly substantial investment in US farmland, the majority (84 percent) of TIAA-CREF's investments have been global, with most of their holdings in Australia, Brazil, and Europe.

Private foreign investors, while viewed as the solution to modernizing the food systems of developing countries, are a disruptive force. Small local farmers bear the brunt of this strategy. In the US, investors and the public face a conflict which determines whether water flows to almond growers or water flows to lawns. Land grabs around the world are a matter of life and death for peasant farmers, and these conflicts occur on a weekly basis:[3]

> Police in Sudan fired tear gas and wielded batons on Friday to break up a protest in Khartoum against government land policies, three witnesses said.
>
> About 500 demonstrators closed two main streets in the eastern al-Jarif district. The protesters, who say they have a right to land that the government has allocated to investors, threw stones at police and burned tyres.
>
> (Reuters, 2015)

Is this conflict an intractable problem? How can developing countries transition to modern industrial farming without creating hardship for a significant proportion of their population whose livelihood depends on farming? Are there alternatives? We look at these questions and possible solutions in Chapter 8.

Conclusion

The financialization process in commodity markets began in the mid-1990s and was formalized through the 2000 Commodity Futures Modernization Act. The 2000 CFMA marks the beginning of the financialization accumulation and food regimes. The financialization regime from 2000 to 2012 was been characterized by slow economic growth, rising and more volatile commodity prices, and M&A activity driven by private equity. In addition, the New Normal of low investment returns, combined with nation-states seeking food security in reaction to the 2008 food riots, has led to a global farmland grab. How have policymakers responded? In the next chapter we look at policy changes in agriculture, trade, and futures markets.

Notes

1 There were rumors of a possible merger between Whole Foods and Publix in 2014.
2 The GRAIN article listed the following countries involved in farmland acquisition: China, India, Japan, Malaysia and South Korea in Asia; Egypt and Libya in Africa; and Bahrain, Jordan, Kuwait, Qatar, Saudi Arabia and the United Arab Emirates in the Middle East.
3 The NGO GRAIN set up a website to monitor global investments in farmland at http://farmlandgrab.org/.

Bibliography

AGProfessional. (2011). The rise of the large operator. Retrieved February 12, 2015 from http://www.agprofessional.com/agprofessional-magazine/the_rise_of_the_large_opera tor_120074514.html

Arrighi, G. (1994). *The Long Twentieth Century: Money, Power, and the Origins of Our Times*. New York: Verso.

Banerjee, D. (2015, January 8). Warburg Pincus hires Pulick to advise on industrial deals. Retrieved June 10, 2015 from http://www.bloomberg.com/news/articles/2015-01-08/ warburg-pincus-hires-pulick-to-advise-on-industrial-deals.

Barton, D., and Wiseman, M. (2015). Short-term profit can cost shareholders dear. *Financial Times*, April 1.

Cecchetti, S. G., and Kharroubi, E. (2012). Reassessing the impact of finance on growth. BIS Working Paper No. 381. Retrieved June 12, 2015 from http://ssrn.com/abstract= 2117753

Ceres Partners. (2014). Retrieved November 18, 2014 from http://cerespartners.com/

Davis, H. (2013). Almonds: harvesting value beyond the farm. *Market Commentary and Investment Insights*. TIAA CREF. Retrieved March 7, 2015 from https://s3.amazonaws. com/s3.documentcloud.org/documents/1310094/tiaacref-almondharvest.pdf

Deininger, K. W., and Byerlee, D. (2011). *Rising Global Interest in Farmland: Can it Yield Sustainable and Equitable Benefits?* Washington, DC: World Bank Publications.

Drean, A. (2014, September 8). The dawn of a new golden age for first-time private equity funds. *Forbes*. Retrieved May 12, 2015 from http://www.forbes.com/sites/ antoinedrean/2014/09/08/the-dawn-of-a-new-golden-age-for-first-time-private-equity- funds/

FAO. Investments in agriculture Retrieved May 18, 2015, from http://www.fao.org/investment- in-agriculture/en/.

Farmland Partners. (2015). Homepage. Retrieved March 23, 2015 from http://www.farm landpartners.com/

GRAIN. (2008). Seized: the 2008 landgrab for food and financial security. Retrieved January 17, 2015 from www.grain.org.

GRAIN. (2012). *The Great Food Robbery*. Cape Town: Pambazuka Press.

Gross, B. (2009). On the "course" to a new normal. *Investment Outlook*. Retrieved May 15, 2015 from http://global.pimco.com/EN/Insights/Pages/Gross percent20Sept percent20 On percent20the percent20Course percent20to percent20a percent20New percent20 Normal.aspx

IMF. (2015). Uneven growth: short- and long-term factors. *World Economic Outlook*: IMF.

Jensen, M. C. (1997). Eclipse of the public corporation. *Harvard Business Review* (Sept.- Oct. 1989), 67(5), 61–74, revised.

Kingsbury, K. (2012, March 19, 2012). Farmland reaps high investment returns. Retrieved March 4, 2015 from http://www.reuters.com/article/2012/03/19/us-column-yourmoney-farmland-investment-idUSBRE82I0SZ20120319

Krugman, P. (2015). Liquidity traps, local and global. [Web log message.] Retrieved May 16, 2015 from http://krugman.blogs.nytimes.com/2015/04/01/liquidity-traps-local-and-global-somewhat-wonkish/?module=BlogPost-Title&version=Blog percent20Main&contentCollection=Opinion&action=Click&pgtype=Blogs&region=Body&_r=0

Kugelman, M. (2012). *The Global Farms Race: Land Grabs, Agricultural Investment, and the Scramble for Food Security*. Washington, DC: Island Press.

Lubove, S. (2011, August 10). Being like Soros in buying farmland reaps annual gains of 16 percent. Retrieved November 11, 2014 from http://www.bloomberg.com/news/articles/2011-08-10/being-like-soros-in-buying-farm-land-lets-investors-reap-16-annual-gains

Massoudi, A. (2015, May 5). Merger and acquisition boom driven by 'jumbo' deals, *Financial Times*.

Megerian, C., Stevens, M., and Boxal, B. (2015, April 1). Brown orders California's first mandatory water restrictions: 'It's a different world', *LA Times*. Retrieved February 16, 2015 from http://www.latimes.com/local/lanow/la-me-ln-snowpack-20150331-story.html#page=1

Nickerson, C., Morehart, M., Kuethe, T., Beckman, J., and Ifft, J. (2012). Trends in US Farmland Values and Ownership. USDA. Economic Research Service. Retrieved November 1, 2014 from http://www.ers.usda.gov/media/377487/eib92_2.pdf

O'Donoghue, E. J., Hoppe, R. A., Banker, D. E., Ebel, R., Fuglie, K., Korb, P. *et al.* (2011). *The Changing Organization of US Farming*. USDA, Economic Research Service.

Olamgroup. (2015). Retrieved March 26, 2015 from http://olamgroup.com/

Palley, T. (2007). Financialization: what it is and why it matters. Political Economy Research Institute Amherst, Working Paper No. 153.

PEGCC. (2015). US private equity investments. Retrieved April 4, 2015 from http://www.pegcc.org/education/pe-by-the-numbers/

Ping, L. (2008, March 7). Hopes and strains in China's overseas farming plan. *The Economic Observer*. Retrieved November 19, 2015 from http://www.eeo.com.cn/ens/Industry/2008/07/03/105213.html

Reuters. (2015). Sudan police teargas protestors in Khartoum – witness. Retrieved June 19, 2015 from http://af.reuters.com/article/sudanNews/idAFL5N0YY3D520150612, 2015

Robaton, A. (2015). Farming REITs. Retrieved April 21, 2015, 2015, from https://www.reit.com/news/reit-magazine/january-february-2015/farming-reits

Roberts, D. (2015, March 25). Here's what happens when 3G Capital buys your company. *Fortune*. Retrieved from http://fortune.com/2015/03/25/3g-capital-heinz-kraft-buffett/.

TIAA-CREF. (2014). Responsible investment in farmland. Retrieved November 29, 2014 from https://www.tiaa-cref.org/public/pdf/Farmland-Sustainability-Report.pdf.

Veblen, T. (1904). *The Theory of Business Enterprise*. New York: Charles Scribners Sons.

7 Food and finance policy

In this chapter we look at recent policy changes related to the food and finance issues discussed in previous chapters. We begin with a brief historical survey to see how policy has evolved over time. US agriculture policy was shaped by a farm crisis which preceded the Great Depression, and the policies established in the 1930s to stabilize farm income did not change dramatically, until recently. A new farm bill passed in 2014 takes a fairly significant departure from previous policy. The 2015 Dietary Guidelines for Americans are also in the final stages of discussions, and battle lines are being drawn over a recommendation to incorporate environmental sustainability. There is also heated debate over two trade bills the Obama administration is trying to "fast-track" through Congress, and, despite passage of the Dodd–Frank Act in 2010, speculative position limit rules are still under review. Policy food fights in the US invariably pit public interest against corporate interest, and the current debates are no different. The important question posed: can ordinary citizens overcome the regulatory capture by corporate interests?

Food policy

US food policy was designed to support the farm sector through price and income support mechanisms. The 1930s depression also provided the impetus for creating nutritional support programs, which, not withstanding, created another outlet for the glut of output generated by US agriculture. While Congress attempted to pass bills in support of farmers during the 1920s, those efforts were either defeated or vetoed. It took the economic crisis of the 1930s to create enough support, and the first major legislation passed in 1933 was the Agriculture Adjustment Act. The essential aspects of the act provided income support and acreage control programs, with the aim of achieving *income parity* with the non-farm sector. Secular decline in agriculture prices relative to manufactured goods meant that the purchasing power of farmers declined over time, so price and income policies were designed to maintain the farm sector's purchasing power, or parity. Other legislation passed during the depression included the 1936 Soil Conservation and Domestic Allotment Act, which established soil conservation programs to reduce acreage planted and help restore the soil depleted of its nutrients from over-planting wheat and corn; and a 1938 Agriculture Adjustment Act which established crop insurance programs, and provided *nonrecourse* loans to finance the production cycle. Nonrecourse loans, issued and managed by the Commodity Credit Corporation (also created in 1933), allowed farmers to repay loans with grain, another factor which would lead to increased government stockpiles. The various farm programs had the desired effect, as farm income increased by 50 percent from 1932 to 1935.

The 1930s farm policies were designed to generate widespread support, and for good reason, as the farm population at the time represented a powerful political force. In 1935 there were more than 6.5 million farms, compared to about 2.1 million today (EPA, 2013).[1] According to Dimitri *et al.*(2005):

> The Federal approach to dealing with these problems – commodity-specific price supports and supply controls – were a product of the farm sector's structure; farms were generally small, diversified operations selling primarily to domestic markets behind high tariff walls. In this environment, the original AAA and subsequent farm legislation into the 1960s relied heavily on price supports and supply controls to increase returns to farmers.
>
> (p. 9)

After World War II, the attempt to reduce surpluses through acreage control was frustrated by the dramatic increase in productivity. Increased mechanization, improved use of fertilizers, and seed breeding (the Green Revolution) generated a significant increase in output even as the number of farmers declined. From 1945 to 1960, farm productivity increased by 54 percent for wheat, 60 percent for corn, 76 percent for cotton, and dairy increased by 47 percent (Bowers *et al.*, 1984).

School lunch and food stamps programs were initiated in the 1930s to improve nutrition for low-income Americans, and the programs also provided an outlet to dispose of surplus crops and livestock. Permanent funding for school lunches would not be secured until the passage of the National School Lunch Act in 1946, and the US Food Stamp Act was passed in 1964. Interestingly, the school lunch program received support from the military because they found that 40 percent of rejected draftees had been turned down due to poor diets, mainly malnourished (Confessore, 2014).

As Nestle (2013) described, US farmers and grain merchants established a symbiotic relationship with the USDA after the war, which formed the basis of the second food regime. With the dramatic improvements in farm productivity, however, US food aid was still unable to reduce surpluses. Given increased government stockpiles of grain, farm policy transitioned from price supports in the 1960s toward income support, and the US Food and Agriculture Act of 1965 formalized this shift. Price floors, which typically resulted in surplus output, were replaced by income support payments (tied to previous price support levels), and farmers received payments as long as they participated in acreage-reduction programs.

The surplus crisis of the early 1960s turned into a scarcity crisis in the 1970s. Between oil shocks and Russian grain deals, farm costs and prices increased, and government stocks were being depleted. The loss of government stockpiles and high prices led to a significant turnaround in US farm policy through the 1973 Agriculture and Consumer Protection Act which focused on expanded production to reduce food prices. This change in US policy led Agriculture Secretary Earl Butz to declare it was "an historic turning point in the philosophy of farm programs in the United States" (Bowers *et al.*, 1984, p. 29). Butz had encouraged farmers to "get big or get out," and the debt-financed expansion by farmers ended in the farm crisis of the 1980s. Despite the problems, US farmers were once again generating surpluses, increasing government stockpiles. US wheat stockpiles had averaged nearly 1 billion bushels through the 1960s, and hit a low of 340 million by the end of the 1973/74 production year. By the mid-1980s, wheat stocks had been restored, and were over 2 billion bushels (USDA Feed Grains).

US farm policy became more market-oriented with the emergence of the neoliberal food regime in the 1980s, and farms "got big, or they got out." The Food Security Act of 1985 established marketing loans to help producers increase exports and reduce the stocks held in government stores; the 1996 Federal Agriculture Improvement and Reform Act replaced price support and supply control programs with a program of direct payments – decoupled from price and production and tied to historical crop production; and it introduced nearly complete planting flexibility. As a USDA report (Dimitri *et al.*, 2005) concluded:

> The structure of farming continues to move toward fewer, larger operations producing the bulk of farm commodities, complemented by a growing number of smaller farms earning most of their income from off-farm sources, all increasingly affected by global events. Although many details of U.S. farm programs have changed over the last 40 years in response to new economic and political circumstances, two key features of commodity programs – commodity specificity and focus on income support – have remained constant. Today, cash receipts for supported commodities (wheat, feed grains, rice cotton, oilseeds, dairy, and sugar) account for only 34 percent of total farm cash receipts. Direct government payments for income support reach only about 500,000 farms (around 25 percent of all farms).
>
> (p. 12)

The US farm sector has typically been a dual system, and is becoming more so, with large farms focused on production of global commodities, and small and medium-sized farms focused on fruits, vegetables, and niche commodities. This is also evidenced by the distribution of farm support dollars, which have always been highly concentrated to the benefit of the global commodity producers. Table 7.1 provides expenditure estimates with some distribution data for US farm support programs compiled by the Environmental Working Group (Mercier, 2011). In fiscal year 2010, the *direct payment* program paid out $4.9 billion to farmers, with the top 10 percent receiving 67 percent of funds distributed; the bottom 80 percent received only 15 percent of support dollars. Crop insurance programs, which subsidize the crop insurance paid by farmers, paid out $5.7 billion during

Table 7.1 Summary of major farm programs

Program title	FY 2010 spending (US$)	Established	Objective	Share of payments to top 10% (%)	Share of payments to bottom 80% (%)	Beneficiaries
Marketing assistance loan	87 million for 2009 crop year	1985 farm bill	Income support	60	19	Producers of all row crops plus honey, wool, and mohair
Countercyclical payment	89 million for 2009 crop year	2002 farm bill	Partially decoupled income support	76	11	All row crop producers with program history
Average Crop Revenue Election(ACRE)	450 million for 2009 crop year	2008 farm bill	Revenue support	50	31	All row crop producers with program history
Direct payment	4.9 billion	1996 farm bill	Decoupled income support	67	15	All row crop producers with program history
Sugar loan and allotments	No direct outlays	Agriculture and Food Act of 1981	Price support	Not applicable	Not applicable	Sugar sector
Dairy price support	40 million in dairy purchases	Agricultural Adjustment Act of 1933	Price support	Not applicable	Not applicable	Dairy farmers
Milk Income Loss Contract	181 million	2002 farm bill	Income support	50	28	Dairy farmers

(Continued)

Table 7.1 (Continued)

Program title	FY 2010 spending (US$)	Established	Objective	Share of payments to top 10% (%)	Share of payments to bottom 80% (%)	Beneficiaries
Crop insurance	5.7 billion for 2009 crop year	1981 Federal Crop Insurance	Insure against crop losses	Not available	Not available	Producers of all insurable crops
Supplemental Revenue Assurance (SURE)	2 billion for 2008 crop year	2008 farm bill	Insure against crop revenue losses	45	34	Producers of all crops
Direct and guaranteed loans	6 billion program level, 147 million cost	Consolidated Farm & Rural Development Act of 1961	Provide operating and capital loans	Not applicable	Not applicable	All farmers; capped amount
Conservation Reserve Program (CRP)	1.9 billion	1985 farm bill	Idle erodible lands	58	25	All farmers; total capped acres
Environmental Quality Incentive Program (EQIP)	1.2 billion	1985 farm bill	Help adoption of conservation practices	40	31	All farmers; annual capped funding
Conservation Stewardship Program (CSP)	$655 million	2002 farm bill	Help adoption of conservation practices	37	41	All farmers; annual capped acres

Source: Mercier (2011). Used with permission from the author and AGree, Washington, DC.

the 2009 crop year. According to an updated blog post by the Environmental Working Group, for the 2011 crop year, the top 10 percent of farms received 54 percent of subsidy benefits. For the period from 1995 to 2011, the top 10 percent received 77 percent of all farm subsidy payments (Sciammacco, 2012).

In a review of US farm support programs, Mercier (2011) stated, "With few exceptions, U.S. farm policy tends to be accretive, with Congress typically choosing to modify existing programs and/or add new programs on top of existing programs rather than subtract programs from the mix" (p. 6). After nearly eighty years, farm policy has changed. The 2014 US Farm Bill created a significant change in policy, eliminating direct payment programs. Where direct payments were made regardless of price, the focus of the 2014 bill is on insurance programs. Two programs were created to provide support when prices or incomes decline beyond given thresholds. Farmers must choose between two insurance programs: the Price Loss Coverage (PLC) program and the Agriculture Risk Coverage (ARC) program. The PLC provides payments for *covered commodities* which include wheat, feed grains (soy and corn), rice, oilseeds, peanuts, and pulses (dry peas, lentils, chickpeas, etc.). With ARC, payments are made when average county revenues drop below 86 percent of a county benchmark based on a 5-year average. There are maximum payment limits of $125,000, and producers are ineligible for payments if their adjusted gross income exceeds $900,000; however, these only apply to the insurance payouts, not the actual insurance subsidies (USDA, 2014b).

As the market for organic produce has increased, the Farm Bill has adapted and increased funding to support organic and local food initiatives, increasing program funding by 50 percent (USDA, 2014a). For example, the Farmers' Market and Local Food Promotion Program increased from $33 million to $150 million, with funding to support farmers' markets, food hubs, and community-supported agriculture (CSA) programs, to name a few. The National Organic Cost Share Certification, which assists organic producers and handlers with the cost of organic certification, increased from $22 million in 2008 to $57.5 million. Funds ($100 million) are also available for programs that promote purchase of local farm products by SNAP, including programs in support of farmers' markets and CSAs.

Despite the recent change emphasizing crop insurance programs, US farm policy is still designed to benefit industrial agriculture interests that produce farm commodities for the global market. While there is positive change and money being directed toward organic farming and promoting programs that directly connect farmers with consumers, it is small potatoes compared to the money subsidizing industrial commodity production. As we discuss in the final chapter, radical change in the incentive program is needed, directed at producing healthy, sustainable agriculture.

Nutrition policy

Nestle (2013) documented the political economy of nutrition and health policy, exposing how food industry interests are intimately tied to outcomes in US nutrition guidelines. There are dollars at stake. Federal food stamp and nutrition

programs like school lunches are influenced by the government's recommendations, and expenditures on those programs directly impact food industry revenues.
For example, the meat industry has successfully fought recommendations to
reduce meat consumption since 1977.

New guidelines are nearing completion, and once again battle lines have been
drawn. The most controversial change recommended is connecting food and
nutrition to sustainability. The secretaries of Health and Human Services and the
USDA established the 2015 Dietary Guidelines Advisory Committee (DGAC)
with the purpose of evaluating the latest research to guide in nutrition recommendations. The *Scientific Report* (DGAC, 2015) recommended:

> Access to sufficient, nutritious, and safe food is an essential element of food
> security for the U.S. population. *A sustainable diet ensures this access for
> both the current population and future generations* [emphasis mine].

> The major findings regarding sustainable diets were that a diet higher in
> plant-based foods, such as vegetables, fruits, whole grains, legumes, nuts, and
> seeds, and lower in calories and animal-based foods is more health promoting
> and is associated with less environmental impact than is the current U.S. diet.
> This pattern of eating can be achieved through a variety of dietary patterns,
> including the Healthy U.S.-style Pattern, the Healthy Mediterranean-style
> Pattern, and the Healthy Vegetarian Pattern. All of these dietary patterns are
> aligned with lower environmental impacts and provide options that can be
> adopted by the U.S. population. Current evidence shows that the average U.S.
> diet has a larger environmental impact in terms of increased greenhouse gas
> emissions, land use, water use, and energy use, compared to the above dietary
> patterns. This is because the current U.S. population intake of animal-based
> foods is higher and plant-based foods are lower, than proposed in these three
> dietary patterns. Of note is that no food groups need to be eliminated com-
> pletely to improve sustainability outcomes over the current status.
>
> (p. 7)

While the DGAC states no food groups need to be eliminated, the focus on
healthier dietary patterns implicitly represents a challenge to the US food industry:

> What has caused such a stir is that it is widely agreed that the scientific com-
> mittee's recommendation represents the opportunity to take a seismic leap
> forward in US food policymaking, informing all federal food, nutrition or
> health programs and affecting $16 billion dollars in spending and 5.5 billion
> lunches in the Federal School Lunch Program alone.
>
> (Wyly, 2015)

Indeed, industry pressure has intensified, and they are using their "influence" to push senators and congressmen from "Big Ag" states to "arm-twist"
the DGAC into backing off environmental and other issues "unfriendly" to the

food industry. For example, Senator John Thune (R-S.D.) sent a letter (Thune, 2015), signed by 29 senators, to USDA Secretary Vilsack stating that they "are concerned about this committee's suggestion to decrease consumption of red and processed meats," and the senators are also questioning the "scientific integrity" of the DGAC. A spokesman for Rep. Robert B. Aderholt (R-Ala.), chairman of the Appropriations Subcommittee which oversees the budget for the Agriculture Department, was quoted in a *Washington Post* article (Ferdman and Whoriskey, 2015), "Chairman Aderholt is skeptical of the panel's departure from utilizing sound science as the criteria for the guidelines...Politically motivated issues such as taxes on certain foods and environmental sustainability are outside their purview."

As the DGAC *Scientific Report* and recent popular (Pollan, 2006) accounts have identified, food, health, climate, and sustainability are interconnected. The DGAC has taken a bold step toward formally recognizing these connections in the new, proposed US Dietary Guidelines. The outcome remains to be seen, as the final decision will be made after this book goes to print.

Trade policy

Trade is another area where public policy has had a significant impact on local and global food systems. The Obama administration is promoting two major trade initiatives, attempting to "fast-track" them through Congress, the Trans-Pacific Partnership (TTP) with eleven other Pacific Rim countries, and the Trans-Atlantic Trade and Investment Partnership (TTIP) with Europe. A fast-tracked bill gets very little public input into the process, and many of the proposals are not made public at all. Given the opacity of the process, very little is known about how the agreements impact food policies, but one change has been leaked to the public, the investor-state dispute settlement (ISDS) mechanism. The ISDS allows corporations to sue a nation if its government takes any action that "harms" profits. Economist Joseph Stiglitz (2015) believes that

> the real intent of these provisions is to impede health, environmental, safety, and, yes, even financial regulations meant to protect America's own economy and citizens. Companies can sue governments for full compensation for any reduction in their future *expected* profits resulting from regulatory changes.

While President Obama scoffed at the notion of the US losing a lawsuit, Stiglitz provided an example. Philip Morris has sued Uruguay and Australia for harmful reduction in sales. Regulations were passed in both countries that required graphic cancer-related pictures on cigarette packages, and they had the desired impact of decreasing smoking, which was harming Philip Morris' cigarette sales. Stiglitz argued the investor-state dispute clause could allow corporations to sue nations for safety and environmental laws that harm corporate profits, including food safety regulations. A foreshadowing of what one can expect was seen in a recent WTO ruling over the US regulation requiring *country of origin* meat labels. The

WTO ruled that the regulation created a disadvantage for meat-packers in Canada and Mexico, and two days after the ruling, the congressional House Agriculture Committee voted in favor of repealing the law.[2]

US trade policies are nearly always designed to expand markets for US business interests, and the TTIP and TTP agreements will be no different. As Patel and McMichael (2009) detailed, the WTO's Agreement on Agriculture was designed to break down government barriers, especially for countries that for years had pursued import-substitution development policies, and

> while countries of the global South were instructed to open their farm sectors, those of the global North retained their huge subsidies. Decoupling subsidies from prices removed the price floor, establishing an artificially low 'world price' for agricultural commodities, which were dumped in Southern markets.
>   (Patel and McMichael, 2009, p. 17)

The emphasis on export-led growth models by the IMF and World Bank arose along with neoliberalism in the 1970s. Emerging economies were encouraged to specialize and gain from the benefits that Ricardo's comparative advantage model claimed – the CASTE system. However, since every trade surplus must have a deficit counterpart, there will be winners and losers if all focus on export-led growth, and there will be a "race to the bottom" to become the most competitive (Palley, 2011). Ben Guriat (2015) evaluated the change in trade strategies for Tunisia and Morocco, and found that the period of export-led growth strategy is associated with lower growth than when both were following import substitution strategies. In addition, chronic current account deficits are creating unsustainable debt situations on the capital account. Export-led strategies also leave countries vulnerable to external supply shocks, and Morocco and Tunisia experienced some demonstrations and rioting during the 2008 food crisis (Schneider, 2008).

Futures markets policy

As a consequence of the global financial crisis and the 2008 commodity price bubble, the US Congress passed the "Wall Street Transparency and Accountability Act" of 2010 (known as the Dodd–Frank Act), and the CFTC was charged to amend the 1936 CEA. The CFTC proposed to "establish speculative position limits for 28 exempt and agricultural commodity futures and option contracts," and "revise the exemptions from speculative position limits, including for bona fide hedging; and extend and update reporting requirements for persons claiming exemption from these limits" (CFTC, 2013, p. 75680). The CFTC adopted the new position limit rules in October 2011; however, the rules were successfully challenged in federal court by the International Swaps and Derivatives Association and the Securities Industry and Financial Markets Association. Essentially the International Swaps and Derivatives Association argued that the CFTC misinterpreted the Dodd–Frank rule, and the CFTC had to establish a *finding of necessity* before it could impose speculative limits. In essence, the CFTC would have to prove that excessive speculative positions caused higher prices, and higher prices created an unnecessary burden on interstate commerce.

The CFTC went "back to the drawing board" and reissued position limit rulings in December 2013 (CFTC, 2013). This time, the CFTC argued it was not the law's intent for the CFTC to establish a *finding of necessity*, rather, Congress had *already* found evidence of speculation in natural gas and wheat markets, and the CFTC was simply following its congressional mandate to impose said position limit rules. The CFTC also cited a change in wording during the development of Dodd–Frank which had originally stated that the CFTC "may" impose limits, with the final version stating that the CFTC "shall" impost limits; further, "To remove all doubt, the House Report accompanying the House Bill also made clear that the House amendments to the position limits bill 'required' the Commission to impose limits" (CFTC 2013, p. 75685). As a way to remove the onus of *finding of necessity*, and based on their review of over one hundred studies on speculation and position limits, the CFTC argued:

> In any case, these studies overall show a lack of consensus regarding the impact of speculation on commodity markets and the effectiveness of position limits. While there is not a consensus, the fact that there are studies on both sides, in the Commission's view, warrants erring on the side of caution. In light of the Commission's experience with position limits, and its interpretation of congressional intent, it is the Commission's judgment that position limits should be implemented as a prophylactic measure, to protect against the potential for undue price fluctuations and other burdens on commerce that in some cases have been at least in part attributable to excessive speculation.
>
> (CFTC 2013, p. 75695)

Given no conclusive evidence, in the CFTC's view, it was preferable to "err on the side of caution." Further, the CFTC stated, "Congress set short deadlines for the limits it 'required,' and directed the Commission to conduct a study of the limits *after* their imposition and to report to Congress promptly on their effects" (CFTC 2013, p. 75682).

The position limits proposed by the CFTC in 2013 were based on data provided by the exchanges. The limits suggested by the CFTC on spot month contracts were 25 percent of "estimated deliverable supply." The spot month limits for CBOT corn and wheat had been 600 contracts, and the new rule would increase them to 1000 and 3,700 respectively; which certainly does not appear restrictive on the surface. Indeed, several public interest organizations complained that the proposed limits were too weak. In their final comments to the CFTC on position limits, the Institute for Agriculture and Trade Policy, an organization that supports family farms, urged the CFTC to take five steps to finalize the rule: (1) set the limits low enough to ensure that commercial participants hold a dominant share of trades; (2) review position limits every six months rather than the proposed two years; (3) define each commodity index fund as a contract subject to position limits; (4) require parity in limits for both physical and cash settled contracts to discourage migration of speculators to cash markets; and (5) do not delegate management of position limits to exchanges in the form of position accountability, as the exchanges did not prevent excessive speculation prior to Dodd–Frank, and they have a conflict of interest in that their profits are related to the volume of trading (Suppan, 2015). Better Markets (2015), in addition to criticizing the 25 percent rule, argued that the proposed rules did nothing to restrain CIFs. As the rules are currently proposed, there are position limits on individual commodities and spreads, but there are no limits on index contracts composed of multiple commodities. The CFTC does not view index contracts as (price) *reference contracts*, hence, in their view, they do not impact price discovery.

Despite the relatively benign limits proposed, the rules have yet to be finalized. In December 2014, current CFTC Chairman Timothy Massad decided to reopen the comment period for the revised December 2013 position limit proposal, citing the need to ensure that position limits did not impact commercial hedgers, and that the process for estimating deliverable supplies – which would determine the spot month limits – was adequate (CFTC, 2014).

All participants in the speculation debate agree that financialization has changed the structure of commodity futures markets, mainly driven by the proliferation of CIFs. Based on this structural change, traditional measures of speculation, and policies to restrain speculation, need to change as well. The issue is finding the right balance of speculation, one that meets liquidity needs of the markets without allowing speculation to dominate price discovery. The evidence is clear: in markets where CIF positions balance commercial short positions, and there are high levels of speculative open interest positions (MMT and other reportables), prices are determined by "speculative opinion," as Working suggested. Market participants and financial publications state that hedge funds drive oil prices. New rules to restrain speculation need to be developed because the markets have changed; they are financialized. As suggested in Chapter 5, a combination of the adjusted Hedge Ratio and a measure of the open interest of the remaining speculators is a starting point.

Given the recent history of finance and regulation, one cannot be certain that meaningful position limit rules will ever be established. However, nearly five years after Dodd–Frank was passed, other regulators as well as politicians are making headway on moving banks out of the physical commodity trading business. The US Senate Permanent Subcommittee on Investigations (Senate, 2014) found that three major Wall Street banks – Goldman Sachs, Morgan Stanley, and JPMorgan – had engaged in physical commodity trading activity that was risky and could potentially create an undue burden on commerce:

> Until recently, Morgan Stanley controlled over 55 million barrels of oil storage capacity, 100 oil tankers, and 6,000 miles of pipeline. JPMorgan built a copper inventory that peaked at $2.7 billion, and at one point, included at least 213,000 metric tons of copper, comprising nearly 60% of the available physical copper on the world's premier copper trading exchange, the

London Metal Exchange (LME). In 2012, Goldman owned 1.5 million metric tons of aluminum worth $3 billion, about 25% of the entire U.S. annual consumption.

(p. 3)

Of course, the evidence for price manipulation, and therefore undue influence on commerce, was not clear cut. Despite the difficulty in proving manipulation, the report did highlighted a concern that trading in physical commodities by Wall Street banks "carried potential catastrophic event risks." The potential for catastrophic risk by banks backed by the FDIC and ultimately the Federal Reserve, led to a caustic Bloomberg editorial (Bloomberg View, 2013):

> The largest U.S. banks are accused of causing problems in markets ranging from energy to aluminum. Regardless of whether they're guilty of market-rigging, as critics say, the charges raise another question: *Why are the banks in these businesses in the first place?* [emphasis mine] Part of the answer is that they're among the country's most subsidized enterprises. The Federal Deposit Insurance Corp. and the Federal Reserve, both backed by taxpayers, provide an explicit subsidy by ensuring that banks can borrow money in times of market turmoil. Banks that are big and connected enough to bring down the economy enjoy an added implicit subsidy: Creditors will lend to them at low rates on the assumption that the government won't let them fail.

Another area of concern raised in the Senate report was related to physical ETFs. Specifically, JPMorgan proposed creation of a physical copper ETF in 2010. ETFs have been created for any and all commodities using futures contracts, but physical ETFs had been restricted to *bullion* metals, like gold and silver. *Base metals* are used in manufacturing and face greater restrictions, for good reason. As the demand for futures-based ETFs increases, more shares are created through purchasing more futures contracts. For a physical ETF based on physical copper, more copper has to be purchased and placed in storage. Physical ETFs drive up the physical demand for copper based upon investor demand, not economic fundamentals.

Since ETFs are traded on stock exchanges, they are overseen by the SEC. Despite industrial end-user complaints, the SEC actually approved JPMorgan's copper ETF in December 2012, but concerns over its registration statement that it did not clarify potential conflicts of interest delayed its release, and "JPMorgan told the Subcommittee that it has placed its copper ETF proposal on indefinite hold" (Senate, 2014, p. 362). Given its concerns over the potential influence of physical ETFs, the report suggested the SEC and CFTC should have regulatory oversight of physical ETFs, and "the CFTC should apply position limits to ETF organizers and promoters, and consider banning such instruments due to their potential in commodity market corners and squeezes" (p. 12).

Federal regulators and politicians have taken notice. Federal Reserve Board member Daniel Tarullo testified to the Senate subcommittee regarding the question of bank ownership of physical commodities, specifically focusing on the *grandfather clause* in the 1999 GLBA. The grandfather clause let bank holding companies continue to engage in the transportation, storage, extraction, and refining of physical commodities if they had done so prior to September 30, 1997. Only two banks qualified, Goldman Sachs and Morgan Stanley. Not only were they allowed to continue activities, but they were given a significant advantage on the cap relative to those imposed on other banks. The GLBA limited finance holding companies to investments in physical commodities up to 5 percent of *tier 1 capital*; however, the restriction for Goldman Sachs and Morgan Stanley was 5 percent of consolidated assets! It should be noted that the Senate report (2014) did include recommendations to eliminate the exclusions for Goldman and Morgan Stanley.

Given that Goldman Sachs and Morgan Stanley were required to become bank holding companies during the global economic crisis, the FRB's Tarullo was also concerned about the catastrophic and liability risks posed by commodity operations of large systemically important banks, and at the time of his testimony to the Senate subcommittee, he stated that the FRB was working on a rule to raise capital standards for banks that trade in physical commodities. Given the increased scrutiny from the FRB, and the 2014 Senate investigation into their physical commodity holdings, banks have been disposing of their physical commodity subsidiaries:

> Goldman Sachs sold its metal-warehouse unit, Metro International Trade Services LLC, to private-equity firm Reuben Brothers ... [and] is winding down a uranium business it owns by not entering into new trades and allowing those coming due to expire. It's also trying to sell the coal-mining business it owns in Colombia.
>
> (Faux, 2014)

Morgan Stanley sold TransMontaigne Inc., its oil storage, marketing, and transportation company, and it just announced a $1 billion sale of most of its remaining oil unit to Castleton Commodities International (Meyer and Braithwaite, 2015). However, Morgan Stanley is not disposing of all their physical assets, as they have retained Heidmar, an oil tanker operator in which Morgan Stanley has a minority stake, because they claim they "will continue trading oil in physical and financial markets for its clients" (ibid.). It is difficult to give up contango profits.

Last but not least, politicians, discontent with the FRB's slow movement on restricting banks' physical commodity trading, have proposed legislation to end physical commodity trading by banks. US Senators Warren (D-Mass) and Vitter (R-La) have introduced a bill which includes a proposal to eliminate the grandfather clause benefits of Goldman Sachs and Morgan Stanley. Specifically, the bill would:

> Reduce the risk of future bailouts and market manipulation by closing the loophole that allows two megabanks to engage in nearly unrestricted activities with physical commodities. The Bailout Prevention Act safeguards

taxpayers from bailing out large financial institutions by repealing section 4(o) of the Bank Holding Company Act, a grandfather clause that allows two firms – Goldman Sachs and Morgan Stanley – to conduct a wide array of commodities-related activities that other financial holding companies cannot. Repealing section 4(o) will level the competitive playing field and reduce systemic risk.

(Warren, 2015, original emphasis)

The political economy of food and finance policy

While there are positive changes in food policy included in the 2014 Farm Bill and the proposed Dietary Guidelines, there is much work to be done. Public policy in the US is dominated by corporate influence. Political campaigns are expensive, and politicians need millions of dollars to fund their campaigns, and there are only two sources of money: corporations and the wealthy. Even when a major crisis creates an opportunity for positive change, change that is beneficial to the public interest rarely occurs.

GMO labeling laws are a case in point. GMO labeling laws are overwhelmingly supported by the American public, and 30 states have introduced bills in support of labeling (Center for Food Safety). To squelch the states' activities, an industry-supported bill was proposed in April 2014 which would create a federal voluntary labeling standard, preempting state laws: "Opponents fear the sway – and vast resources – of the bill's industry backers. Groups representing major agriculture and biotechnology interests have poured millions of dollars into battles over state proposals to create mandatory labeling laws" (Wheeler, 2015).

Even when laws are passed, rules can take years before they are finalized, as in the case of position limits recommend by Dodd–Frank, or they become watered down through industry pressure.

Worse, is *regulatory capture*. The theory of regulatory capture states that regulatory agencies are eventually dominated by the very industries they are charged with regulating. This is evidenced by the "revolving door" of government, as prominent leaders of industry and finance take leadership positions in the regulatory agencies that provide oversight to the industries from which they come. Some examples include former CEO of Goldman Sachs Hank Paulson was Secretary of the Treasury during the financial crisis, and former Monsanto vice president of public policy Michael Taylor is deputy commissioner of foods for the FDA. The door is revolving, so public servants usually end up right back in the industry. For example, after Wendy Gramm stepped down as chair of the CFTC, she accepted a position on Enron's Board of Directors.

The Gramm name is remindful of another form of regulatory capture, through the judicial system. An October 19, 2010 Washington Post article quoted retiring CFTC judge George Painter that his colleague made a promise to Gramm, while she was chair of the CFTC, that he would never rule in favor of an investor's complaints:

On Judge Levine's first week on the job, nearly twenty years ago, he came into my office and stated that he had promised Wendy Gramm, the Chairwoman of the Commission, that we would never rule in a complainant's favor .... A review of his rulings will confirm that he fulfilled his vow," Painter wrote.

(Hilzenrath, 2010)

The article concluded with a statement that the judge in question was the subject of a *Wall Street Journal* article in which it was stated, "he never ruled in favor of an investor."

Is all lost in this food fight? Have monied corporate interests captured government? While there are some positive changes in the 2014 Farm Bill, and a handful of US politicians (Senators Warren and Sanders) are supporting public causes, it is not enough. Is there a solution? Ironically, the solution may be money, though in this case, how we consumers choose to spend it. In the final chapter of this work we discuss some of the global, national, and local movements that are reacting against the financialized, globalized, industrialized food system.

Notes

1 The population-to-farm ratio in 1927 was about 20, and it has increased to roughly 142 in 2013.
2 The bill has yet to receive Senate approval.

Bibliography

Ben Guriat, M. (2015). Export-led growth models and the balance of payments constrained economies of Tunisia and Morocco. Working Paper, Laurentian University.

Better Markets. (2015). Position limits for derivatives and aggregation of positions. Comments to CFTC. Retrieved May 16, 2015 from http://www.bettermarkets.com/sites/default/files/documents/CFTC%20-%20CL-%20Position%20Limits%20for%20Derivatives%20and%20Aggregation%20of%20Positions%20-%201-22-2015.pdf

Bloomberg View. (2013). The wrong business for big banks. Retrieved May 12, 2015 from http://www.bloomberg.com/bw/articles/2013-08-01/bloomberg-view-the-wrong-business-for-big-banks

Bowers, D., Rasmussen, W., and Baker, G. (1984). History of agricultural price-support and adjustment programs, 1933–84. Agriculture Information Bulletin No. 485. Washington, DC: USDA Economic Research Service.

CFTC. (2013). *Position Limits for Derivatives*. Federal Register. Retrieved May 16, 2015 from http://www.cftc.gov/ucm/groups/public/@lrfederalregister/documents/file/2013-27200a.pdf.

CFTC. (2014). *Position Limits for Derivatives and Aggregation of Positions*. Federal Register. Retrieved May 16, 2015 from http://www.cftc.gov/ucm/groups/public/@lrfederalregister/documents/file/2014-28482a.pdf.

Confessore, N. (2014, October 7). How school lunch became the latest political battleground. *New York Times Magazine*. Retrieved from http://www.nytimes.com/2014/10/12/magazine/how-school-lunch-became-the-latest-political-battleground.html?_r=0 June 10, 2015.

DGAC. (2015). Scientific Report of the 2015 Dietary Guidelines Advisory Committee. Retrieved April 22, 2015 from http://www.health.gov/dietaryguidelines/2015-scientific-report/

Dimitri, C., Effland, A. B., and Conklin, N. C. (2005). *The 20th Century Transformation of US Agriculture and Farm Policy.* Washington, DC: USDA.

EPA. (2013). Ag101 demographics. Retrieved April 4, 2015, from http://www.epa.gov/agriculture/ag101/demographics.html

Faux, Z. (2014). Goldman sells metals unit to billionaire Reubens after probe. Retrieved May 27, 2015, from www.bloomberg.com

Ferdman, R. A. and Whoriskey, P. (2015, February 19). Think of Earth, not just your stomach, panel advises. *The Washington Post.* Retrieved May 27, 2015 from http://www.washingtonpost.com/business/economy/think-of-earth-not-just-your-stomach-panel-advises/2015/02/19/b3aab734-b876-11e4-aa05-1ce812b3fdd2_story.html

Hilzenrath, D. S. (2010, October 19). Commodity Futures Trading Commission judge says colleague biased against complainants. *The Washington Post.* Retrieved June 6, 2015 from http://www.washingtonpost.com/wp-dyn/content/article/2010/10/19/AR2010101907216_pf.html

McMichael, P. (2009). The world food crisis in historical perspective. *Monthly Review, 61*(3), 32.

Mercier, S. (2011). *Review of US Farm Programs.* Washington, DC: AGree.

Meyer, G., and Braithwaite, T. (2015, April 15). Morgan Stanley offered $1bn for oil unit. *Financial Times.* Available at: http://www.ft.com/intl/cms/s/0/2a64c480-e2f4-11e4-aa1d-00144feab7de.html#axzz3cPfYpAAr

Nestle, M. (2013). *Food Politics: How the Food Industry Influences Nutrition and Health* (Vol. 3). Stanford: University of California Press.

Palley, T. I. (2011). The rise and fall of export-led growth. Levy Economics Institute of Bard College Working Paper (675).

Patel, R., and McMichael, P. (2009). A political economy of the food riot. *Review (Fernand Braudel Center),* 9–35.

Pollan, M. (2006). *The Omnivore's Dilemma: A Natural History of Four Meals.* Harmondsworth: Penguin.

Schneider, M. (2008). We are hungry! (D. Sociology, Trans.). Retrieved June 10, 2015, from http://www.academia.edu/238430/_We_are_Hungry_A_Summary_Report_of_Food_Riots_Government_Responses_and_State_of_Democracy_in_2008

Sciammacco, S. (2012). Farm subsidies still concentrated in the hands of the most successful. Retrieved June 10, 2015, from http://www.ewg.org/agmag/2012/06/policy-plate-farm-subsidies-still-concentrated-hands-most-successful

Senate, US (2014). *Wall Bank Street Involvement with Physical Commodities.* Permanent Subcommittee on Investigations.

Stiglitz, J. E. (2015). The secret corporate takeover of trade agreements. Retrieved may 14, 2015, from http://www.commondreams.org/views/2015/05/14/secret-corporate-takeover-trade-agreements

Suppan, S. (2015). The last hurrah for speculative postion limits? Retrieved May 28, 2015, from http://www.iatp.org/blog/201504/the-last-hurrah-for-speculative-position-limits

Thune, J., R-SD. (2015). Thune leads call for USDA, HHS to include lean red meat in 2015 dietary guidelines. Press release. Retrieved June 10, 2015 from http://www.thune.senate.gov/public/index.cfm/press-releases?ID=2cbe42da-eac8-48c1-a820-44a392b57195

USDA. *Feed Grains Database.* Retrieved March 12, 2015 from: http://www.ers.usda.gov/data-products/feed-grains-database/

USDA. (2014a). Agricultural Act of 2014: highlights and Implications. Retrieved April 15, 2015 from http://www.ers.usda.gov/agricultural-act-of-2014-highlights-and-implica tions/crop-commodity-programs.aspx

USDA. (2014b). Crop commodity programs. Retrieved April 23, 2015, 2015, from http://www.ers.usda.gov/agricultural-act-of-2014-highlights-and-implications/crop-commodity-programs.aspx

Warren, E., D-MA. (2015). Warren, Vitter introduce Bailout Prevention Act. Press release. Retrieved May 21, 2015, 2015, from http://www.warren.senate.gov/?p=press_release& id=818

Wheeler, L. (2015). GMO Bill intensifies federal food fight. Retrieved June 7, 2015, from http://thehill.com/regulation/237268-gmo-bill-intensifies-federal-food-fight

Wyly, C. (2015). US dietary guidelines: historic battle for people and planet. Retrieved April 14, 2015, from http://www.huffingtonpost.com/christiana-wyly/embargoed-until-may-8-die_b_7236916.html

8   The global food chain reaction

Industrialized food. Globalized food. Financialized food. These forces constitute what we have characterized as the neoliberal food regime, which has significantly shaped the US and global food systems since the late 1970s. Through financialization of commodity markets, private equity takeovers, and investments in global farmland, financialization has been the dominant force influencing food systems since 2000.

If capitalism is the commodification of all things, financialization is the capitalization of all things. Under industrial capitalism in the mid-nineteenth century, food became a tradable, fungible commodity. Under financialized capitalism at the turn of the new millennium, food became an asset, no different than stocks and bonds.

There is a contradictory relationship between food as a commodity and food as nourishment for life. Under capitalism, labor is viewed as an input, a commodity that feeds the industrial production process. Food is also an input, a commodity, which is necessary to feed and nourish labor – food is fuel. We must *eat* to replenish labor power. Food as a commodity under capitalism follows the same logic as goods; it is mass-produced and costs are constantly driven down to maximize profits. As corporeal human beings, however, food is the centerpiece of our social and cultural experiences. We don't eat, we *dine*. We *break bread*, which is to share a meal with others, and we are raised sharing meals with our family and friends. Food is life, and most of us want to enjoy it.

During the development of industrial capitalism in Britain, wheat, as the main source of food, was the most important commodity input required for reproduction of labor power. The history of industrial capitalism is also the history of wheat: cheap wheat kept wages low and profits high. Twentieth century capitalism was characterized by surplus, and capitalism had to adapt by developing mechanisms to regulate demand to ensure enough consumption for the surfeit of goods produced. Food was also produced in surplus, and surplus agriculture products doled out as aid became a mechanism through which the US influenced countries in the developing world. However, this stable and regulated post-war system gave rise to volatility, which created the conditions for a re-emergence of the power of markets and trade, managed by the tentacles of finance. Finance transforms physical "things" into tradable paper assets, and asset prices are more volatile, and volatility is profitable for finance. Food, farmland, climate, and water are being financialized by a leviathan in search of profit and yield.

The search for yield is global. The capital accumulation process driven by profit is global, and, despite what simple textbook models claim, the profit motive often leads to outcomes detrimental to social welfare. Unregulated capitalism creates negative externalities, additional costs that are borne by the rest of society. For example, the perceived benefits of free trade are used by international institutions to encourage nations to liberalize agriculture markets so corporations, Sovereign Wealth Funds, and investors can fund global expansion of the industrial farming model, but this global land grab creates additional costs in the form of millions of peasant farmers losing their land.

In the US, the food system is dominated by industrialized farming methods that use high doses of pesticides, hormones, and antibiotics to raise production levels. At the other end of the food chain, food conglomerates focus on finding the "bliss point," the precise amount of salt, sugar, and fat to produce maximum pleasure (or addiction) for the consumer (Moss, 2013). As US food corporations strive to increase profits, they have created significant external costs to our health which are borne by the rest of society. How can the US have the most expensive healthcare system in the advanced world and also have the worst health? The answer should be obvious.

We have reached the turning point. Food as a reproducible commodity produced *anywhere* by a globalized, industrialized, financialized food system becomes "food from nowhere" (McMichael, 2009). We want to know where our food comes from and what it contains. We want food that has taste and a sense of place. The industrial food system is killing us, and it has set off a global food chain reaction.

Global reactions

The world's population is becoming increasingly urban: about 30 percent of the population lived in urban areas in 1950; currently about 55 percent live in urban areas; and the UN projects two-thirds will live in urban regions by 2050 (United Nations, 2014). Global population is expected to increase by 34 percent by 2050, topping the 9 billion mark, so that 6 billion people are expected to live in cities. To feed this larger, urban population, the FAO estimates that annual investments of $83 billion in agriculture production are needed (FAO, n.d., a). The strategy pushed by the World Bank is to liberalize markets so that global corporations, private equity, and sovereign wealth funds provide the needed investment in farmland. This solution proposed by the World Bank is more of the same: expansion of the industrialized food system sourced by genetically engineered seeds because it is the only way to "deliver the goods." However, this strategy creates a serious conflict. Feeding the world requires more farmland for big industrial farms, but most of the available arable land is in the poor countries of the developing world, farmed by peasants on small farms. A policy that depends on industrial farming will cause millions to be displaced. Globalization driven by trade liberalization has already caused the displacement of rural farmers by large-scale industrial farming; by some estimates, 20–30 million farmers lost their land in the first several decades of the neoliberal food regime (McMichael, 2009). Given the global land grab over the past ten years, the number of peasant farmers who have lost their land has most likely accelerated (GRAIN, 2014). TINA: there is no alternative. Or is there?

The global land grab and push for industrial farming have set off a global reaction. There are millions who believe *there is an alternative.* One of the most well-known is the *food sovereignty* movement started in the early 1990s by *La Via Campesina,* an international organization composed of peasants and small farmers. La Via Campesina defined food sovereignty as:

> The right of peoples to healthy and culturally appropriate food produced through sustainable methods and their right to define their own food and agriculture systems. It develops a model of small scale sustainable production benefiting communities and their environment. It puts the aspirations, needs and livelihoods of those who produce, distribute and consume food at the heart of food systems and policies rather than the demands of markets and corporations.
>
> Food sovereignty prioritizes local food production and consumption. It gives a country the right to protect its local producers from cheap imports and to control production. *It ensures that the rights to use and manage lands, territories, water, seeds, livestock and biodiversity are in the hands of those who produce food and not of the corporate sector.* Therefore the implementation of genuine agrarian reform is one of the top priorities of the farmer's movement.
>
> (Via Campesina, 2011)

Since its inception, the movement has grown significantly. The International Planning Committee for Food Sovereignty claims that over 800 organizations and 300 million small food producers are part of an autonomous and self-organized global movement that includes rural workers' organizations and community-based social movements (Food Sovereignty, n.d.). Through the use of public pressure, NGOs like La Via Campesina, GRAIN, and Oxfam are making inroads. For example, Oxfam America has used petitions and social media to pressure PepsiCo, Coca-Cola, and Nestle to support land rights of small farmers.

> In November 2013, Coca-Cola – the world's largest purchaser of sugar – announced major commitments to respect and protect the land rights of rural and indigenous communities. PepsiCo declared similar commitments in March 2014. Then, in August 2014, Nestle followed suit with a bold commitment to "zero tolerance" for land grabs in its supply chains. "In plain and simple language, the company has committed to ensure that its ingredients

don't come from land that has been illegally, underhandedly, or unfairly taken from poor people.

(Oxfam, n.d.)

While it is important to restrain the global land grab and ensure that peasant farmers retain their land, the process will continue unless an alternative solution emerges. Is there an alternative to industrial farming? In a *New York Times* debate on the population–food question, author Fred Pearce (Pearce, 2015) argued the issue is not so much population, as it is projected to level out sometime this century; rather, he stated that the main issues are our consumption patterns and how we produce what we consume. Pearce believes it is possible to create a sustainable food system and feed the world through technological advancements and fixing the massive inefficiencies in food production. The most glaring inefficiency is waste, as up to one-third of all food is spoiled or squandered before it is consumed by people (FAO, n.d, b). The American diet also contributes significantly to inefficiencies in global food systems as acknowledged by the Dietary Guidelines Advisory Committee, "current evidence shows that the average US diet has a larger environmental impact in terms of increased greenhouse gas emissions, land use, water use, and energy use, compared to the above dietary patterns" (Dietary Guidelines Advisory Committee, 2015).

Can sustainable, small-scale agriculture deliver the goods to meet the global population needs by 2050? A report by the Special Rapporteur on the right to food for the United Nations, suggested *agroecology* is one technology with significant potential (De Schutter, 2010). Agroecology is the "application of ecological science to the study, design and management of sustainable agroecosystems" (p. 6). Agroecology uses science to mimic natural systems to generate higher yield using sustainable agriculture practices. The UN report found that agroecology initiatives in 57 different countries experienced yield increases of 80 percent on average, and more recent projects doubled output within a 3-10-year period. Additional evidence comes from "down under." Experimentations in Australia suggest that new methods using traditional grain seeds can generate significant increases in yield. According to South Australia's Agriculture Minister Leon Bignell, "Instead of using the top five centimetres of the soil, you go down to 50cm or even deeper .... You put clay in it when it's needed, you put organic matter where it's needed as well .... We're seeing [yield] increases of 50 per cent, 100 per cent, even 300 per cent in some of the cases" (Grindlay, 2015). Australian farmers are motivated to use non-GE seeds because the Chinese are increasingly distrustful, and Australians are positioning themselves for this lucrative market.

The ability to meet the food and nutrient needs of the world population is more a political issue than economic, which is evidenced by current efforts to reduce hunger. The problem, as FAO data and experts note, is that meeting current (and future) food needs is mainly a distribution problem (Koba, 2013). The world produces enough food to feed the current population, but "the principal problem is that many people in the world still do not have sufficient income to purchase (or land to grow) enough food" (Worldhunger, 2015). Bolivia is a good example. Under President Evo Morales, Bolivia implemented policies to establish food sovereignty, food independence, and, most important, reduce hunger and malnutrition. According to the FAO (2014), Bolivia has made significant progress in a short amount of time:

> Bolivia has established processes and institutions that include all stakeholders, particularly previously marginalized indigenous peoples. The strong focus on pro-poor food security policies resulted in hunger decreasing rapidly by 7.4 percent during 2009–11 and 2012–14. Chronic undernourishment in children less than three years of age fell from 41.7 percent in 1989 to 18.5 percent in 2012.
>
> (p. 6)

There is no magic bullet. The solution to feeding the world and reducing hunger requires a combination of strategies:

> Hunger reduction requires an integrated approach, and needs to include: public and private investments to raise agricultural productivity; better access to inputs, land, services, technologies and markets; *measures to promote rural development* [emphasis mine]; social protection for the most vulnerable, including strengthening their resilience to conflicts and natural disasters; and specific nutrition programmes, particularly to address micronutrient deficiencies in mothers and children under five.
>
> (FAO, 2014, p. 1)

This statement by the FAO does not preclude any strategies moving forward, and it correctly suggests an emphasis on rural development. The strategy advocated by international institutions is self-serving: pursuing the industrial farming model ensures the necessity of it. Expanding the industrial farming model forces people off the land, and into urban areas; and the only way to feed large, urban populations is with industrial farming. Q.E.D.

Evidence indicates there is an alternative. Currently, the majority of food produced in the non-industrialized world is produced on small farms, oftentimes, with higher levels of productivity than industrial methods (GRAIN, 2014, p. 13). The alternative solution is the exact opposite of the World Bank model. In a world where capital-intensive production requires less labor, funneling more people into ever larger urban areas serves no purpose; a better solution is to promote rural development as the FAO suggests.

Technology and incentives can promote the needed developments toward sustainable global agriculture production, and the renewable energy industry suggests a model. Improved solar panel technology has increased efficiency, and tax credits have increased demand, allowing solar producers to expand scale of production, reducing costs. Solar is now competitive with fossil fuels, and it is literally putting heat on the market share of traditional utility companies. In 2013, global energy producers added more energy capacity from investment in (all) renewables than fossil fuels (Randall, 2015). A similar transformation can and should happen in global food production. The technology to produce high yields with sustainable farming methods and traditional seeds is available; the difficult step is changing the politicized subsidy system which provides billions of dollars per year in support of the production of commodities for the global market. One way to restrain global production is suggested by the food sovereignty movement: prioritize local food production and consumption.

Local reactions

The regional food movement in the US traces its roots back to the 1970s, started by restaurants like *Chez Panisse* in San Francisco, California which began to source food from regional producers and cook locally inspired cuisine. This form of regionalism was driven by high-end restaurants offering fresh ingredients that tasted better than produce shipped from afar. The current movement was motivated by the publication of books like Eric Schlosser's *Fast Food Nation* (2001) and Michael Pollan's *The Omnivore's Dilemma* (2006) which raise issues of sustainability, health and safety, and environmental impact from an increasingly globalized food system. Questioning the environmental impact and healthiness of the food system is no longer relegated to hippies and peaceniks, it has gone mainstream. In this section we look at some of the trends and developments in the regional and urban food movements, and, for the most part, we do so through the lens of Buffalo, New York, my hometown.

As consumers have rediscovered a taste for real food, they are making direct connections with producers through farmers markets, CSAs (Community Supported Agriculture), field-to-fork experiences, food hubs, and more. In addition, as the population of de-industrialized cities like Buffalo have declined, and vacant houses have been torn down, community gardens and urban farms are reclaiming these empty spaces, and, as urban farming expands, the distinctions between rural and urban have become blurred. Similar experiences in cities across America have led to the development of Food Policy Councils (FPC) which help local governments design policies to handle this growing intersection of rural and urban. Figure 8.1 provides data on the growth of Food Policy Councils in North America. In 2005 there were 32 FPCs in the US, and there are now more than 200. The Buffalo–Erie Food Policy Council was formed in May 2013 to work in an advisory capacity and inform public agencies and policy makers in Buffalo and Erie County on matters pertaining to food policy. Membership is reflective of all constituents and includes politicians, policy experts, activists, farmers, and residents.

The Buffalo–Erie FPC was cultivated through a collaboration between community organizations and university researchers, and it exemplifies the growing movement in US urban agriculture (Raja *et al.*, 2015). The Massachusetts Avenue Project (MAP) is one of the community organizations that were involved with organizing the FPC. MAP works with urban youth to educate on issues of health and food, and it provides hands-on training in organic farm methods. MAP's mission is to "nurture the growth of a diverse and equitable local food system and

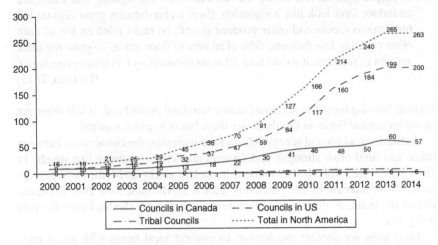

Figure 8.1 Food Policy Councils in North America.

Source: Center for a Livable Future, Johns Hopkins Bloomberg School of Public Health.

promote local economic opportunities, access to affordable, nutritious food and social change education" (MAP, 2015). It is located on the west side of Buffalo in an area populated by low-income, working-class citizens, and a growing refugee population. MAP trains and educates urban youth to grow and manage urban farms operating on 13 reclaimed vacant lots. Their organic produce is marketed and distributed to restaurants and retail establishments, and a "mobile market" delivers produce to communities lacking access to fresh produce. According to its 2013 Annual Report, MAP:

> Produced and distributed 15,000 lbs of organic produce, including 72 varieties of fruits, vegetables, herbs, eggs and fish …. Composted nearly 500,000lbs of food waste, removing it from the municipal waste stream …. Improved nutritious, affordable food access to over 2,300 low-income households through our farm stand and Mobile Market sites …. Provided training, technical assistance and farm tours to over 4,800 individuals, schools and organizations.
>
> (MAP, 2013)

Working with urban youth and low-income communities, MAP helps overcome the notion that healthy fresh food is only for those who can afford it.

New technology will change the scale of urban farming from small community gardens to sophisticated vertical systems that can produce for commercial markets. Vertical farming has the potential to generate commercial levels of high-nutrient output:

> Ecopia Farms is a vertical indoor farm in the San Francisco area founded in an 8,000-square-foot warehouse by a group of Silicon Valley veterans.

In purple light thrown off by the red and blue LED lighting that can make an indoor farm look like a nightclub, these techie-farmers grow organic lettuce, micro greens and other produce in soil, on racks piled on top of each other covering less than one-fifth of an acre of floor space. To grow the same amount of produce, it would take 30 acres outdoors and 30 times more water.

(Lawson, 2015)

Vertical farming turns the notion of scarce farmland on its head. While there are two-dimensional limits to farmland, are there limits to going vertical?

As the demand for and access to fresh food increases, the connections between urban and rural grow stronger, and farmers markets have grown like weeds. In 2004 there were 3,706 farmers markets in the US, and by 2014, the number grew to 8,268, an increase of 123 percent (Figure 8.2). Buffalo, New York is indicative of the trend, as the number of farmers markets have doubled over the past 5–6 years.

Food hubs are another mechanism to connect local farms with urban markets. Food hubs are facilities where small and medium-sized farms can aggregate product for marketing and distribution on a scale they could not achieve independently. The Buffalo region's first food hub was announced in 2013 and it is in the final stages of development.

One of the largest outlets for local farm produce is the Lexington Co-Operative Market, the largest retail food co-op in Western New York. Established in the early 1970s in one of Buffalo's most vibrant neighborhoods, the co-op has focused on

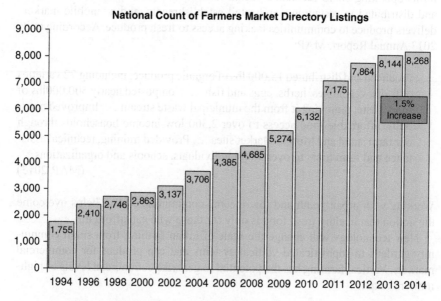

Figure 8.2 Number of farmers' markets in the US.

Source: USDA.

supplying local produce, organic and sustainable products to its membership. As the population in Western New York has been in decline for years, the growth of the co-op is a good barometer of the local food chain reaction in the US. Despite the demographic trend, co-op membership has grown at an annual rate of 16 percent per year for the past 15 years; there were 628 members in 2000, and in early 2015 the co-op was celebrating the addition of its 10,000th member. With increased membership, sales have grown rapidly, increasing at an annual rate of 20 percent from 2000 to 2014, and given its rapid growth, it will open a second location in 2016.

Another program that directly connects consumers to farmers is Community Supported Agriculture. In a CSA, consumers pay a fixed, up-front cost and receive a weekly delivery of farm products throughout the growing season. It is a mutually beneficial arrangement as consumers tend to pay a lower per pound cost for fresh produce, and farmers receive a guaranteed amount of income at the beginning of the season. There are currently 16 CSAs available in the Western New York region, and the USDA estimates there are over 12,000 CSAs nationwide.

The local initiatives in Buffalo are emblematic of the national, and international reactions to food from nowhere produced by global corporations, and these trends are hitting corporations where it hurts, the bottom line:

> Sales of Campbell's condensed soup slipped 3 per cent year on year during its last six months of reported results. During the most recent quarter, North American revenues for Kellogg's cereals and other morning foods fell 7.7 per cent, while Kraft Foods, the North American grocery business of the old consumer giant, reported a 6.6 per cent sales decline for meals and desserts, including its macaroni and cheese in a box.
>
> (Silverman, 2015)

Consumers have spoken with their wallets, and global food corporations are "listening." In the spring of 2015, Tyson and McDonald's announced they would stop using human antibiotics in chicken; PepsiCo announced it would stop using aspartame; Chipotle stated it will no longer use GMO-sourced food in its ingredients; Kraft said it will stop using yellow dye in its macaroni and cheese, using natural ingredients instead; and Panera announced a "No No List" of 150 artificial additives it would eliminate from its products.[1] While food corporations are bending to public pressure, what of finance?

Finance

We return to one of the original questions. Is finance a benign force that simply intermediates the savings of individuals to the efficient allocation of productive investment? Or is it a giant vampire squid abusing its government-licensed financial power to suck more and more income from the productive sector? The thousands of small and medium sized community banks may be a benign force, but big global banks, big finance, has exceeded its utility. One hundred years ago large Wall Street banks extended their tentacles to control equally large oligopolistic industries. Hilferding (Hilferding and Bottomore, 1990) described the process and the *Pecora Commission* exposed the fraud and overlapping relationships, leading to financial regulations and stability for nearly forty years. Financial interests are intertwined with commercial interests yet again. Food has been financialized; farmland is being financialized; and water is being financialized (Bayliss, 2014). What is left to control? Public assets. With local finances stretched, more and more governments are privatizing public assets, with financial interests providing the funds (Rosner, 2013):

> Today, there are few financial assets classes left to support growth of the size necessary to generate returns proportional to our largest banks' needs. Seeking new returns, our largest and most systemically interconnected banking firms, under the guise of infrastructure development, are turning their focus to an expansion of their control of nonfinancial assets.
>
> The Asset Management units of several of these firms are seeking "controlling interests" nonfinancial assets without ownership of those assets. To effect these goals the firms are pitching pension and other investors on investments in the leasing, operation and control of infrastructure assets. To date, these firms have attained "controlling interests" and have "active control strategies" – in the U.S. and abroad. They currently control ports, airports, electric utilities, water utilities, sewer utilities, wind power farms, parking meters, solar power generation, parking garages, rail leasing, charter schools and other assets.
>
> (pp. 9–10)

During 2014, private equity funds accumulated nearly $300 billion to purchase public infrastructure assets (Cotterill, 2015), and, as Rosner noted, the marketing materials of the banks indicate that these investments are attractive because of their monopolistic and quasi-monopolistic nature. Monopolies and needs are ideal qualities that allow finance to extract more rent.

Wall Street banks have lost their social purpose. In an era of low returns from productive investments, large banks have directed their credit-creating privileges toward control of the things that people need. Unregulated rentier finance gains at the expense of workers and industry, too often illegally. This is not empty rhetoric. The *Financial Times* maintains an ongoing database of fines paid by global banks, and they began collecting the information on May 30, 2007 (Bank Fines, 2015). As of April 23, 2015, 60 banks have been levied fines with 231 individual cases totaling $150 billion.[2] While a significant number of fines were related to the housing bubble, a significant amount were not. The cases receiving the most publicity since the housing crisis were the LIBOR/EURIBOR and foreign exchange riggings, but additional offenses run a gamut of markets, including energy market manipulation, municipal bond rigging, misleading credit unions on investments, and selling unsuitable investments to school districts. JPMorgan leads the pack with 36 fines totaling $31.3 billion, although Bank of America, with "only" half the fines (18), has the highest penalty total at $58 billion.

In the US, evidence suggests the size of the financial sector has exceeded its social utility (Cecchetti and Kharroubi, 2012): additional growth of the financial sector leads to slower growth. Finance must be reined in, but what are the solutions? Former Citigroup CEO John Reed suggested the big banks need to be broken up and Glass–Steagall should be reinstated; a Financial Transactions Tax has been proposed in the EU and the US; and others have called for expansion of public banking, specifically the creation of a national infrastructure bank (Likosky, 2015).

Sometimes the market feeds back on itself. In the futures market, while position limit rules have been delayed for years, market reactions have created a restraint on commodity prices, much like Petzel (2009) suggested. High commodity prices that may not reflect underlying demand encourage more supply, and contango markets reduce returns on index investments. Commodity prices have been on a downward trend since 2012, and agriculture ETFs were the worst performing ETFs in 2013, some down over 30 percent (Cummans, 2014). However, despite this market reaction, financialized commodity markets mean prices will rebound quickly at any hint of recovery. Financial traders need to be restrained in food commodity markets, but policy makers are captured.

In the US, one of the most difficult issues to overcome is the influence corporations have on the democratic process. Lobbying and the need to finance campaigns cause politicians to bend to the wishes of corporate interests. Regulatory capture is there if politicians aren't. American political factions, who often support similar issues, are *balkanized*, and an apathetic electorate fails to vote. In fact, voter turnout in the 2014 national election (a non-presidential election year) was the lowest since 1942 (DelReal, 2014). The system is broken. Are there issues to galvanize support and create change? Position limits on speculators does not make for a good rallying cry.

A food-based political movement?

The recent announcements by corporations to adopt sustainable policies and eliminate "junk" from food sparked a blogosphere debate among food policy analysts, food writers, and activists in the US. The debate began when Professor Marion Nestle posted the following question on her blog, "Is the food movement winning?" (Nestle, 2015). Her post engendered this response from *New York Times* food editor Mark Bittman (Bittman, 2015): "I'm not even sure such thing as a food movement exists." Bittman lamented the lack of movement on issues he has been writing on for years. He suggested that there might be a few issues that people could unite behind in a national movement, but they require strong organizations to back them, real funding, and learning how to fight.

Shortly after Bittman's response, food activist Winona Hauter responded on her blog (Hauter, 2015):

The real challenge has been translating that movement into building political power. For the most part, food activism has been focused on cultural changes and buying habits, not on building power to hold elected officials accountable for how their votes affect food policy. The emphasis has been on using dollars to vote for better food or corporate campaigns focused on making junk food a little less bad for you .... The best way to build this political power is to organize around issues that resonate with people, engage those folks, and begin to develop long term change.

This food fight is more semantics than substance. Bittman and Hauter would like to see a broad national movement on the back of the food movement, but what food-related issues might galvanize political support? Bittman (2015) provided a list of the issues he has been writing about for years:

- end subsidies to processed food;
- break up the Department of Agriculture and empower the Food and Drug Administration;
- outlaw concentrated animal feeding operations;
- encourage and subsidize home cooking;
- tax the marketing and sale of unhealthful foods;
- mandate truth in labeling;
- remove the routine use of antibiotics from food production;
- radically improve and expand the school lunch program;
- ensure that there is land for people who want to grow real food on it.

As Hauter pointed out, there is widespread public support for GMO labeling, and more people are aware of the excessive use of antibiotics in food production. While food and health are galvanizing issues, are any of those on Bittman's list enough to generate a national movement? Given the level of apathy by US electorate, I am skeptical.

We all want access to fresh, healthy food. If a national movement is unlikely, then it will take more of what *is* working: continue to vote with our wallets and continue to advocate for local changes that expand the connections between producers and consumers. With respect to food, local is global. Prioritizing local food production and consumption impacts global sales, and consumer buying power has shown to be a powerful force. The work of popular writers, bloggers, and activists is influencing the debate, despite Bittman's lament. Small is beautiful. Local food movements can and are changing the global food system "one meal at a time."

Notes

1 Panera's "No No List" can be found at https://www.panerabread.com/en-us/company/food-policy-no-no-list.html.
2 The data were updated on May 22, 2015, and the total is now $160 billion.

Bibliography

Bank Fines. (2015). *Financial Times*. Retrieved April 4, 2015 from http://blogs.ft.com/ftdata/2015/05/22/bank-fines-data/

Bayliss, K. (2014). The financialization of water. *Review of Radical Political Economics*, *46*(3), 292–307.

Bittman, M. (2015, May 6). Let's make food issues real. Editorial. *The New York Times*. Retrieved May 17, 2015 from http://www.nytimes.com/2015/05/06/opinion/lets-make-food-issues-real.html?_r=0

Cecchetti, S. G., and Kharroubi, E. (2012). Reassessing the impact of finance on growth. Retrieved June 12, 2015 from http://ssrn.com/abstract=2117753

Cotterill, J. (2015, May 22). Demand for assets loads up infrastructure risks. *Financial Times*.

Cummans, J. (2014). The best & worst commodity ETFs of 2013. Retrieved June 1, 2015, from http://etfdb.com/2013/the-best-worst-commodity-etfs-of-2013/#WorstPerformers

De Schutter, O. (2010). Report submitted by the special rapporteur on the right to food (H. R. Council, Trans.). United Nations.

DelReal, J. A. (2014, November 10). Voter turnout in 2014 was the lowest since WWII. *The Washington Post*. Retrieved June 16, 2015 from http://www.washingtonpost.com/blogs/post-politics/wp/2014/11/10/voter-turnout-in-2014-was-the-lowest-since-wwii/

Dietary Guidelines Advisory Committee. (2015). *Scientific Report of the 2015 Dietary Guidelines Advisory Committee*. Washington, DC: US Dept of Health and Human Services and US Dept of Agriculture.

FAO. (n.d., a). Investments in agriculture. Food and Agriculture Organization of the United Nations.Retrieved May 18, 2015, from http://www.fao.org/investment-in-agriculture/en/

FAO. (n.d., b). Food loss and food waste. Food and Agriculture Organization of the United Nations. Retrieved June 19, 2015, from http://www.fao.org/food-loss-and-food-waste/en/

FAO. (2014). State of food insecurity in the World 2014 in brief. *The State of Food Insecurity in the World*. Food and Agriculture Organization of the United Nations. Available at: http://www.fao.orgFood Sovereignty. (n.d.). Retrieved February 18, 2015, from http://www.foodsovereignty.org/about-us/

GRAIN. (2014). Hungry for land: small farmers feed the world – with less than a quarter of all farmland. Retrieved March 27, 2015 from https://www.grain.org/article/entries/4929-hungry-for-land-small-farmers-feed-the-world-with-less-than-a-quarter-of-all-farmland

Grindlay, D. (2015, March 16). SA Agriculture Minister says soil program porves utilising 'God's gifts' can boost yields better than GM technology. Retrieved April 9, 2015 from http://www.abc.net.au/news/2015-03-17/genetic-modification-grain-canola-agriculture-minister-bignell/6325276

Hauter, W. (2015). Another view on Mark Bittman's recent note to food activists. [Web log message.] Retrieved June 3, 2015 from http://www.foodandwaterwatch.org/blogs/another-view-on-mark-bittmans-recent-note-to-food-activists/

Hilferding, R., and Bottomore, T. B. (1990). *Finance Capital: A Study in the Latest Phase of Capitalist Development*: London: Routledge.

Koba, M. (2013). A hungry world: lots of food, in too few places. Retrieved June 12, 2015, from http://www.cnbc.com/id/100893540

Lawson, C. (2015). Vertical farming: a hot new area for investors. Retrieved June 7, 2015, from http://www.cnbc.com/id/102557803

Likosky, M. (2015). A national bank with one goal, infrastructure. *The New York Times*. Retrieved Retrieved June 18 from http://www.nytimes.com/roomfordebate/2013/10/01/should-states-operate-public-banks/a-national-bank-with-one-goal-infrastructure

MAP. (2013). Massachusetts Avenue Project, Annual Report 2013. Retrieved June 14, 2015 from http://mass-ave.org/wp-content/uploads/2011/06/MAP-2013-Annual-Report.pdf

MAP. (2015). Massachusetts Avenue Project. Retrieved June 19, 2015, from http://mass-ave.org/about/

McMichael, P. (2009). The world food crisis in historical perspective. *Monthly Review, 61*(3), 32.

Moss, M. (2013). *Salt, Sugar, Fat: How the Food Giants Hooked Us*. New York: Random House.

Nestle, M. (2015). Is the food movement winning? [Web log message.] Retrieved June 3, 2015 from http://www.foodpolitics.com/2015/04/is-the-food-movement-winning/

Oxfam (n.d.). The truth about land grabs. Retrieved May 18, 2015, from http://www.oxfamamerica.org/take-action/campaign/food-farming-and-hunger/land-grabs/?gclid=CjwKEAjw9PioBRDdpqy0-ofG3DgSJAACe5NEy9JtlZIv3tB3MNONsMpGJP5mek5nOzOn1jhU7qtvOxoCwjLw_wcB

Pearce, F. (2015, June 8, 2015). Overconsumption is a grave threat to humanity. *The New York Times*. Retrieved May 28, 2015 from http://www.nytimes.com/roomfordebate/2015/06/08/is-overpopulation-a-legitimate-threat-to-humanity-and-the-planet/overconsumption-is-a-grave-threat-to-humanity

Petzel, T. (2009). Testimony before the CFTC: July. Retrieved December 18, 2014 from http://www.cftc.gov/ucm/groups/public/@newsroom/documents/file/hearing072809_petzel2.pdf

Pollan, M. (2006) *The Omnivore's Dilemma: A Natural History of Four Meals*. NewYork: The Penguin Press.

Raja, S., Picard, D., Baek, S., and Delgado, C. (2015). Rustbelt radicalism: a decade of food systems planning practice in Buffalo, New York. *Journal of Agriculture, Food Systems, and Community Development, 4*(4), 173–189.

Randall, T. (2015). Fossil fuels just lost the race against renewables. *Bloomberg*. Retrieved June 2, 2015 from http://www.bloomberg.com/news/articles/2015-04-14/fossil-fuels-just-lost-the-race-against-renewables

Rosner, J. (2013). *Examining Financial Holding Companies: Should Banks Control Power Plants, Warehouses, and Oil Refineries?* Committee on Banking, Housing, and Urban Affairs: US Senate.

Schlosser, E. (2001) *Fast Food Nation: The Dark Side of the All-American Meal*. NewYork: Houghton Mifflin.

Silverman, G. (2015, March 16). Craft versus Kraft. *Financial Times*.

United Nations. (2014). World's population increasingly urban with more than half living in urban areas. Retrieved May 15, 2015, from http://www.un.org/en/development/desa/news/population/world-urbanization-prospects-2014.html

Via Campesina. (2011). The international peasant's voice. Retrieved May 18, 2015, from http://viacampesina.org/en/index.php/organisation-mainmenu-44

Worldhunger.org. (2015). 2015 World hunger and poverty facts and statistics. Retrieved June 14, 2015, from http://www.worldhunger.org/articles/Learn/world%20hunger%20facts%202002.html

Index